BIG BOOK OF
KNOWLEDGE

Penguin
Random
House

FIRST EDITION 1994

General Editor Sarah Phillips
General Art Editors Ruth Shane, Paul Wilkinson
Subject Editors Francesca Baines, Val Burton,
Deborah Chancellor, Roz Fishel, Hilary Hockman,
Rosemary McCormick, Sarah Miller, Seán O'Connell,
Jean Rustean, Anne de Verteuil
Subject Art Editors Flora Awolaja, Liz Black,
Amanda Carroll, Richard Clemson, Ross George,
Sarah Goodwin, Sara Nunan, Ron Stobbart,
Andrew Walker, Sonia Whillock
Designers Wayne Blades, Alison Greenhalgh,
James Hunter, Marianne Markham, Tuong Nguyen,
Alison Verity, Samantha Webb
Picture Researchers Lorna Ainger,
Caroline Brook, Venetia Bullen, Anna Lord,
Miriam Sharland, Paul Snelgrove
Subject Consultants Dr Michael Benton, Nicholas Booth,
Martyn Bramwell, Roger Bridgman, Eryl Davies,
Liza Dibble, John Farndon, Adrian Gilbert, Alan Harris,
Paul Hillyard, Dr Malcolm MacGarvin, Diana Maine,
Margaret Mulvihill, Dr Fiona Payne, Chris Pellant,
Dr Richard Walker, Shane Winser
Production Manager Ian Paton
Production Assistant Harriet Maxwell
Editorial Director Jonathan Reed
Design Director Ed Day

THIS EDITION 2019

Produced for DK by
Dynamo Limited
Second Floor, Exeter Bank Chambers, 67 High
Street, Exeter EX4 3DT

Project Editor Ben Ffrancon Davies
US Editor Karyn Gerhard
Subject Consultants Peter Chrisp,
Penny Johnson, Susan Pattie, Kristina Routh,
Chris Woodford, John Woodward
Jacket Editor Emma Dawson
Jacket Designer Prarthana Dixit,
Surabhi Wadhwa-Gandhi
DTP Designer Rakesh Kumar
Jackets Editorial Coordinator Priyanka Sharma
Managing Jackets Editor Saloni Singh
Jacket Design Development Manager
Sophia MTT
Producer, Pre-production Robert Dunn
Producer Meskerem Berhane
Managing Editor Lisa Gillespie
Managing Art Editor Owen Peyton Jones
Publisher Andrew Macintyre
Associate Publishing Director Liz Wheeler
Art Director Karen Self
Publishing Director Johnathan Metcalf

This American Edition, 2019
First American Edition, 2002
Published in the United States by DK Publishing
1450 Broadway, 8th Floor, New York, NY 10018

Published in Great Britain by Dorling Kindersley Limited
A catalog record for this book is available from the Library of Congress
ISBN: 978-1-4654-8041-5

DK books are available at special discounts when purchased
in bulk for sales promotions, premiums, fund-raising, or educational use.
For details, contact: DK Publishing Special Markets,
1450 Broadway, 8th Floor, New York, NY 10018
SpecialSales@dk.com
Printed and bound in Malaysia

A WORLD OF IDEAS:
SEE ALL THERE IS TO KNOW

www.dk.com

ACKNOWLEDGMENTS

Photographers: Peter Anderson, Steve Bartholomew, Peter Chadwick, Tina Chambers, Andy Crawford, Colour Company, Geoff Dann, John Downes, Michael Dunning, John Edwards, Lynton Gardiner, Steve Gorton, Colin Keates, Tim Kelly, Gary Kevin, Chris King, Dave King, Cyril Laubscher, Kevin Mallett, Ray Moller, David Murray, Tim Ridley, David Rudkin, Karl Shone, James Stevenson, John Swift, Harry Taylor, Andreas von Einsiedel, Jerry Young. **Illustrators:** Graham Allen, Norman Barber, David Bergen, Roby Braun, Peter Bull, Joanna Cameron, Jim Channell, Bob Corley, Sandra Doyle, David Fathers, Roy Flooks, Tony Gibbons, Mike Gillah, Tony Graham, Peter Griffiths, Terry Hadler, Edwina Hannah, Charlotter Hard, Kaye Hodges, Keith Hume, Ray Hutchins, Aziz Khan, Pavel Kostal, Norman Lacey, Stuart Lafford, Kenneth Lilly, Linden Artists, Steve Lings, Mike Loates, Chris Lyon, Alan Male, Richard Manning, Janos Marffy, Josephine Martin, Annabel Milne, Sean Milne, Patrick Mulray, Richard Orr, Alex Pang, Darren Pattenden, Liz Pepperell, Jane Pickering, Gill Platt, Maurice Pledger, Sebastian Quigley, Christine Robins, Eric Rome, Michelle Ross, Simon Roulstone, Colin Salmon, John Searl, Pete Serjeant, Rob Shone, Clive Spong, Roger Stewart, John Temperton Grose Thurston, Graham Turner, Brian Watson, Phil Weare, Sonia Whillock, John Woodcock, Michael Woods. **Models:** Celia Allen, Roby Braun, Atlas Models, Cheltenham Cutaway Exhibits Ltd, Crystal Palace Park, London, Arril Johnson, Donks Models, Centaur Studios, Norrie Carr Model Agency, Peter Griffiths, John Holmes, Scallywags Model Agency, Truly Scrumptious Child Model Agency.

DK

BIG BOOK OF
KNOWLEDGE

Contents

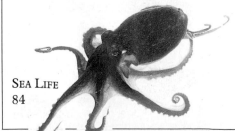

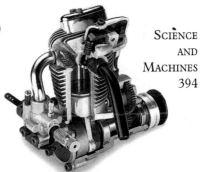

How to Use This Book

It's easy to use the *Big Book of Knowledge*. Start by looking at the contents page. There you will see that the book has four chapters, which are divided into different subject areas. Find a subject or a picture that interests you, and turn to that page. If you can't find what you want on the contents page, look it up in the index at the back. This is an alphabetical list of everything covered in the book. After each entry, there is a list of all the pages on which that topic is mentioned.

See how the index works by looking up "butterflies." Turn to all the pages listed after the entry until you find the main page for Butterflies shown here.

This page uses a picture of that section to tell you about some of the regular features you will find in the *Big Book of Knowledge*.

BUTTERFLIES

Butterflies are perhaps the most beautiful of all insects. It is amazing to think that a fat, leaf-eating caterpillar can become a brightly colored, fluttering creature of the air. The change happens in the butterfly chrysalis. The caterpillar's body is broken down and completely changed. After about four weeks, a fully formed butterfly emerges.

Time to wake up
The butterfly comes out of the chrysalis in three stages. During this time it is very open to attack by hungry birds or spiders.

1. No longer a caterpillar, a beautiful butterfly comes out of the chrysalis with its wings crumpled up.

Monarchs on the move
Most butterflies are born, live, and die in one place. But when winter comes to the eastern and western coasts of North America, thousands of monarchs fly south to the warmth of California and Mexico. When warm weather returns to their first home, they fly north again.

116

Title and Introduction
Each double page deals with a different subject. The title tells you exactly what the subject is, and the introduction gives you some basic information about it.

BUTTERFLIES

Butterflies are perhaps the most beautiful of all insects. It is amazing to think that a fat, leaf-eating caterpillar can become a brightly colored, fluttering creature of the air. The change happens in the butterfly chrysalis. The caterpillar's body is broken down and completely changed. After about four weeks, a fully formed butterfly emerges.

Time to wake up
The butterfly comes out of the chrysalis in three stages. During this time it is very open to attack by hungry birds or spiders.

1. No longer a caterpillar, a beautiful butterfly comes out of the chrysalis with its wings crumpled up.

2. The butterfly must stay still for many hours, as blood is pumped into the wing veins to stretch the wings. Later it holds its wings apart to let them harden.

3. When its wings have hardened, the butterfly is ready to fly off to find its first meal of nectar.

Captions
Most double pages feature one large, exciting picture. All around it, captions point out important details. They will help you to look carefully at the picture and understand it.

Measurements

In most cases, units of measurement are spelled out, but in some places you will come across the following abbreviations.

cm	=	centimeters
m	=	meters
km	=	kilometers
km/h	=	kilometers per hour
l	=	liters

In the background
Some butterflies make a tasty meal for birds. But if they are able to blend in with their background, they may avoid being eaten. The open wings of the Indian leaf butterfly have a striking orange pattern. But when its wings are closed, the butterfly looks exactly like an old, dry leaf.

Stories in a Box

Amazing facts or stories appear in a box. Sometimes boxes suggest experiments to try, or things to do that will help you understand the subject better.

Picture Catalogs

On some pages, you will find a row of small pictures that are similar to the large one. Try to figure out the differences between them.

Brilliant butterflies

Wallace's golden birdwing

Glass swallowtail butterfly

88 butterfly

Cramer's blue morpho butterfly

Happy landings
A clouded yellow butterfly comes in to land on a thistle. Butterfly flight is more controlled than it looks. The insect is able to change course instantly and make sudden landings.

Butterflies feed through a tube called a proboscis. This is coiled up when not in use.

Butterflies have clubbed antennae.

Wings open.

Wings closed, resting on leaf.

In the background
Some butterflies make a tasty meal for birds. But if they are able to blend in with their background, they may avoid being eaten. The open wings of the Indian leaf butterfly have a striking orange pattern. But when its wings are closed, the butterfly looks exactly like an old, dry leaf.

2. The butterfly must stay still for many hours, as blood is pumped into the wing veins to stretch the wings. Later it holds its wings apart to let them harden.

3. When its wings have hardened, the butterfly is ready to fly off to find its first meal of nectar.

Brilliant butterflies

Wallace's golden birdwing

Glass swallowtail butterfly

88 butterfly

Scaly wings
The wings of both butterflies and moths are covered with tiny scales, which overlap like the tiles on a roof. Bright colors can either be used to attract a mate, or to warn predators that the butterfly, or moth, is not good to eat.

Cramer's blue morpho butterfly

117

Close-ups

Occasionally, you will find an image that shows you something in more detail. This picture, for instance, shows you what a butterfly's wing looks like up close!

Scaly wings
The wings of both butterflies and moths are covered with tiny scales, which overlap like the tiles on a roof. Bright colors can either be used to attract a mate, or to warn predators that the butterfly, or moth, is not good to eat.

CHAPTER 1

EARTH AND SPACE

To us, our planet Earth seems enormous, but if we were able to gaze at it across the vastness of space, it would look like a tiny speck. It is one of the eight planets that are constantly hurtling around a star—our sun—along individual elliptical paths called orbits.

Together, the sun and its planets are known as the solar system. This, in turn, is part of a cluster of millions of stars and planets, called a galaxy. Our galaxy, which is shaped like a spiral, is called the Milky Way. It is so huge that a jet would take more than 100 billion years to fly across it. Scientists think that there are at least 200 billion different galaxies in our universe.

Stars are made from layers of burning gas around a dense core. Some planets are also mostly gas, but other planets and moons are rocky, like Earth.

Earth
Space

EARTH

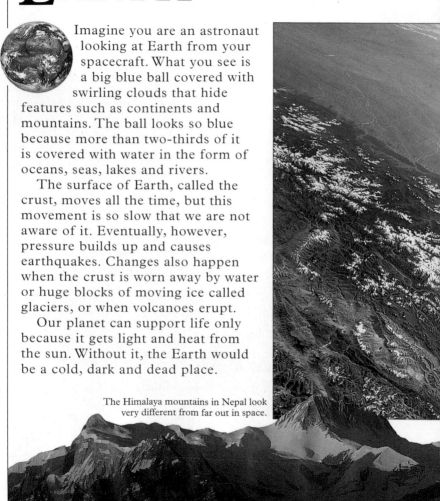

Imagine you are an astronaut looking at Earth from your spacecraft. What you see is a big blue ball covered with swirling clouds that hide features such as continents and mountains. The ball looks so blue because more than two-thirds of it is covered with water in the form of oceans, seas, lakes and rivers.

The surface of Earth, called the crust, moves all the time, but this movement is so slow that we are not aware of it. Eventually, however, pressure builds up and causes earthquakes. Changes also happen when the crust is worn away by water or huge blocks of moving ice called glaciers, or when volcanoes erupt.

Our planet can support life only because it gets light and heat from the sun. Without it, the Earth would be a cold, dark and dead place.

The Himalaya mountains in Nepal look very different from far out in space.

Stalactites form in caves.

Sandstone

Pumice

Green marble

Uluru in Australia is made of sandstone.

Earth photographed from a satellite

EARTH'S CRUST

Just like you, Earth has a very thin skin. It is so thin that if you compare it to the whole Earth, it is thinner than the skin of an apple.

Earth's skin, or crust, is made up of rock, built up in layers over millions of years. The layers look like blankets on a bed, with lots of lumps and bumps in them.

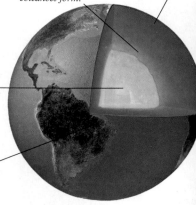

The crust is a thin layer of rock between 3.7 and 43.5 miles (6 and 70 kilometers) thick

The mantle is the layer below the crust. Parts of it are molten where volcanoes form.

The outer core is made of iron and nickel that have melted to form a liquid.

The inner core is a ball of iron and nickel. It is hotter here than at the outer core, but the ball stays solid.

How mountains are made
Many mountains are made when the Earth's crust is pushed up in big folds or forced up or down in blocks. The different shapes made are given different names.

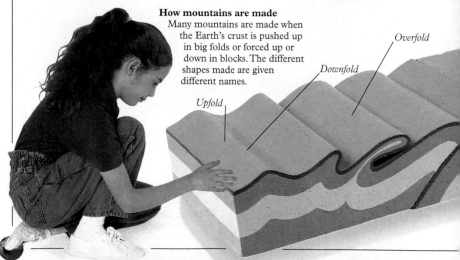

Overfold

Downfold

Upfold

The sea lies on top of the oceanic crust. Some of it is found underneath the edge of the continental crust.

The land is made out of the continental crust. It is thickest where mountains are found.

Under the oceans the crust is as little as 3.7 miles (six kilometers) thick, but under the continents it is up to 43.5 miles (70 kilometers) thick.

The mantle

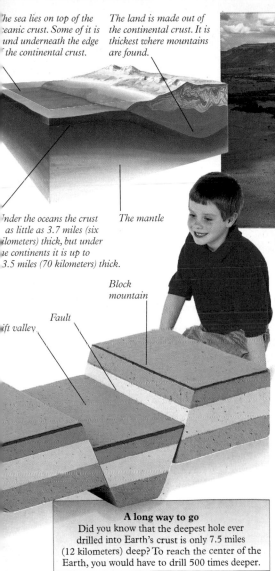

Block mountain

Fault

Rift valley

A long way to go
Did you know that the deepest hole ever drilled into Earth's crust is only 7.5 miles (12 kilometers) deep? To reach the center of the Earth, you would have to drill 500 times deeper.

Going down
This is a rift valley. It was made when a block of land sank down between two long breaks, called faults, in the Earth's crust.

Going up
Here the land has been pushed into giant folds by movements in the Earth's crust. You can see how the crust is made up of lots and lots of layers of rock.

MOVING PLATES

The Earth's surface is not one unbroken piece. It is made up of many pieces that fit together like a giant jigsaw puzzle. These pieces, called plates, move as the mantle slowly moves beneath them. The movement of the plates can cause spectacular effects—earthquakes split the crust, volcanoes form, new land is made, and huge mountain ranges are pushed skyward.

All scrunched up
Sometimes, two plates push against each other and then crumple the land to make huge mountain ranges.

Going down
Sometimes, one plate slides under another. It is pushed down into the mantle and melts.

Doing the splits
Sometimes, two plates split apart and lava bubbles up to fill the gap. It hardens and makes new land.

Slip sliding away
Sometimes, two plates slip past each other. This is another kind of movement that causes earthquakes.

On the move
The plates are never still, they are always moving. In one year they can move about 1 inch (2.5 centimeters), about as much as your fingernails grow in the same amount of time.

The red dots show you the places where earthquakes happen.

Continent

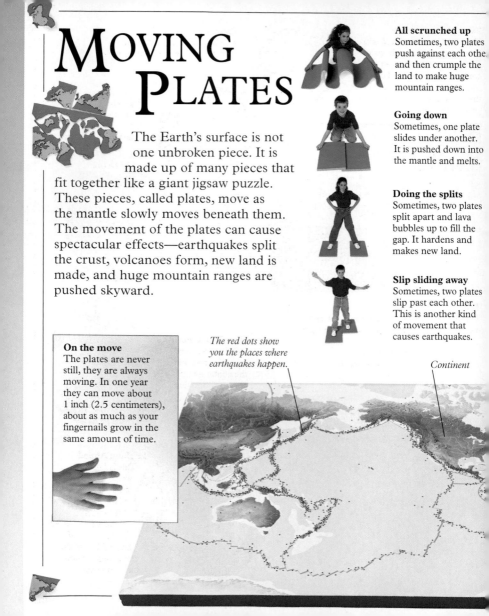

Past, present, future
Have you ever wondered what Earth looked like in the past? These pictures show you how the continents have moved over the last 300 million years, and how the world may look 50 million years from now.

300 MILLION YEARS AGO

Changing places
The land is coming together to make one gigantic continent.

250 MILLION YEARS AGO

PANGAEA

All together
The supercontinent has come together. It is called Pangaea.

200 MILLION YEARS AGO

LAURASIA

GONDWANALAND

Worlds apart
The land is drifting apart again. Pangaea is splitting into two, Laurasia and Gondwanaland.

The restless Earth
This spot in Iceland is where two plates are moving apart, forming new land in the gap.

These lines show where two plates meet.

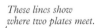

TODAY

Familiar ground
Today, the world looks like this, but the continents are still moving.

50 MILLION YEARS' TIME

Looking Ahead
This is how the world may look in 50 million years. Can you spot how the land has changed its shape? To start you off, find Africa on the globe and see how it has joined up with Europe.

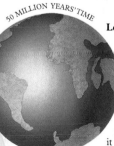

15

VOLCANOES

When you shake up a can of soda pop and open it, the contents shoot out with a great whoosh! Some volcanoes act a bit like this. With tremendous force, molten (melted) rock bursts through weak parts in the Earth's crust and is hurled high into the sky. This molten rock is called magma when still inside the Earth, and lava after it has erupted.

Volcanoes can be quiet and not erupt for a long time.

Hot springs are often found near volcanoes.

Nature's fireworks
This volcano is putting on its own spectacular fireworks display. The explosions of red-hot lava and ash from the crater look like gigantic "Roman Candles."

The spotter's guide to volcano shapes

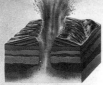

Spreading out
The lava from shallow shield volcanoes is runny, so it spreads out in a thin sheet.

Short and plump
Cinder cones are a bit bigger. They are made of ash, which is lava that has turned to dust.

Going up
Composite volcanoes have pointed cones. Their lava is thick and sticky.

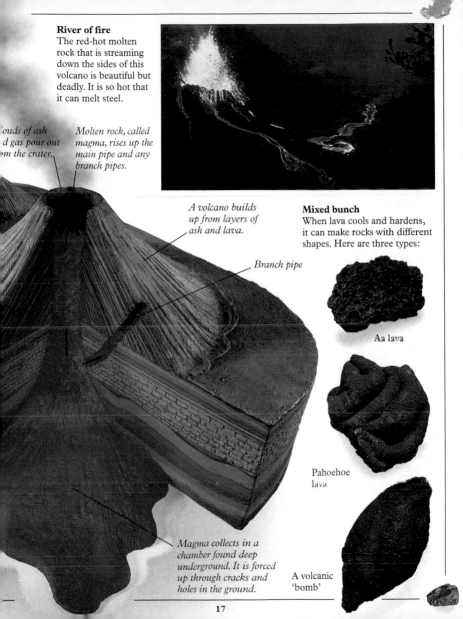

River of fire
The red-hot molten rock that is streaming down the sides of this volcano is beautiful but deadly. It is so hot that it can melt steel.

louds of ash
d gas pour out
m the crater.

Molten rock, called magma, rises up the main pipe and any branch pipes.

A volcano builds up from layers of ash and lava.

Branch pipe

Mixed bunch
When lava cools and hardens, it can make rocks with different shapes. Here are three types:

Aa lava

Pahoehoe lava

A volcanic 'bomb'

Magma collects in a chamber found deep underground. It is forced up through cracks and holes in the ground.

EARTHQUAKES

Our planet is a restless place. Several hundred times a day, the ground suddenly rumbles and trembles. Most of the movements are so slight that they are not felt. Others bring disaster. Big cracks appear in the land, streets buckle, and buildings crumble. Whole towns and cities can be destroyed. Then everything settles down but is totally changed. Earth has shaken and an earthquake has happened.

Fires are started by broken gas pipes and broken electrical cables.

Telephone lines brought down

Cars are smashed and they settle at crazy angles.

Unsafe ground
This is the San Andreas Fault in California. Earthquakes regularly happen here.

Terror from the sea
Earthquakes under the sea can cause long, giant, destructive waves called tsunamis.

On this side of the fault the land has moved toward you.

An earthquake occurs along a fault in the seabed.

Tsunamis can travel many miles across the ocean.

18

Why earthquakes happen

You may think that your feet are firmly on the ground, but Earth's crust is moving all the time. It is made of moving parts called plates. When the plates slide past or into each other, the rocks jolt and send out shock waves.

Shaken up

The Mercalli Scale measures how much the surface of the Earth shakes during an earthquake. There are 12 intensities, or grades. At intensity 1, the effects are not felt, but by intensity 12, the shock waves can be seen and there is total destruction.

What to do in an earthquake

Indoors, lie down under a bed or heavy table, or stand in a doorway or a corner of a room. After a minute, when the tremors will usually have finished, go outside, away from buildings, to a wide-open space.

Earthquake words

The place within the Earth where an earthquake starts is called the focus. The earthquake is usually strongest at the epicenter. This is the point on the Earth's surface directly above the focus. The study of earthquakes and the shock waves they send out is called seismology.

Destructive force

A tsunami piles up and gets very tall before it crashes onto the shore. It is so powerful that it can smash harbors and towns and sweep ships inland.

Fault line

On this side of the fault the land has moved away from you.

A tsunami can be more than 98 feet (30 meters) high and can travel as fast as a jet.

ROCKS

Movements in the Earth's crust are slowly changing the rocks that make up the surface of our planet. Mountains are pushed up and weathered away, and the fragments moved and made into other rocks. These rocks may be dragged down into the mantle and melted by its fierce heat. When a volcano erupts, the melted rock is thrown to the surface as lava, which cools and hardens as rock. This is broken down by weathering, and so the cycle starts again.

Limestone

Conglomerate

Sedimentary rocks
These are made from b of rock and plant and animal remains. They are broken into fine pieces and carried by rivers into the sea. They pile up in layers and press together to make solid rock.
The Painted Desert, in Arizona, is made of sedimentary rocks.

Red sandstone

In the beginning
Rocks belong to three basic types. Igneous rocks are made from magma or lava. The word igneous means "fiery." Sedimentary rocks are made in layers from broken rocks. Metamorphic rocks can start off as any type. They are changed by heat and weight and the word metamorphic means "changed."

In time, material moved by rivers and piled up in the sea will become sedimentary rocks.

Rock fragments called sediments are carried by rivers, glaciers, the wind, and the sea.

Recently formed sedimentary rocks

Igneous rocks

These are made from magma or lava. It cools and hardens inside the Earth's crust or on the surface when it erupts from a volcano. Sugarloaf Mountain in Brazil was once igneous rock under the crust. The rocks above and around it have been worn away.

Metamorphic rocks

These are igneous or sedimentary rocks that are changed by underground heat, underground weight, or both. This marble was once limestone, a sedimentary rock. It was changed into marble by intense heat.

Marble

Granite

Obsidian

Slate

Surface rocks are broken down by the weather and by the scraping effect of tiny pieces of rock carried in the wind or in the ice of glaciers.

Glacier

Some rocks are thrust up as mountain ranges when the crust moves and makes giant folds.

Volcano

Magma that erupts from a volcano becomes lava, and forms extrusive igneous rock.

Molten rock that cools and hardens inside the Earth is called intrusive igneous rock.

Metamorphic rocks

Folded rocks

Magma

CAVES

Caves are hollows beneath the surface of the Earth. The biggest ones are all found in rock called limestone and some are huge. The world's biggest cave, in Sarawak, is so large that you could fit 800 tennis courts in it. Yet these caves began simply as cracks or holes in the rock that, over thousands of years, were made bigger by rainwater trickling into them and dissolving the surrounding rock.

Water dripping from the ceiling of a cave leaves behind a mineral called calcite. Very slowly, this grows downward in an icicle shape that is called a stalactite.

The stream disappears underground into a pothole

This pothole, or tunnel, leads straight down through the rock. It was made by a stream wearing away the rock.

Limestone is a very common rock. It is made from the skeletons and shells of tiny sea creatures that died millions of years ago.

Drip . . .
The rainwater that seeps into the ground is very slightly acidic and begins to dissolve the limestone.

Drip . . .
The rainwater continues to dissolve the rock. It widens the cracks into pits, passages and caves

Drip
Over thousands of years, the passages and caves may join up to make a huge underground system.

nnel of lava
ves are found in rocks other than limestone. This
e is made of lava and is inside a volcano in Hawaii.

racks in the rock are
dened when rainwater
eps along them.

Limestone pavements are
made when the rock
dissolves along joint lines.

Caving in
Sometimes a cave turns into a gorge.
This happens when the roof falls in to
reveal underground caverns and, far
below, the river that carved them.

Cliff

Gallery

Cave
mouth

Stream

Going up
Where water drips onto
the cave floor, columns of
calcite, called stalagmites,
grow upward.

OCEANS

With oceans and seas making up 71 percent of the Earth's surface, more than two-thirds of our planet is covered with water. Beneath the waves lies a fascinating landscape. Much of the ocean floor is a vast plain, but there are also trenches, cliffs, and mountains, all larger than any found on dry land.

Sun

Earth

Moon

Ebbing and flowing
Tides are made by the sun and moon pulling on the oceans. When the sun, Earth, and moon are in a line, there are large spring tides.

Ocean currents
These show the directions in which water flows.

Cold currents

Warm currents

Underwater canyons are cut by currents flowing over the seabed like rivers.

These underwater islands are called guyots.

Trenches can be deeper than the highest mountains on land.

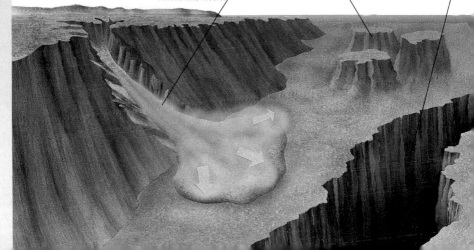

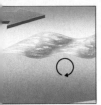

...ing . . .
...he water inside a
...ve moves around and
...ound in a circle. It is
...e wind that drives the
...ve forward.

Going . . .
Near the shore, the
circular shape of the
wave is changed and
it becomes squashed.

Gone
The top of the wave
becomes unstable.
When it hits the beach,
it topples and spills over.

Surface

Lighted zone,
up to 660 feet
(200 meters)

Dark zone, up
to 13,000 feet
(4,000 meters)

Deepest zone,
a trench of
36,200 feet
(11,034 meters)

The dark depths
Even in clear water,
sunlight cannot reach
very far. The oceans
become darker and
darker the farther down
you go, until everything
turns inky black.

Ocean currents
The direction in which currents
move depends on winds and the
Earth's spin. Winds blow the top
of the oceans forward, but the
Earth's spin makes the water
below go in a spiral.

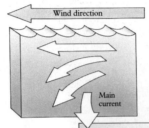

Wind direction

Main
current

*his island is a volcano
...at has erupted from
...e ocean floor.*

*A long, wide
ocean ridge*

*Water, heated by
...ot rocks, shoots
...ack into the sea.*

*...olten rock rises
...o, cools, and
...rms new
...abed.*

Frozen worlds
In Antarctica and the
Arctic, the oceans freeze.
Icebergs break away from
glaciers flowing into the
water. Only a tiny part of
an iceberg is seen above
the surface of the ocean.

COASTLINES

Have you ever built a sand castle and then watched the sea come in, knock it down, and flatten it? This is what happens to the coastline, the place where the land and the sea meet. The coastline changes all the time because, every few seconds of every day, waves hit the land and either wear it away or build it up into different shapes.

Some waves carry sand and pebbles from one part of the coast and leave them at another. This makes a new beach.

Headland

Going, going, gone
When caves made on both sides of a headland meet, an arch is formed. If the top of the arch falls down, a pillar of rock, called a stack, is left.

An arch

A cave is made when seawater gets into cracks and holes in a cliff and makes them bigger.

A stack

Some beaches are made in bays between headlands where the water is shallow and the waves are weak.

Pounding away
Waves pound the coastline like a giant hammer until huge chunks of rock are broken off. The chunks are then carried away by the sea and flung against the coastline somewhere else.

From rocks to sand
Waves roll rocks and boulders backward and forward on the shore. The boulders break into pebbles and then into tiny grains of sand. This change takes hundreds or thousands of years.

Shifting sands
Dunes are made of sand blown into low hills by the wind.

An estuary is the place where a river flows into the sea.

Sea cliffs are one of the best places to see the different layers of rock.

Mud flats and marshes

Waves can build sand, mud, and pebbles into a long strip of new land. It is called a spit.

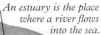

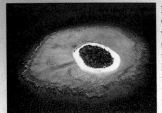

Living rock
Coral is found in warm, sunny, shallow seas. It is made by tiny sea creatures that look like flowers. Over thousands of years, their skeletons build up into huge coral reefs and islands.

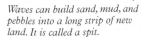

GLACIERS

Mountains

Glaciers begin huge snowfields

A glacier is like a huge river of ice that starts its life as a tiny snowflake. As more and more snow falls and builds up, in time it gets squashed under its own weight and turns to ice. A glacier moves very slowly downhill. Because it is very heavy, it can push rock along like a bulldozer. It can wear away the sides of mountains, smooth off the jagged bits from rocks, and move giant boulders over dozens of miles.

The snow collects in hollows and turns to ice under its own weight.

Glaciers usually move downhill very slowly, no more than a few inches each day.

The ice begins to move and rub away the sides and bottom of the hollow. Little by little, it changes the shape of the land and makes it into a U-shaped valley.

Close-up view
The pilot in this plane is watching a wall of ice break away from a glacier and begin to crash into the water below.

Ice power
When the water in this bottle freezes and turns to ice, it takes up more room and breaks the bottle. When the water that makes up the ice of a glacier freezes, it takes up more room and pushes away the rock.

Rubble is carried along by the glacier.

Shaping the land
When you see a valley like this, you can tell from its U shape that it was once filled with the ice of a glacier.

*elted ice
ws as streams
d rivers beneath
ost glaciers.*

*umps in the rock
n be smoothed
t by the ice
oving downhill.*

Out of place
This giant boulder of hard rock was moved by a glacier and left on soft limestone. Then, most of the limestone was weathered away, leaving a small block under the boulder.

Where a glacier flows into water, chunks of ice break off and float away.

*cks carried along by
e glacier pile up when the
cier starts to melt and
ps pushing them.*

The lower end of the glacier is called the "snout."

When the glacier melts, it makes new rivers.

RIVERS

Rivers are very powerful, so powerful that the force of the moving water is able to change the shape of the land. As they flow through mountains and over plains, rivers carry away huge amounts of rock, sand, and mud. They then dump it somewhere else, usually on riverbanks or in the sea, to make new land.

A river usually begins in mountains or hills. Its water comes from rain or melted snow.

Where the rock i[s] hard, the river makes rapids or waterfalls.

Glacier

Over the top
When a river tumbles over the edge of a steep cliff or over a hard, rocky ledge, it is called a waterfall. This one is in Brazil, South America.

As the river flows quickly down steep slopes, it wears away the rock to make a V-shaped valley.

Oxbow lake

Sand, mud, and gravel is left by the water as sediment.

River deep
A gorge is a deep, narrow valley carved by a river. The Colorado River has made the largest gorge in the world—the Grand Canyon. It is 1 mile (1.6 km) deep and 227 miles (446 km) long.

River's end
This swampy land is part of the Yukon Delta in Alaska.

A wide bend or meander goes across flat country.

As it reaches the sea, the river divides into small streams, leaving a mass of sand, mud, and rock fragments, called a delta.

Round the bend
When a river reaches flat land, it slows down and begins to flow in large loops. It leaves behind sand, gravel, and mud, called deposits. This changes the river's shape and course.

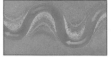

The river leaves deposits on the inside bend and eats away the outer bend.

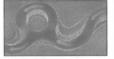

The deposits change the shape of the bend. In time, the neck of the bend narrows and the ends of the neck join up.

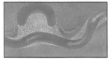

The river leaves behind a loop. It is called an oxbow lake because of its shape.

Record rivers
The Nile, in Africa, is the longest river in the world. It is 4,130 miles (6,650 km) long. The largest delta covers 40,500 square miles (105,000 sq km). It is made by the Ganges and Brahmaputra rivers, in Bangladesh and India.

DESERTS

Did you know that deserts come in many different forms? They can be a sea of rolling sand, a huge area of flat and stony ground, or mountainous areas of shattered rock. There are hot deserts and cold deserts. So what do these very different areas have in common?

The answer is that they are all very dry and they all get less than 10 inches (25 cm) of rain each year. This rain may not fall regularly. Instead, it may all come in a single day and cause a dramatic flash flood.

Sea of sand
A desert may be hard to live in, but it can be stunning to look at. These dunes are in Saudi Arabia.

Tail dunes

Wind

Crescent dunes

Linear dunes

Star dunes

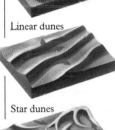

Wind power
Wind blows the sand into hills which are called dunes. These have different shapes and names.

A cuesta is a step of hard rock.

A large, steep-sided area with a flat top is called a mesa.

Natural rock arch

A butte is a small, flat-topped hill.

Dunes

Hard rock that has been worn into a pinnacle is called a chimney or pipe rock.

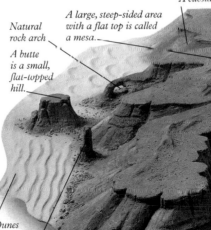

On the move

Imagine the hairdryer is the wind. It blows the sand up the gentle slope of the dune. When the sand gets to the top, it tumbles down the steep slope. As more and more sand is moved from one slope to another, the whole dune moves forward.

...eavy rain makes ...sh floods. These rush ...er the land, loaded with ...nd and stones, and cut ...ep channels in the surface ... the desert.

Broken rocks slide downhill and collect in gullies.

Water power

The tremendous power of water has made this deep ravine near an oasis in Tunisia.

Where the rock is hard, ridges will stand out in the landscape.

Shaping the land

Wind-borne sand blows against the rocks and wears them into beautiful and surprising shapes.

Steep slopes of broken rock

Outwash fan

Hot and cold

This is one of the Devil's Marbles in the Northern Territory, Australia. The rock's outer layers have started to peel off because of the desert's very hot and very cold temperatures.

SPACE

The universe is made up of galaxies, stars, planets, moons, and other bodies scattered throughout space. A galaxy is a group of billions of stars: our galaxy, which is shaped like a spiral, is called the Milky Way.

On a clear night, it is possible to see thousands of stars, which appear as twinkling points of light. The Earth's moon is usually clear, and sometimes you can also see five of the planets: Mercury, Venus, Mars, Jupiter, and Saturn. These do not twinkle, but look like small steady discs of light. Earth is the third planet from the sun, which is about 93 million miles (150 million kilometers) away from us. People have always been curious about the things they could see in the sky. It is only quite recently, though, that science has developed the advanced technology needed to send people into space.

Space shuttle

Milky Way

SATUR

NEPTUNE

URANUS

34

SUN

MERCURY

VENUS

EARTH

MARS

Asteroid belt

JUPITER

Rings

35

ROCKETS

Rockets were invented in China a long time ago. They looked a bit like arrows and worked by burning gunpowder, which burns up very quickly, so the rockets did not travel very far. Since then, people have tried many ways of sending rockets up into space. Modern rockets usually use two liquid fuels. They mix together and burn. Then the hot gas shoots out of the tail, pushing the rocket up and away.

V-2 Rocket 1945   Gemini Titan 1964

The Fly!
In 1931 Johannes Winkler launched his HW-1 rocket. It went 6.5 feet (two meters) into the air, turned over, and fell back to the ground. A month later he tried again and this time it climbed to 300 feet (90 meters) and landed 650 feet (200 meters) away.

3, 2, 1, fire!
A hundred years ago, soldiers used rockets like this. They were called Congreve rockets.

Saturn power
Saturn V is one of the biggest rockets ever built. It is as tall as a 30-story building! It was used in the Apollo program, which carried the first American astronauts to the moon.

Fuel tank

See it go!
If you blow up a balloon and let it go without tying a knot in the neck, the air will rush out very quickly. When the air goes out one way, it pushes the balloon the other way—just like a rocket!

The stabilizing fins keep the rocket on course.

Five rocket engines

Up, up . . .
How far can you throw a ball? About 50 or 60 feet? It doesn't go on forever because the Earth's gravity pulls it back down again.

Quest for power
As rockets have become more powerful their shapes have changed. The latest ones carry shuttles into space.

Soyuz
1967

Space Shuttle
1981

Rocket engine

Launch Escape System

Service Module

Command Module

Lunar Module

SATURN V

Five rocket engines

Overpowering
See just how enormous Saturn V's engines are compared to these people!

. . . and away
To escape from Earth by rocket you have to travel at 25,000 miles (40,000 kilometers) per hour—more than 40 times faster than a jet.

Safe landing
The Falcon 9 rocket can leave Earth and soar into outer space before returning safely to Earth afterward and doing it all over again.

MOON MISSION

The moon is the Earth's nearest neighbor in space, but it still takes three days to get there by rocket. It would take 200 days by car! When astronauts first went to the moon no one could be sure it would be safe to land there. But now American astronauts have been to the moon on Apollo missions six times and they all returned safely to Earth. The first moon trip was in 1969 and the last in 1972.

The second stage drops off when its five engines run out of fuel.

The Command and Service Modules turn, join onto the Lunar Module, and pull it out of the third stage.

Astronauts who are going to the moon crawl through a tunnel from the Command Module to the Lunar Module.

Second stage

We have liftoff!
The first stage of the Saturn V rocket has five huge engines. When these run out of fuel they fall back to Earth. Then the second stage takes over.

This air recycling unit keeps the air fresh in the cabin.

Lunar Module

CSM = Command and Service Modules
LM = Lunar Module
CM = Command Module

CSM docks with LM

CSM in orbit

LM back to CSM

Moon

LM descends to moon

CSM back to Earth

liftoff

Earth

splashdown

CM splashes down

Moon trail
The Apollo missions to the moon followed a path in the shape of a figure eight.

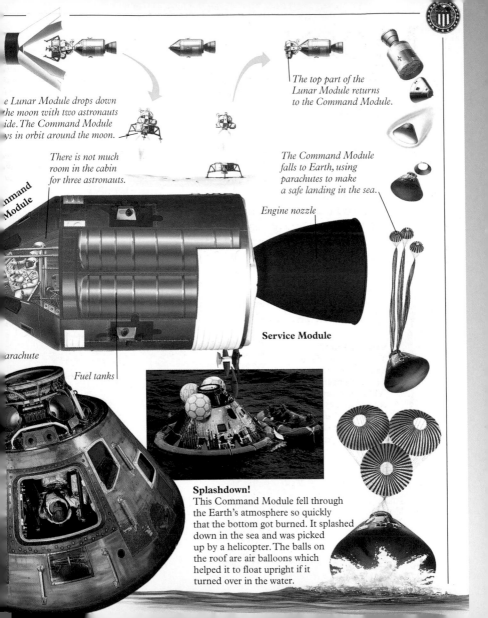

The Lunar Module drops down the moon with two astronauts ide. The Command Module ys in orbit around the moon.

The top part of the Lunar Module returns to the Command Module.

There is not much room in the cabin for three astronauts.

ommand Module

The Command Module falls to Earth, using parachutes to make a safe landing in the sea.

Engine nozzle

Service Module

arachute

Fuel tanks

Splashdown!
This Command Module fell through the Earth's atmosphere so quickly that the bottom got burned. It splashed down in the sea and was picked up by a helicopter. The balls on the roof are air balloons which helped it to float upright if it turned over in the water.

LUNAR LANDING

Mission patch A lunar landing is a moon landing. If you went to the moon you would find nothing living at all, no air, and no water.

If you stayed for a lunar "day"—about 28 Earth days—you would have two weeks of baking sun followed by two weeks of freezing night. The first men on the moon went down in the Lunar Module, named "Eagle."

The Apollo 11 crew
Neil Armstrong and Edw "Buzz" Aldrin were the first men to walk on the moon. Michael Collins stayed in orbit in the Commmand Module.

Hanging out the laundry?
No, just setting up a panel to collect dust! The moon is covered in dusty soil and scattered rocks.

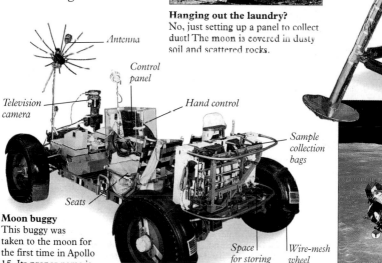

Antenna

Control panel

Television camera

Hand control

Sample collection bags

Seats

Moon buggy
This buggy was taken to the moon for the first time in Apollo 15. Its proper name is the lunar roving vehicle.

Space for storing equipment

Wire-mesh wheel

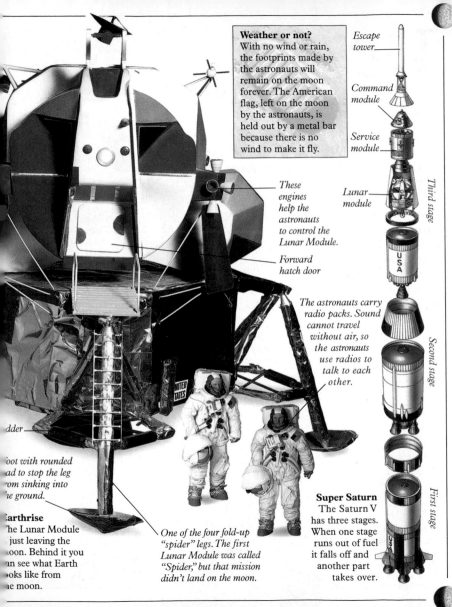

Weather or not?
With no wind or rain, the footprints made by the astronauts will remain on the moon forever. The American flag, left on the moon by the astronauts, is held out by a metal bar because there is no wind to make it fly.

These engines help the astronauts to control the Lunar Module.

Forward hatch door

The astronauts carry radio packs. Sound cannot travel without air, so the astronauts use radios to talk to each other.

dder

oot with rounded
ad to stop the leg
om sinking into
ie ground.

:arthrise
he Lunar Module
 just leaving the
.oon. Behind it you
an see what Earth
ooks like from
ie moon.

One of the four fold-up "spider" legs. The first Lunar Module was called "Spider," but that mission didn't land on the moon.

Escape tower

Command module

Service module

Lunar module

Third stage

USA

Second stage

First stage

Super Saturn
The Saturn V has three stages. When one stage runs out of fuel it falls off and another part takes over.

MERCURY AND VENUS

Between the Earth and the sun are two planets called Mercury and Venus. They are very hot because they are the sun's nearest neighbors. Venus is the brightest object in the night sky. Mercury is the smallest planet in the solar system. Photographs from space probes tell us more about these planets.

Crust

Iron core

Magellan

Hard center
If you could slice Mercury like a peach, you would find it had a core made of iron.

Mariner 10

Antenna

Hello, goodbye!
Mariner 10, intended to explore Mercury and Venus, was the first probe to visit two planets in a row. It worked for 17 months before breaking down. Launched in 1973, it is now in orbit around the sun.

The solar detector made sure that the solar panels were always facing the sun.

Solar pan

Television cameras sent pictures back to Earth.

Dish antenna

Star detector

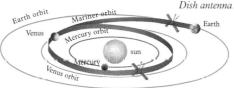

The Journey of Mariner 10

Happy new year
Mercury travels fast through space and is the closest planet to the sun. The Earth orbits the sun every 365 days— one Earth year. Mercury's year is 88 days.

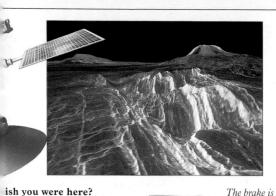

The space probe was in a capsule on the Venera spacecraft.

Venera 9 Venus landing

The capsule fell through the atmosphere of Venus.

The heat shield covers separated and fell off.

The brake is shaped like a disk to help slow down the space probe.

ish you were here?
he Magellan probe used
dar cameras to take pictures
rough the thick fog around
nus. Computers made this
D image of the volcanoes.

nus Venera
veral Russian missions
nt to Venus between
61 and 1984 in
program called Venera.
e spacecraft sent pictures
ck to Earth. This is
e part of Venera 9
at went down to
nus by parachute.

Instrument container

The probe was slowed down by a small parachute.

The landing ring helped to make the landing soft.

VENUS

Hot orange
Venus has a dense
atmosphere that traps heat
from the sun. It is the
hottest planet of all—so
hot it could melt lead!
It has a bright orange
sky with flashes of
lightning. Earth
spins around once
every 24 hours, but
Venus spins very slowly
—once every 244 days!

Three larger parachutes were used for the final stage.

After a safe landing, the television cameras and instruments were switched on.

THE RED PLANET

Mars is called the Red Planet because its soil and rocks are red. Light winds blow dust around, which makes the sky look pink. People once thought there was life on Mars, but nothing living has been found so far.

The Viking spacecraft were sent to Mars to find out what it is like. Two missions, Viking 1 and Viking 2, made the journey. Perhaps one day people may go to live on Mars because it is the planet most like our own.

The Viking lander is folded into a capsule on the spacecraft.

Viking spacecraft

It leaves the orbiter and begins its journey down to Mars.

The television camera takes a series of pictures as it moves around.

It moves so fast that it gets very hot.

A parachute is used to slow it down, and then the heat shield drops off.

This remote control arm is used to collect samples of Mars soil.

Tight fit
The Viking lander fits into a capsule on the spacecraft. With its legs folded up, it looks a bit like a tortoise inside its shell.

The legs unfold, and rockets are used as brakes for a soft landing.

The Viking lander

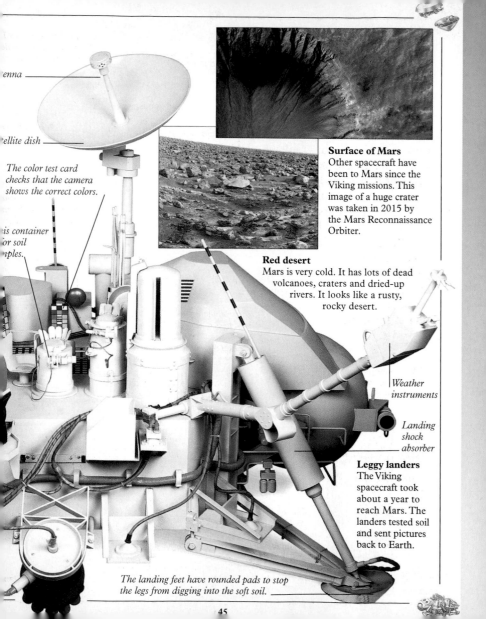

enna

ellite dish

The color test card checks that the camera shows the correct colors.

is container or soil ples.

Surface of Mars
Other spacecraft have been to Mars since the Viking missions. This image of a huge crater was taken in 2015 by the Mars Reconnaissance Orbiter.

Red desert
Mars is very cold. It has lots of dead volcanoes, craters and dried-up rivers. It looks like a rusty, rocky desert.

Weather instruments

Landing shock absorber

Leggy landers
The Viking spacecraft took about a year to reach Mars. The landers tested soil and sent pictures back to Earth.

The landing feet have rounded pads to stop the legs from digging into the soft soil.

JUPITER AND SATURN

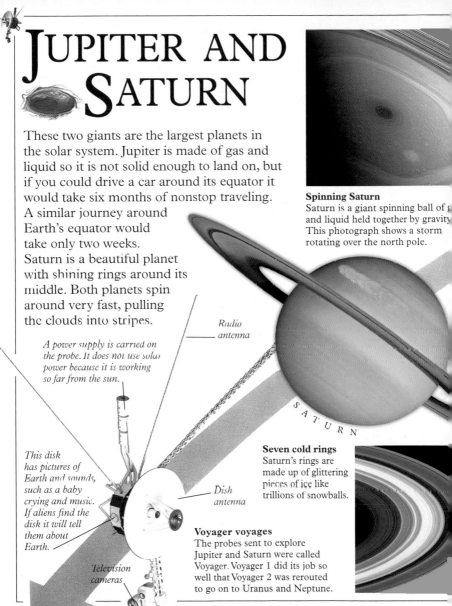

These two giants are the largest planets in the solar system. Jupiter is made of gas and liquid so it is not solid enough to land on, but if you could drive a car around its equator it would take six months of nonstop traveling. A similar journey around Earth's equator would take only two weeks. Saturn is a beautiful planet with shining rings around its middle. Both planets spin around very fast, pulling the clouds into stripes.

A power supply is carried on the probe. It does not use solar power because it is working so far from the sun.

Radio antenna

This disk has pictures of Earth and sounds, such as a baby crying and music. If aliens find the disk it will tell them about Earth.

Dish antenna

Television cameras

Spinning Saturn
Saturn is a giant spinning ball of g and liquid held together by gravity. This photograph shows a storm rotating over the north pole.

Seven cold rings
Saturn's rings are made up of glittering pieces of ice like trillions of snowballs.

Voyager voyages
The probes sent to explore Jupiter and Saturn were called Voyager. Voyager 1 did its job so well that Voyager 2 was rerouted to go on to Uranus and Neptune.

Pioneer picture
The program for sending unmanned spacecraft to Jupiter was called Pioneer. Pioneer 10 succeeded, so 11 went on to Saturn. Both sent back lots of pictures.

Power supply

Asteroid and meteor detector

Pioneer

Dish antenna

Sun sensor

Mega moons
Jupiter has 79 moons circling around it. The largest is called Ganymede. It is bigger than Mercury.

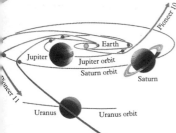

Pioneer 10

Earth

Jupiter

Jupiter orbit

Saturn orbit

Saturn

Pioneer 11

Uranus

Uranus orbit

Voyager 2

ne-way ticket
he journeys of Pioneer 10 and 11 and of Voyager 1 and 2 passed several of the planets. These spacecraft are now heading for the stars.

Neptune

J U P I T E R

Red storm
Jupiter, like Saturn, has a small, rocky core surrounded by liquid. It has icy clouds and a giant red spot which is the center of a huge storm.

Swirling winds blow Jupiter's clouds into a hurricanelike storm.

THE OUTER PLANETS

URANUS

Uranus and Neptune are the farthest planets from the sun so they are called the outer planets. They are very cold. Uranus was the first planet to be discovered using a telescope because you cannot see it from Earth just with your eyes. Pluto orbits outside Neptune and used to be classed as the ninth planet of the solar system until 2006, when it was reclassified as a dwarf planet. There are many other dwarf planets in the solar system, including Cerea, Eris, Haumea, and Makemake.

The rings of Uranus are made of rocks. The widest ring is 62 miles (100 kilometers) across

Outer solar syst

Ellipses
The planets move around the sun in squashed circles called ellipses. This girl is drawing ellipses.

Order of orbits
The word planet means wanderer. The planets travel around the sun in paths, called orbits. The ones nearer the sun have shorter orbits than the ones farther away. One way of remembering the order of the planets in the solar system is to remember the sentence "My Very Educated Mother Just Served Us Noodles."

This diagram shows the orbits of the planets and their places in the solar system. It does not show their sizes.

NEPTUNE

Blue Neptune
The Voyager 2 spacecraft took photographs of Neptune's clouds and its storm, called the Great Dark Spot.

Inner solar system

PLUTO

Cold dwarf!
The dwarf planet Pluto is smaller than our moon. At night it is 10 times colder than a freezer!

Light from the sun takes three minutes to reach Mercury, eight minutes to reach Earth, but more than four hours to reach Neptune!

The sun
Orbit of Mercury
Orbit of Venus
Orbit of Earth
Orbit of Mars

Pluto is sometimes nearer to the sun than Neptune, but three other dwarf planets are always farther away.

Orbit of Jupiter
Orbit of Saturn
Orbit of Uranus
Orbit of Neptune

SKY WANDERERS

Between Mars and Jupiter there is a belt of rocks in orbit called the asteroid belt. The chunks of rock are called asteroids. Sometimes these pieces crash into each other and pieces fall down toward Earth.

Also in orbit around the sun are lumps of rock and ice, called comets. When comets get near the sun they shine like 'hairy stars' which is what people used to call them long ago. The most famous comet is Halley's Comet, named after the man who first studied it.

Path of Halley Comet

Wind from sun blows the d and gas around Halle Comet into an enormous t Comets' tails alwo point away fr the sun and c be millions miles lo

Solar system

Halley's comet

Earth comets
Because they are made of rock and ice, comets are often called "dirty snowballs." Make your own comet next time it snows!

The comet's center is made of ice. As it gets near the sun some of the ice melts.

A belt you cannot wear
There are thousands of asteroids in the asteroid belt. Some are tiny specks of dust, and others are nearly 620 miles (1,000 kilometers) across.

Regular visitor
We see Halley's Comet from Earth once every 76 years because it takes that long to orbit the sun. It was shown on a picture, called the Bayeux Tapestry, over 900 years ago!

Comet head
This is a photograph of the head of Halley's Comet. Computer colo show the bright center and the layers round it

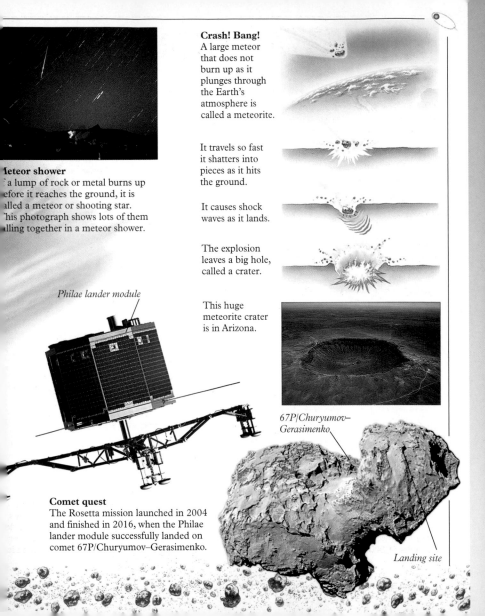

Crash! Bang!
A large meteor that does not burn up as it plunges through the Earth's atmosphere is called a meteorite.

It travels so fast it shatters into pieces as it hits the ground.

It causes shock waves as it lands.

The explosion leaves a big hole, called a crater.

This huge meteorite crater is in Arizona.

Meteor shower
If a lump of rock or metal burns up before it reaches the ground, it is called a meteor or shooting star. This photograph shows lots of them falling together in a meteor shower.

Philae lander module

67P/Churyumov–Gerasimenko

Landing site

Comet quest
The Rosetta mission launched in 2004 and finished in 2016, when the Philae lander module successfully landed on comet 67P/Churyumov–Gerasimenko.

SKY WATCHING

If you look up at the sky on a clear night you can see hundreds of stars and, sometimes, the moon. But if you use binoculars or a telescope you can see even more—for example, the planets and the craters on the moon.

When astronomers study the universe they use huge radio telescopes, some with dishes, to help them to see far, far away, and to gather information from space. The Hubble Space Telescope is the largest telescope to be put into space. It can take clear pictures of stars and galaxies because it orbits 340 miles (547 kilometers) above the Earth's atmosphere.

Clearly Venus
This photograph of Venus was taken by the Pioneer Venus Orbiter. It used radar to get a clear picture through the thick clouds around Venus. The signals were sent back to Earth to a radio telescope where this picture was produced.

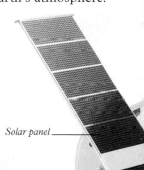

Solar panel

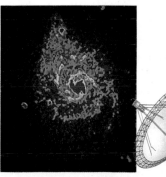

Whirligig
This radio map of the Whirlpool galaxy was taken by a radio telescope. The added colors show the spiral arms of the galaxy.

Radio telescope

ar belt
his photograph shows part
the constellation of Orion
also called "The Hunter."

Head in the stars
A nebula is a cloud of
dust and gas lit from
inside by newly born
stars. This picture
of the Horsehead
nebula was taken
by the Hubble
Space Telescope.

Flap door —

Small mirror

Star cluster
This photograph
was taken by the
Hubble Space
Telescope and
it shows star
clusters colliding.

Star light
This picture
of the Orion
nebula was
taken by the
Spitzer Space
Telescope.

Antenna

Double Hubble
The Hubble has
two mirrors—
the largest is 8 feet
(2.4 meters) wide
and 12 inches (30
centimeters) thick.

Look out
Observatories
are places where
astronomers work.
These are usually
away from big
cities where there
are no street lights
and the air is clear.

STARS AND GALAXIES

Stars look like tiny points of light from Earth but really they are huge, hot balls of burning gas deep in space. They are forming, changing, and dying all the time. There are big stars called giants, even bigger ones called supergiants, and small ones called dwarf stars. Our sun is just one of about a hundred thousand million stars that all belong to a galaxy called the Milky Way. A galaxy is a group of millions of stars, held together by a strong force called gravity.

Starry, starry night
On a clear night do not forget to look up at the sky! You will see hundreds of twinkling stars, like tiny sparkling diamonds, far above you.

The gas and dust pack tightly together, getting smaller and very hot.

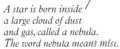

A new star is very bright. It shines steadily for many years.

A group of growing stars is called a cluster.

As it cools, the star gets bigger and forms a red giant.

A star is born inside a large cloud of dust and gas, called a nebula. The word nebula means mist.

Near the end of its life the core of a red giant may cave in and give off layers of gas.

Sky lights
There are many new stars in the gas and dust of this pink nebula. A new young star on its own shines blue.

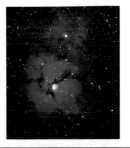

Sometimes a giant star explodes and is blown to pieces. This is called a supernova.

A supernova explosion sometimes results in a pulsar. A pulsar is a rapidly spinning star that gives off pulses of radio waves.

A black hole is not really a hole but a very tightly packed object with gravity so strong that not even light can escape.

Some dying stars grow into huge red supergiants.

Massive stars shine very brightly, but do not live as long as smaller stars.

If seen through a telescope the star, with its gas shell, now looks like a planet, so it is called a planetary nebula.

Some stars gradually get smaller and whiter, until they become white dwarf stars.

Star spinner

Our galaxy, called the Milky Way, is a barred spiral galaxy. Our solar system is about two-thirds of the way out from the center, in one of the spiral arms. There are lots of galaxies in the universe and they have different shapes.

Our solar system is here.

Galaxies

A spiral galaxy

An elliptical galaxy

A barred spiral galaxy

CHAPTER 2

THE NATURAL WORLD

When the Earth was brand-new, more than 4,500 million years ago, there were violent storms, lightning bolts, and fiery volcanoes on its surface, but there was no life. In time, oceans formed, and it was here that the first life appeared in the form of simple organisms called bacteria and algae. Soon, more complex life-forms developed and, by about 600 million years ago, the seas were alive with soft-bodied animals. Later, other animals developed hard shells and skeletons, and small plants began to grow on the shores.

Insects and similar creatures were the first animals on land, followed by amphibians (which live in water and on land), then reptiles, birds, and mammals. It was not until quite recently—about four million years ago—that the first upright-walking ancestors of humans appeared.

Plant Life
Sea Life
Insects and Spiders
Dinosaurs
Birds
Mammals
The Human Body

PLANT LIFE

Plants grow everywhere, from the icy Arctic to the tropics—any place where there is air, light, and water.

In deserts, where it rarely rains, plants have to save moisture. Some, like cacti, have pleated stems that expand to store water when there is a shower. Where the climate is hot and humid, plants grow very quickly all year round to make lush rainforests. In temperate places—where it is not too hot and not too cold, with a medium amount of rain—most plants flower and fruit in summer, but may lose their leaves or stop growing in winter. Plants usually grow in soil, but some absorb what they need directly from the water. Without plants, our world would be very different; from plants we get food, clothes, paper, and lots of other things. Most important of all, they provide oxygen, which all living creatures need to breathe.

Water hyacinth

The growth of a blackberry from flower to fruit

Stag's horn sumach

Cobra lily

Larch cones

Tropical rainforest

Acorns

Oak leaf

Oak tree in winter and in summer

59

WHAT IS A PLANT?

The leaves are used for making food.

An apple tree and a cactus do not look much like each other. But they have more in common than you might think. They are both plants. Like all other plants they make their own food, and during the course of their lifetime, they can produce many new plants. To do these things they use their roots, stems, leaves, and flowers. You will find that no matter how different one plant may look from another, each one is using these parts in much the same way, in order to live and grow.

Look, no hands
Some plants do not need soil—they prefer to perch in trees. A stag's horn fern gets a good grip by wrapping its large fronds around a branch.

Apples and other fruit contain seeds.

Hitching a lift
Some plants use other plants for support. This passion flower can climb very high by winding itself around the trunks and branches of trees.

Trees have a main stem and many branches.

The flowers make seeds for new plants.

The flexible stems can bend and twine.

Fresh fruit
Apple trees are not best known for their flowers. But if they did not have flowers first, we would not have apples to eat.

Good fronds
Fern leaves are called fronds. They often grow straight out of the ground, from stems under the soil.

Feather duster
Pampas grass has long, sharp leaves, and those feathery plumes are its flowers.

This bud will open into a flower.

Eye-catching
You can't miss these blooms. Like other plants that flower, orchids want to make sure that insects visit them. So they advertise themselves with colors and scents that are attractive to insects.

Don't touch!
This cactus has a stem with branches but where are its leaves? The prickles are really special leaves.

Nonflowering plants
Most plants flower, but not all. Ferns, mosses, and liverworts don't. The earliest plants to colonize the Earth— over 400 million years ago—were nonflowering. These plants are their descendants. Instead of seeds, they produce tiny spores which become new plants.

Fern

Liverwort

The curling tendrils hang on tight.

Moss

LEAVES

Leaves work very hard for plants. They make food, and they also help plants to cope with serious problems like how to survive the cold or get enough water. Leaves come in all sorts of shapes and sizes—large and small, thick and thin. In fact, you can tell quite a lot about a plant and where it grows just by looking at its leaves.

Weatherproof
Scots pine trees need to be tough to survive long, cold winters. They have thousands of tiny, needlelike leaves. The needles have a waterproof coating to protect them from rain and snow.

Water store
Agave plants grow in hot places where it may not rain for weeks on end. They are able to store water in their large, thick leaves.

Wind blows through the needles without damaging them.

Their leaves can grow up to 6.6 feet (two meters) long.

Open sesame
Leaves have tiny holes called stomata, which the plant can open and close. When the stomata are open, they let air in and out, and water out. When they are closed, water can't escape from the leaves.

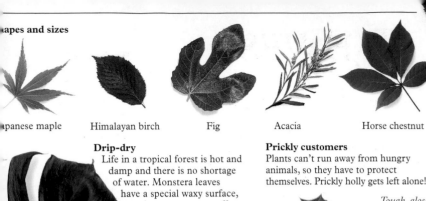

Japanese maple   Himalayan birch   Fig   Acacia   Horse chestnut

Drip-dry

Life in a tropical forest is hot and damp and there is no shortage of water. Monstera leaves have a special waxy surface, so the water can run off.

Monstera plants grow in the shade of trees that constantly drip moisture.

Prickly customers

Plants can't run away from hungry animals, so they have to protect themselves. Prickly holly gets left alone!

Tough, glossy leaves are a good defense against wind and weather.

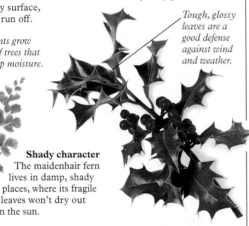

Shady character

The maidenhair fern lives in damp, shady places, where its fragile leaves won't dry out in the sun.

ater signals

aves can't talk, but they can sometimes d a message. The leaves of this cyclamen are limp and drooping as if the plant is unhappy. The soil in the pot is dry, and the message is, "Water me."

Do plants sweat?

Plants are constantly losing water through their leaves as part of a process called transpiration. Most of the time you can't see it happening. But if you put a plant inside a plastic bag and tie it, after a while you will see waterdrops on the inside of the bag. The moisture you can see is coming from the leaves of the plant.

HOW PLANTS MAKE FOOD

Hungry animals can go out hunting for their food—but plants cannot. Instead, they make their own food in their leaves by using light from the sun, water from the soil, and carbon dioxide from the air. A plant's way of making food is called photosynthesis. It takes place during the day when the leaves are absorbing sunlight.

Reach for the sun
These palms grow in the shade of tall trees. Their leaves are arranged like fans to help them catch all the light they can.

The leaves of all plants contain a special pigment that gives them their green color. It is called chlorophyll, and it is essential for photosynthesis.

Colorful cover-up
All leaves contain green chlorophyll. But in some leaves the green is hidden from sight by other, stronger colors.

The roots take up water from the soil. It is drawn up the stem to the leaves.

The leaves take in light from the sun.

Plants store some of their sugary food in their leaves.

Carbon dioxide from the air enters the leaves.

When plants make food they release oxygen into the atmosphere.

Some food becomes sap. It flows around the plant from the leaves to the roots, and provides energy for growing.

Rest time
Without sunlight, plants cannot make food. When it is dark they shut down for the night by closing their stomata.

Photosynthesis
Chlorophyll in the leaves absorbs sunlight. sunlight provides the plant with energy to turn water and carbon dioxide into food.

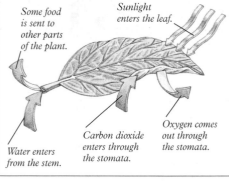

Some food is sent to other parts of the plant.

Sunlight enters the leaf.

Water enters from the stem.

Carbon dioxide enters through the stomata.

Oxygen comes out through the stomata.

Tree in summer leaf

Bare tree in winter

Slowing down
In winter there is less light and the water often freezes in the ground. It is difficult to make food, so plants grow very little. Many plants shed their leaves or even die back at this time of year.

CARNIVOROUS PLANTS

Watch out! These plants are meat-eaters and they have some very cunning devices for trapping their victims. Unlucky insects, attracted by the plant's scent and color, discover too late that they have been tricked. It is a nasty end for an insect, but a ready-made, nutritious meal for the plant.

The lid can close to keep rainwater out.

Gruesome gruel
Flies lose their footing on the slippery rim of the hanging pitcher plant and tumble into the water below. They gradually dissolve into a kind of fly broth.

Rim with nectar

Pitcher for collecting water

Remains of flies

Water jugs
A pitcher plant has several pitchers, so it can catch a lot of flies.

Venus flytrap
The instant an unsuspecting insect lands, the venus flytrap snaps into action.

To a fly, this pad looks like a safe landing place.

Swamped
Most carnivorous plants, such as these cobra lilies, grow in boggy places where the minerals they need are in short supply. The insects they catch are a vital addition to their diet, because they are rich in the missing minerals.

1. A passing damselfly lands on a pad.

The middle of the leaf forms a hinge.

An open trap waiting for a visitor.

2. It touches the sensitive hairs that trigger the hinge.

Sensitive hairs

3. In less than a second, the sides of the trap begin to close.

The trap is closed—there is something inside.

Pointed teeth lock together to make a cage.

4. There is no escape. The teeth close and the damselfly is firmly locked in. It takes two weeks for the venus flytrap to digest its meal.

Glued to the spot

The glistening, golden leaves of the butterwort are a deadly glue trap. Flies get stuck when they land. But no matter how hard they struggle, the leaf edges keep curling inward and the butterwort begins its lunch.

Hair-raising story

Any fly that lands on the hairy leaves of the sticky sundew is in for a nasty surprise. In no time at all it finds its legs are hopelessly entangled in the glue produced by the hairs.

STEMS

Roots, shoots, leaves, and flowers are all connected to the plant's stem. Although it may not always stand as straight, the stem is kind of like your backbone, holding all the different parts together. Being in the center of everything means it is in the perfect position to carry water and food to every part of the plant.

Clever creature
This aphid knows just where to go for food supplies! It takes less than a second to pierce the soft part of the stem, which is full of nutritious sap.

This young tree is two years old.

Sun worshippers
The stems of sunflowers turn so their flowers can always face the sun.

Branches grow from the stem and hold the leaves out to the light.

As the tree gets older and taller, the main stem will thicken to form a trunk.

Clinging on
In its rush toward the light, the sweet pea has no time to grow strong stems. Instead it uses twirling tendrils to wrap around other plants. They will support its fast climb to the top.

The widest spread on Earth
Just one banyan tree can make a forest! Their branches throw down special aerial roots. These grow into the ground and expand into trunks. A single tree in Kolkata, India, has more than 2,600 of these trunk look-alikes.

Water and minerals travel up the stem from the roots.

Supporting role
The strong, hard stems of bamboo are called canes. In some parts of the world they make great thickets 23 feet (seven meters) high.

Weak at the knees
Gourd stems don't even attempt to stand up to support their fruit, which may weigh several pounds. They just trail gracefully over the ground.

The branches are slender and not yet very strong.

The inside of a bamboo cane is hollow.

Keep off!
It is very difficult to get near a prickly thistle, but most animals that do won't be back for a second bite.

Food is made in the leaves and travels down to the roots.

Close-up of thistle stem

Section through cactus

Conservation
Desert cacti hold water reserves in their thick stems. Thirsty animals know that. But the barricade of fierce spines means no free drinks.

Water diet
African baobab trees have a special way of surviving. During the rainy season their trunks store so much water that they visibly swell up. These reserves get them through the hot, dry times, when their slimmer shape slowly returns.

ROOTS

Roots are not pretty or colorful like leaves and flowers, but plants couldn't do without them! Anchored in the soil, they hold plants upright against wind and weather. They also grow out and down in search of water and minerals which are drawn all the way up to the leaves. Think how tall a tree can grow, and you can see it needs strong roots to keep it supported.

There are pockets of in the soil. Without a roots woul wither and

Roots can fit themselves into tiny spaces.

When earthworms burrow they help to add air to the soil.

The roots of the tree grow outward to balance the spread of the branches above.

Knobbly knees
Avicennia has roots that grow above ground. Also known as black mangrove, they grow in boggy ground, where there is not enough air. The roots are called pneumatophores, and supply the plants with air.

Strong intent
Roots don't let much stand in their way. These roots are growing toward the drain in the road, where there is a useful supply of water.

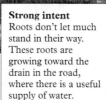

Rootless wonder
Draped like strange beards over the branches of trees, the extraordinary Spanish moss plant survives with no roots at all. Spanish moss grows in subtropical climates where the air is very wet. It absorbs all the moisture it needs through its fine, threadlike leaves.

Rock climbers
Alpine plants grow against rock faces, to protect themselves from high winds and icy squalls. Their tiny roots wriggle into cracks in the rock.

Most roots grow in the top 12 inches (30 centimeters) of soil. This part contains most of the important minerals the tree needs.

Every root grows a mass of tiny hairs near its tip to absorb water from the soil.

Water crops
Plants need water, minerals, and some support for their roots. But they do not necessarily need soil. Today many food crops are grown entirely in water with special pebbles. They are given liquid minerals to replace those in the soil.

INSIDE A FLOWER

Hibiscus

When you look at flowers you notice many colors, shapes, and sizes. Some plants have a single flower, others have so many it is impossible to keep count. But stop and take a closer look—this time inside. However different they may look, flowers all have the same basic parts. This is because all plants produce flowers for the same purpose: to make seeds so another plant can grow.

The male part of a flower is called the anther. Each one of these produces masses of tiny pollen grains.

Insects leave pollen on the female part, which is called the stigma.

New beginnings
The process of making new seeds is called reproduction. The male and female parts in the center of this lily are its reproductive parts.

Lily

Mistaken identity
You could be confused by this poinsettia. What look like bright red petals are actually a kind of leaf, called a bract. The real flowers are the tiny green dots in the center.

Grand finale
Not all plants flower every year, but there is no other plant that is as slow as the *Puya raimondii* from South America. It takes 150 years to produce a massive flower spike, up to 33 feet (10 meters) tall. Exhausted, it then dies, but luckily, not before it has produced a few seeds.

Mighty magnolias

Giant dinosaurs may have munched on magnolias like these. Magnolia trees are among the oldest flowering plants— they have been around for more than 100 million years.

The petals are brightly colored, with special markings to attract insects.

Flower arrangement

All of these flowers have the same basic parts, but they are arranged on the stem in different ways.

These bell-shaped flowers hang down.

Is this a flower?

Tropical orchids like this one often look more like strange insects than flowers.

Hundreds of small flowers grow in a single spike.

The flowers of the spider orchid can be up to 24 inches (60 centimeters) long.

Daisy petals are arranged like the rays of the sun.

Each of these tightly packed flowers is called a floret.

Poppy petals open out to the light.

This flower resembles a pom pom.

| Snake's head fritillary | Echinops | Mullein | Transvaal daisy | Poppy | Yarrow |

FLOWERS AND THEIR POLLINATORS

Most plants cannot make seeds without some outside help. The first job is to move pollen from the anther of one flower to the stigma of another. This is called pollination. Plants cannot travel, but their flowers produce sweet nectar, which animals love. As the animal feeds on the nectar, some pollen rubs onto its body. Each time it moves on to another flower, it leaves some pollen behind and picks up a new supply.

Honey hunters
As it feasts on nectar, the Australian honey possum gets pollen on its fur.

Pollen stop
Bees flit from flower to flower all day, feeding on nectar. Each time they stop, they pick up some pollen.

A flower, not a fly!

This bee is having a good pollen bath.

Clever tricks
Fly orchids look and smell like the real thing. Male flies looking for a mate are easily tricked. They buzz off in disgust, taking the orchid's pollen with them.

Pollen from the anthers of the flower sticks to the butterfly's body.

Pollen galore
Some plants rely on the wind to carry pollen between flowers. These catkins, for example, produce masses of pollen to make sure some will end up reaching the tiny stigmas of its female counterparts.

Nectar gatherers
Brightly colored flowers attract butterflies looking for nectar.

Special collection
When a hummingbird pushes its long beak deep inside the flower to collect the nectar, some pollen brushes off onto its body.

Inside story
Not many insects would ever find the flowers of the fig tree. They actually grow inside the figs! They are pollinated by special fig wasps that live inside the fig. When the flowers are producing pollen, some of the wasps leave home. They move into another fig, carrying pollen with them on their bodies.

Pollen is brushed onto the bat's fur as it moves from flower to flower.

The bat's long tongue is perfect for whisking out the nectar.

Tropical favorite
The bird of paradise flower grows in the tropics. It is pollinated by bats as well as by birds.

On its nightly nectar hunt, one bat can pollinate several flowers.

Bats find it easy to pick out the spiky shape of the bird of paradise flower at night.

FLOWERS BECOME FRUITS

After they have been pollinated, flowers produce seeds and fruits. The fruits protect the seeds and keep them safe until the time comes for them to grow. Like flowers, fruits come in all sorts of shapes and sizes. Horse chestnuts make chestnuts, dandelions make parachutes, and plum trees make plums. Every fruit has its own kind of seed. Some are light enough to be blown away on the wind, others are armor-plated so they can be swallowed by animals and pass out in their droppings without being damaged!

From rose to hip
Bees are attracted to this rose by its sweet smell and the promise of nectar.

1. The swelling beneath the flower is called the receptacle, and it will become the fruit.

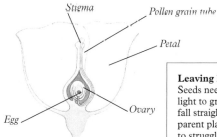

Stigma

Pollen grain tube

Petal

Ovary

Egg

Fertilization
When an insect leaves some pollen on the stigma of a flower, fertilization can take place. Each tiny pollen grain grows a long tube. The tube grows down until it reaches the ovary where eggs are produced. Now a male gamete from the pollen tube joins with an egg from the ovary, and a seed is born.

Leaving home
Seeds need space and light to grow. If they fall straight off the parent plant, they have to struggle to grow in its shadow. So plants use all sorts of clever devices for making sure their seeds are carried away from them by wind or animals. Some have exploding pods that catapult the seeds into the air.

Poppy seeds are spread by the wind.

Vetch pods explode when they are dry.

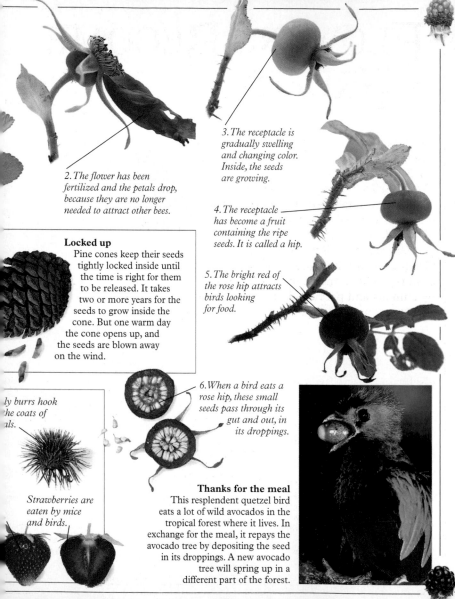

2. The flower has been fertilized and the petals drop, because they are no longer needed to attract other bees.

3. The receptacle is gradually swelling and changing color. Inside, the seeds are growing.

4. The receptacle has become a fruit containing the ripe seeds. It is called a hip.

5. The bright red of the rose hip attracts birds looking for food.

Locked up
Pine cones keep their seeds tightly locked inside until the time is right for them to be released. It takes two or more years for the seeds to grow inside the cone. But one warm day the cone opens up, and the seeds are blown away on the wind.

6. When a bird eats a rose hip, these small seeds pass through its gut and out, in its droppings.

ly burrs hook he coats of als.

Strawberries are eaten by mice and birds.

Thanks for the meal
This resplendent quetzel bird eats a lot of wild avocados in the tropical forest where it lives. In exchange for the meal, it repays the avocado tree by depositing the seed in its droppings. A new avocado tree will spring up in a different part of the forest.

SEEDS BECOME PLANTS

Below ground, a seed is waiting to start life. But until it gets the right signals, a seed will remain just a seed. As soon as the soil becomes warm and damp, the seed can begin to absorb moisture. This makes it swell and the seedcase splits open. Germination has begun—and the seedling starts to grow toward the light.

Wall flowers
Some seeds land in odd places—and there they grow!

The leave unfold in a fan sha

Peanuts

Peanut bush

Cof bush

Coffee beans

Seed and plant
You may recognize these seeds, but do you know what they grow into?

Oak tree

Lemon seeds

Acorns

Lemon tree

Roots grow do through the h of the coco

Eggshells

Fast food
Mustard and watercress seeds are quick and easy to grow. Put some damp cotton balls in clean egg shells and sprinkle a few seeds on top. Look at the seeds each day and keep the cotton balls damp. In about 10 days you will have your own home-grown salad!

Seeds

Damp cotton balls

On the beach
A coconut can travel long distances by sea, until it is washed up onto the shore. In the warm sand, it sprouts and starts to grow.

Some like it hot
Some seeds must literally go through fire and water before they can germinate. In the arid Australian outback, fierce fires can rip across the land. They awaken the dormant seeds of these acacia trees.

The stem is formed from the stalks of the leaves.

As the shoot gets longer and thicker, the first leaves open.

The coconut contains liquid, so the seedling has its own water supply for a while.

Inside the bean, you can see the part that is the future root.

A first sign of life—the root pushes through the skin of the bean.

The shoot appears above ground. This is the stem.

Roots and shoots
When the soil gets warm in spring, this broad bean germinates and begins to grow.

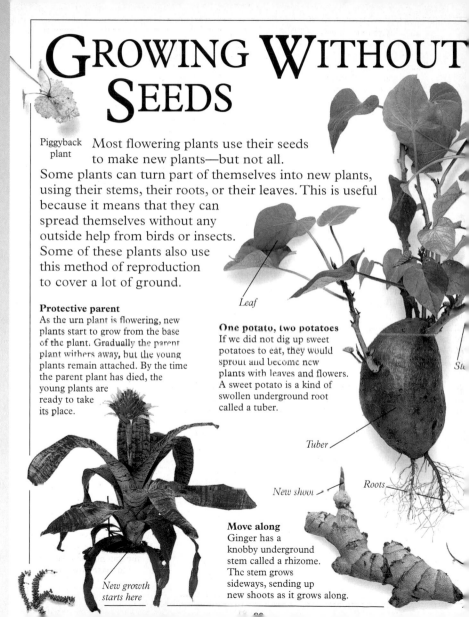

GROWING WITHOUT SEEDS

Piggyback plant

Most flowering plants use their seeds to make new plants—but not all. Some plants can turn part of themselves into new plants, using their stems, their roots, or their leaves. This is useful because it means that they can spread themselves without any outside help from birds or insects. Some of these plants also use this method of reproduction to cover a lot of ground.

Leaf

Protective parent

As the urn plant is flowering, new plants start to grow from the base of the plant. Gradually the parent plant withers away, but the young plants remain attached. By the time the parent plant has died, the young plants are ready to take its place.

One potato, two potatoes

If we did not dig up sweet potatoes to eat, they would sprout and become new plants with leaves and flowers. A sweet potato is a kind of swollen underground root called a tuber.

Ste

Tuber

New shoot

Roots

New growth starts here

Move along

Ginger has a knobby underground stem called a rhizome. The stem grows sideways, sending up new shoots as it grows along.

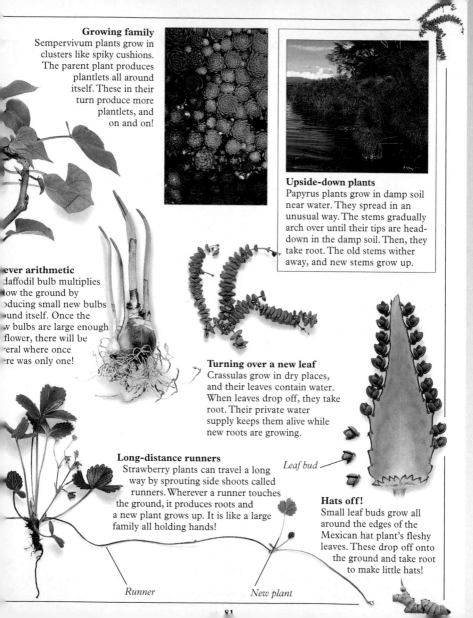

Growing family
Sempervivum plants grow in clusters like spiky cushions. The parent plant produces plantlets all around itself. These in their turn produce more plantlets, and on and on!

Upside-down plants
Papyrus plants grow in damp soil near water. They spread in an unusual way. The stems gradually arch over until their tips are head-down in the damp soil. Then, they take root. The old stems wither away, and new stems grow up.

...ever arithmetic
...daffodil bulb multiplies ...low the ground by ...ducing small new bulbs ...und itself. Once the ...w bulbs are large enough ...flower, there will be ...veral where once ...re was only one!

Turning over a new leaf
Crassulas grow in dry places, and their leaves contain water. When leaves drop off, they take root. Their private water supply keeps them alive while new roots are growing.

Leaf bud

Long-distance runners
Strawberry plants can travel a long way by sprouting side shoots called runners. Wherever a runner touches the ground, it produces roots and a new plant grows up. It is like a large family all holding hands!

Hats off!
Small leaf buds grow all around the edges of the Mexican hat plant's fleshy leaves. These drop off onto the ground and take root to make little hats!

Runner   *New plant*

TREES

The heartwood is the oldest part of the tree. It is no longer living, but it is very strong.

Trees are the longest living of all plants. They grow strong, woody trunks so that they can tower above other plants and get plenty of light. There are trees that lose all their leaves in one shot when the weather gets cold. They are known as deciduous trees. Others are evergreen and shed a few leaves at a time throughout the year.

Monkey puzzle tree

Bark is very important. It protects all the living, working parts of the trunk.

Fiery finale
Before they fall, the leaves of many deciduous trees change color. The green chlorophyll disappears, revealing other colors that were hidden. Chemicals in the leaves deepen these colors to fiery golds and reds.

Silver birch

Bark
As trees grow, their trunks expand. The bark cracks to make lots of different patterns.

This part of the trunk is still alive and busy, carrying water and food to the rest of the tree.

Paperbark maple

Tibetan cherry

Holding on
Over the years, wind has shaped and battered the branches of this tree. But its trunk and strong roots keep it standing.

Deciduous trees

Spanish oak

American mountain ash

Weeping willow

Cross section

Every year a tree adds a new layer of growth to its trunk and branches. Look at this slice from a tree's trunk, and you will see lots of rings. Each ring shows the growth made by the tree in one year. By counting the rings you can tell how old a tree is.

A wide ring shows that the tree grew a lot in this year.

A bad year for growth! Thin rings show how trees sometimes grow very slowly.

Shagbark hickory

Cork oak

Snakebark maple

Evergreen trees

Deodar

Mountain gum

Black spruce

The incredible hulk

What size waist do you have? The trunk of this giant redwood in California measures 103 feet (31 meters) all the way around, and stands nearly 275 feet (84 meters) high. It is so famous it has even been given a name—General Sherman!

SEA LIFE

Nearly three-quarters of the Earth is covered by oceans and seas. These billions of gallons of salty water are home to silent sharks, playful dolphins, enormous whales, huge marine turtles, fascinating octopuses with their eight long arms, masses of shellfish, and fish of all shapes and sizes. Beautiful underwater gardens of brightly colored coral provide a home for stinging sea anemones, showy sea slugs, giant clams, and spiny sea urchins.

Many parts of the world's seas and oceans are too deep, dark, and cold to support a lot of life, although the animals that live there are among the strangest on the planet. We are just beginning to explore this mysterious, watery world using special deep-sea submersibles. Almost every visit reveals forms of life that scientists have never seen before.

Leatherback turtle

Coral reef

Blue whale

Tropical sundial she

Flounder with camouflage coloring

Female angler fish with males underneath

Edible crab

Harbor seal pup

Common starfish

PLANKTON

Seawater is full of billions of very tiny living things called plankton. Most are less than 0.04 inches (one millimeter) long, but without them, very little else could live in the sea! Clouds of microscopic algae called phytoplankton drift around at the mercy of tides and currents. They are eaten by swarms of tiny animals called zooplankton, and these are then eaten by fish, whales, and even seabirds.

This curved feeler is covered in fine senso[r] hairs which help the copepod find food.

Zooplankton are tin[y] animals, but they ar[e] much bigger than most phytoplankton.

Phytoplankton...eaten by...zooplankton...eaten by...fish...eaten by...seabirds

Bucket full!
Copepods are a type of zooplankton. They are so small that more than one million could fit into a bucket of seawater.

Food for everyone
Seabirds, turtles, and seals all eat other animals, such as fish and shellfish, that eat plankton. They would all starve if there were no plankton in the sea.

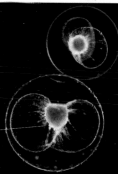

Part-time plankton
Some animals begin their lives as tiny plankton, but then they grow much, much bigger.

Microscopic phytoplankton absorb the energy of the sun as they float along.

Crab

Starfish

Octopus

Sun lovers
Like land plants, phytoplankton use sunlight to make their food.

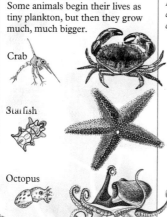

There are many different sorts, or species, of copepods. This male is flashing bright blue to attract a female.

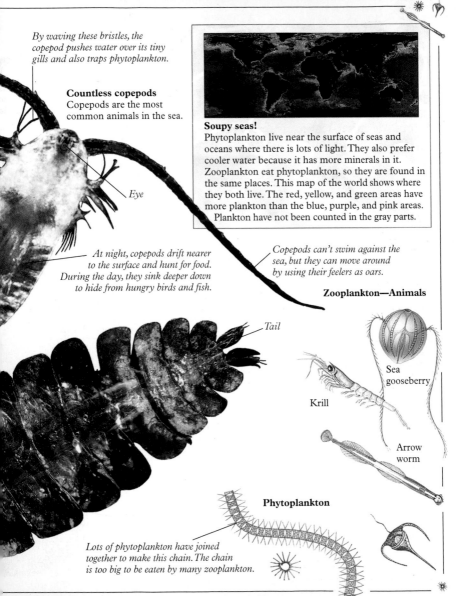

By waving these bristles, the copepod pushes water over its tiny gills and also traps phytoplankton.

Countless copepods
Copepods are the most common animals in the sea.

Eye

At night, copepods drift nearer to the surface and hunt for food. During the day, they sink deeper down to hide from hungry birds and fish.

Soupy seas!
Phytoplankton live near the surface of seas and oceans where there is lots of light. They also prefer cooler water because it has more minerals in it. Zooplankton eat phytoplankton, so they are found in the same places. This map of the world shows where they both live. The red, yellow, and green areas have more plankton than the blue, purple, and pink areas. Plankton have not been counted in the gray parts.

Copepods can't swim against the sea, but they can move around by using their feelers as oars.

Zooplankton—Animals

Tail

Sea gooseberry

Krill

Arrow worm

Phytoplankton

Lots of phytoplankton have joined together to make this chain. The chain is too big to be eaten by many zooplankton.

SHELLFISH

The shells that you find on a beach are the empty homes of small animals called shellfish. These soft-bodied creatures need hard shells to protect them from starfish, crabs, fish, and birds. The most common types of shellfish are gastropods and bivalves. Gastropods are underwater snails. They grow coiled shells and slide around on a slimy foot. Bivalves have two, flatter shells that cover their whole body.

Eggs   Larva

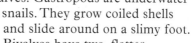

Growing up
Unlike crabs, shellfish never shed their shells. Each baby, or larva, has a tiny shell that gets bigger as it grows.

Because their shells are light, bubble shells can use their mantles as flippers to help them swim.

Mantle

The animal inside
Bivalves, gastropods, and all other shellfish have soft bodies and no backbones. Most, such as this scallop, have shells.

These feelers help the animal find food.

Worm

Water in

Water out

Eye

Swimming scallops
By taking in water and then shooting it out of its back end, a scallop is able to jump through the sea.

Buried alive
Tusk shells and many bivalves spend most of their life buried in sand. Bivalves dig a hole with their foot, then poke tubes, or siphons, into the sea. The siphons take water into the bivalve's gills and catch food.

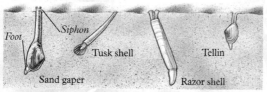

Foot   Siphon
Tusk shell   Tellin
Sand gaper   Razor shell

Eye on a stalk

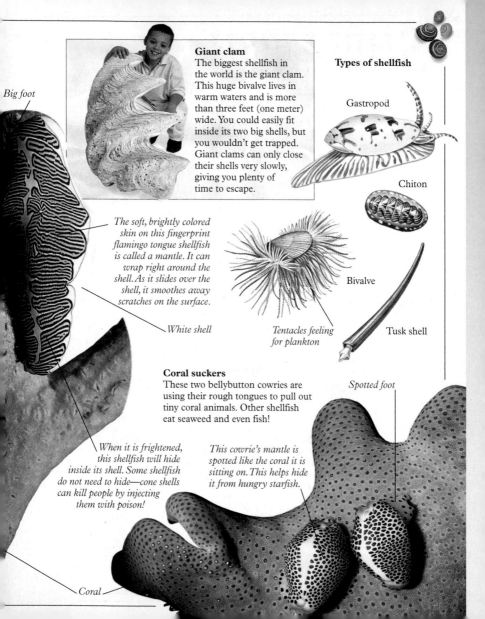

Big foot

Giant clam
The biggest shellfish in the world is the giant clam. This huge bivalve lives in warm waters and is more than three feet (one meter) wide. You could easily fit inside its two big shells, but you wouldn't get trapped. Giant clams can only close their shells very slowly, giving you plenty of time to escape.

Types of shellfish

Gastropod

Chiton

The soft, brightly colored skin on this fingerprint flamingo tongue shellfish is called a mantle. It can wrap right around the shell. As it slides over the shell, it smoothes away scratches on the surface.

White shell

Bivalve

Tentacles feeling for plankton

Tusk shell

Coral suckers
These two bellybutton cowries are using their rough tongues to pull out tiny coral animals. Other shellfish eat seaweed and even fish!

Spotted foot

When it is frightened, this shellfish will hide inside its shell. Some shellfish do not need to hide—cone shells can kill people by injecting them with poison!

This cowrie's mantle is spotted like the coral it is sitting on. This helps hide it from hungry starfish.

Coral

CRABS

Crabby face

Antennae
Eye
Mouth

What lives in the sea or on land, can be any color, has its eyes on stalks, swims and walks sideways, and carries its own house? Would you have guessed a crab? Crabs live in all parts of the sea, from the very deepest oceans to wave-swept shores.

Crabs use their back four pairs of legs to scuttle sideways.

The crab uses its strong claws to crush and tear up food, such as hard-shelled shellfish and fish.

Under this spine, there are two feelers, called antennae. The crab uses tiny hairs along the antennae to touch, smell, and taste.

The shell is often called the carapace.

When crabs get too big for their shells they split them open and shed them. Underneath the old suit of armor there is a new, soft shell. It can take up to three days to harden.

Crabs can grow new legs if they are torn off.

This spiny spider crab is protected from most of its enemies by its shell.

Crab eaters
Crabs make a tasty meal for fish, birds, octopuses, seals, and people!

Crabs breathe through five pa of gills. These are insi the shell, near t top of each

Joint

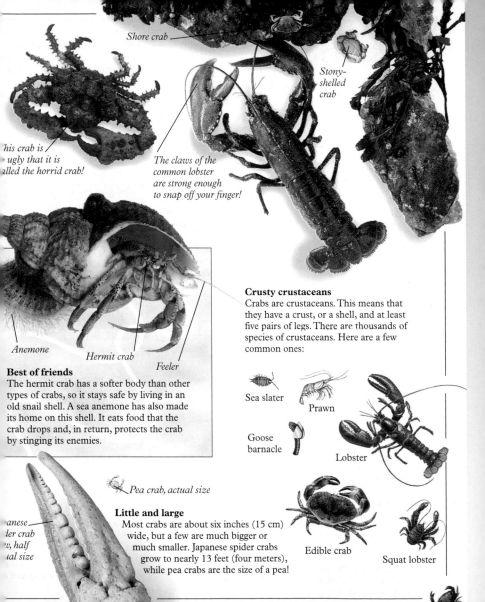

Shore crab

Stony-shelled crab

his crab is ugly that it is lled the horrid crab!

The claws of the common lobster are strong enough to snap off your finger!

Anemone

Hermit crab

Feeler

Best of friends
The hermit crab has a softer body than other types of crabs, so it stays safe by living in an old snail shell. A sea anemone has also made its home on this shell. It eats food that the crab drops and, in return, protects the crab by stinging its enemies.

Crusty crustaceans
Crabs are crustaceans. This means that they have a crust, or a shell, and at least five pairs of legs. There are thousands of species of crustaceans. Here are a few common ones:

Sea slater

Prawn

Goose barnacle

Lobster

Pea crab, actual size

Little and large
Most crabs are about six inches (15 cm) wide, but a few are much bigger or much smaller. Japanese spider crabs grow to nearly 13 feet (four meters), while pea crabs are the size of a pea!

anese
ler crab
, half
ual size

Edible crab

Squat lobster

STARFISH

Starfish are star-shaped, but they are not fish—they are echinoderms. This means that they have spiny skin. They cannot swim, but they are very good at crawling! They can walk up strands of seaweed and climb down the sides of rocks. Even in the deepest, darkest parts of the sea, there are starfish creeping around.

This crimson-knobbed starfish, like most starfish measures less than eight (20 cm) from tip to tip. But some species are as as a small car!

Starfish don't have any eyes. Instead, they have eyespots on the tips of their arms. These special cells cannot see shapes, but they can tell whether it is light or dark.

These bumps are actually spines.

Central disk

Burrowing starfish

Starfish's arms are very bendy because their skeleton is made up of lots of tiny spines that can move in any direction.

Starfish breathe through their feet and also through tiny tubes that are found all over their body.

Cushion star

Common starfish

Stomach this
Starfish eat clams and mussels. When it finds one, it pulls open the shell with its tiny tube feet, pushes its whole stomach inside and slowly digests the animal's soft body.

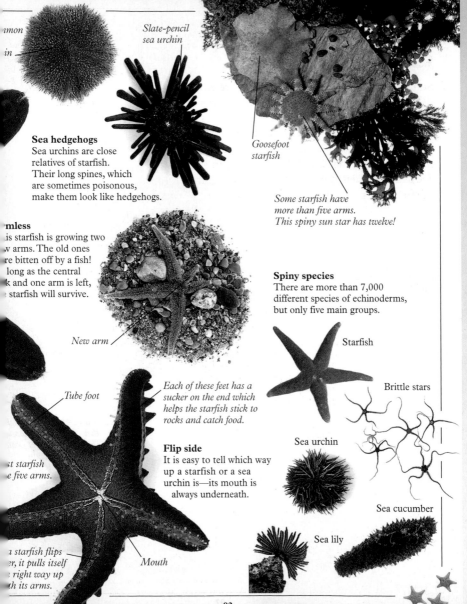

Slate-pencil sea urchin

Goosefoot starfish

Sea hedgehogs
Sea urchins are close
relatives of starfish.
Their long spines, which
are sometimes poisonous,
make them look like hedgehogs.

*Some starfish have
more than five arms.
This spiny sun star has twelve!*

mless
is starfish is growing two
w arms. The old ones
re bitten off by a fish!
long as the central
k and one arm is left,
e starfish will survive.

New arm

Spiny species
There are more than 7,000
different species of echinoderms,
but only five main groups.

Starfish

Brittle stars

Tube foot

*Each of these feet has a
sucker on the end which
helps the starfish stick to
rocks and catch food.*

Flip side
It is easy to tell which way
up a starfish or a sea
urchin is—its mouth is
always underneath.

Sea urchin

st starfish
e five arms.

Sea cucumber

Sea lily

a starfish flips
r, it pulls itself
right way up
h its arms.

Mouth

OCTOPUSES

Did you know that octopuses are related to snails? But unlike most other mollusks, they don't have shells to protect them. Instead, these eight-armed animals squeeze their soft bodies into small cracks or holes in rocks. Once they are safely hidden, it is very hard for conger eels, sharks, seals, and people to find and eat them.

Bunch of eggs
Inside each of these soft-shelled eggs there is a baby octopus.

With their large eyes, octopuses can see shapes and colors very well.

Web

Gone fishing
Octopuses hunt for their food. They pounce on fish, starfish, and crabs. Some have webs between their arms which help them net even more animals.

Tentacle

This common octopus measures only four inches (10 centimeters) from tip to tip. The largest octopus ever found was more than 30 feet (nine meters) wide!

An octopus can shoot ink, called sepia, out of its siphon. This black cloud hangs in the water and hides the octopus from its enemies.

Jet-propelled
If an octopus is frightened, it does not crawl away slowly—it jets off! By forcing water out through its siphon, it can shoot through the sea.

Siphon

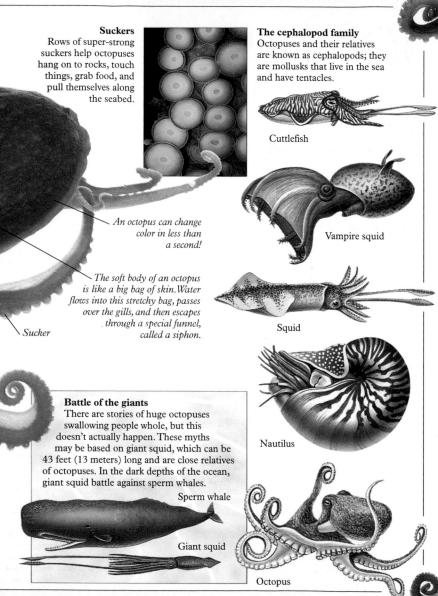

Suckers
Rows of super-strong suckers help octopuses hang on to rocks, touch things, grab food, and pull themselves along the seabed.

An octopus can change color in less than a second!

The soft body of an octopus is like a big bag of skin. Water flows into this stretchy bag, passes over the gills, and then escapes through a special funnel, called a siphon.

Sucker

The cephalopod family
Octopuses and their relatives are known as cephalopods; they are mollusks that live in the sea and have tentacles.

Cuttlefish

Vampire squid

Squid

Nautilus

Battle of the giants
There are stories of huge octopuses swallowing people whole, but this doesn't actually happen. These myths may be based on giant squid, which can be 43 feet (13 meters) long and are close relatives of octopuses. In the dark depths of the ocean, giant squid battle against sperm whales.

Sperm whale

Giant squid

Octopus

FISH

Almost all living things need a gas called oxygen to survive. You cannot see it, but it is found in air and water. You use your lungs to take in oxygen by breathing in air. If you swim under water, you either have to hold your breath or use a snorkel. Fish don't have to do this. They can take their oxygen straight out of the water.

Fish eggs
Most fish lay jellylike eggs. Some guard their eggs until they hatch. Others, like cod, just squirt millions of tiny eggs into the sea. This is called spawning.

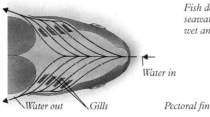

Dorsal fin

Fish do not need eyelids— seawater keeps their eyes wet and free of dirt.

Water in

Water out   *Gills*

Pectoral fin

Breathing under water
Water flows into the fish's mouth, over red flaps called gills, and out through the gill openings. The gills take the oxygen out of the water.

There are four sets of gills behind this flap.

Bony fish have a "balloon" inside them called a swim bladder. It can be filled with air to help them float.

The pectoral and pelvic fins help the fish move up, down, left, or right.

Pelvic

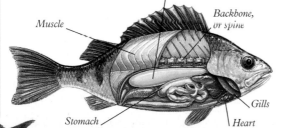

Muscle

Backbone, or spine

Gills

Stomach

Heart

Inside story
Most of the important parts of a bony fish are in the lower half of its body. The top half is full of muscles, which move the tail.

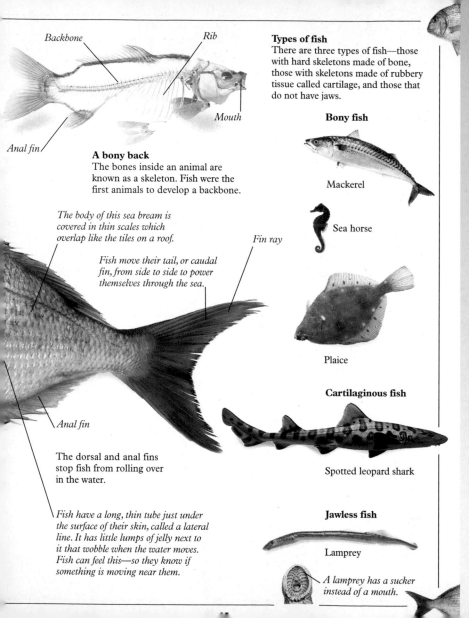

Backbone

Rib

Mouth

Anal fin

Types of fish
There are three types of fish—those with hard skeletons made of bone, those with skeletons made of rubbery tissue called cartilage, and those that do not have jaws.

Bony fish

Mackerel

A bony back
The bones inside an animal are known as a skeleton. Fish were the first animals to develop a backbone.

The body of this sea bream is covered in thin scales which overlap like the tiles on a roof.

Sea horse

Fin ray

Fish move their tail, or caudal fin, from side to side to power themselves through the sea.

Plaice

Anal fin

Cartilaginous fish

The dorsal and anal fins stop fish from rolling over in the water.

Spotted leopard shark

Fish have a long, thin tube just under the surface of their skin, called a lateral line. It has little lumps of jelly next to it that wobble when the water moves. Fish can feel this—so they know if something is moving near them.

Jawless fish

Lamprey

A lamprey has a sucker instead of a mouth.

SHARKS

Sharks are the best hunters in the sea. With their terrible teeth and huge jaws, they can tear up seals, turtles, fish, and even wooden boats! Tiger sharks and great white sharks sometimes bite people, but most sharks are more scared of us and soon swim away.

See how big this jaw is!

Sharks are like a swimming nose. They can smell injured animals and other food that is hundreds of yards away.

All living animals produce a small amount of electricity. You cannot sense it, but sharks can. Little dimples on their head work like television aerials to tell them where animals are hiding.

Five gill slits on each side of the head let water pass through the shark's gills.

Teeth as sharp as knives
Shark teeth can cut through skin and crunch up bones, but they soon get dull. Each tooth only lasts for a few weeks, then it falls out and is replaced by a new one. Basking sharks eat plankton so they don't need any teeth!

Dorsal fin

Pectoral fin

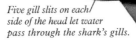

Super swimmer
A typical shark swims by bending from side to side. First it moves its head, then its body, and last of all its long tail. This wave travels down its body, pushing the shark through the sea.

Shark attack!
Just before they bite, sharks bend their noses up and move their teeth forward.

Great white shark

Sand tiger shark

Blue shark

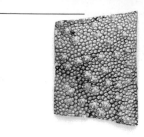

Close-up of shark skin

Watch your hands
Shark skin feels like rough sandpaper—it is covered in tiny teeth.

Tail, or caudal fin

Anal fin

Like most sharks, this school shark has a second dorsal fin.

The top of a shark's tail is larger than the bottom. This odd shape helps to lift the shark up in the water when it is swimming.

Pelvic fin

Shark shapes
Not all sharks look like the ones you see in films; some are tiny and others are quite odd shapes.

Cookiecutter shark

Hammerhead shark

Prickly dogfish

Wobbegong

Great white shark

Sink or swim
Sharks, like many fish, are heavier than water, so they should sink to the bottom of the sea. Bony fish have inflatable swim bladders to stop this from happening, but sharks have oily livers instead. The oil helps them float because it is lighter than water. There is enough oil inside a basking shark's liver to fill five big buckets!

Liver

Some great white sharks are 26 feet (eight meters) long.

Pelagic thresher shark

Porbeagle shark

Graceful shark

Oceanic whitetip shark

RAYS

Rays are cartilaginous fish closely related to sharks but with flattened, diamond-shaped bodies. Some of these shy, gentle animals can be glimpsed using their winglike fins to glide gracefully through open water, but others spend most of their time feeding on the seabed.

These sharp spines protect the ray. Stingr[ays] also have one very lar[ge] poisonous spine whic[h] they use to stab their enemies.

Like sharks, rays have skeletons made of cartilage.

Gill slit

Mouth

Thornback ray

Upside down
On the underside of a ray, there are ten gill slits and a mouth that is full of flat teeth.

Small pelvic fin

When a ray is lying on the sea bottom, its mouth is blocked, so it sucks in water through a tiny hole, called a spiracle, behind each eye.

Mighty manta
Most rays are less than 6.5 feet (two meters) wide, but a manta ray can grow to more than 30 feet (nine meters) in width. Luckily for divers, it only eats plankton and small fish.

By flapping their fins, rays disturb the sand and uncover crabs—a tasty snack for a ray.

Underwater flying
A ray is one of the mo[st] graceful swimmers in [the] sea. Flapping its broa[d] fins, it "flies" like an underwater bird.

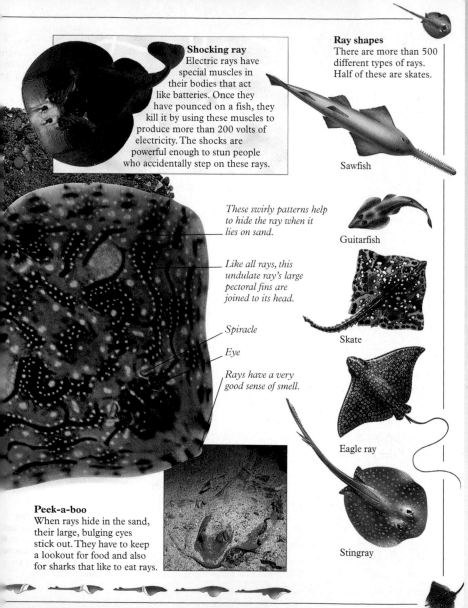

Shocking ray
Electric rays have special muscles in their bodies that act like batteries. Once they have pounced on a fish, they kill it by using these muscles to produce more than 200 volts of electricity. The shocks are powerful enough to stun people who accidentally step on these rays.

Ray shapes
There are more than 500 different types of rays. Half of these are skates.

Sawfish

These swirly patterns help to hide the ray when it lies on sand.

Like all rays, this undulate ray's large pectoral fins are joined to its head.

Spiracle

Eye

Rays have a very good sense of smell.

Guitarfish

Skate

Eagle ray

Peek-a-boo
When rays hide in the sand, their large, bulging eyes stick out. They have to keep a lookout for food and also for sharks that like to eat rays.

Stingray

WHALES

Millions of years ago whales used to walk. Since then, they have changed a lot. They have grown bigger and bigger, their back legs have disappeared, and their front legs have turned into flippers. They can't live on land anymore, but they are still mammals. This means that they breathe air and feed their babies milk.

There are two sorts of whales: those that have teeth and those that do not. Whales that have no teeth are called baleen whales.

Krill for supper
Baleen whales eat krill, a kind of plankton. A large whale can eat two tons a day—half the weight of an elephant!

The whale moves its tail up and down to push itself through the sea. The fastest whale is the sei. It can reach speeds of 40 miles (64 kilometers) an hour, 10 times faster than a person can swim.

There she blows!
When a whale surfaces to fill its lungs with fresh air, warm air escapes from its blowhole. This escaping air mists up, just like your breath on a cold day, and forms a tall spout called a blow.

No animal has longer flippers than a humpback whale—they are about 16 feet (five meters) long, almost the height of a giraffe.

Deep throat grooves let a baleen whale's mouth stretch so that it can hold vast amounts of water and krill.

Whales have thick fat, called blubber.

Jumping for joy
Humpback whales love to leap right out of the water. This is called breaching. When they crash back into the sea, they make a huge splash!

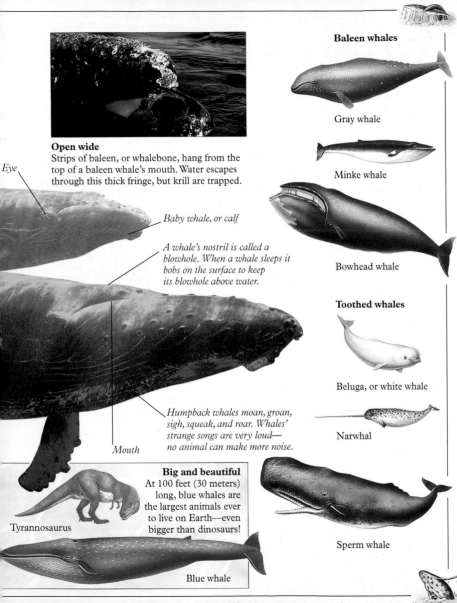

Baleen whales

Gray whale

Minke whale

Bowhead whale

Toothed whales

Beluga, or white whale

Narwhal

Sperm whale

Open wide
Strips of baleen, or whalebone, hang from the top of a baleen whale's mouth. Water escapes through this thick fringe, but krill are trapped.

Eye

Baby whale, or calf

A whale's nostril is called a blowhole. When a whale sleeps it bobs on the surface to keep its blowhole above water.

Humpback whales moan, groan, sigh, squeak, and roar. Whales' strange songs are very loud— no animal can make more noise.

Mouth

Big and beautiful
At 100 feet (30 meters) long, blue whales are the largest animals ever to live on Earth—even bigger than dinosaurs!

Tyrannosaurus

Blue whale

DOLPHINS

Dolphins are small, toothed whales. Some people think that these slim, smooth-skinned mammals are as intelligent as we are. They learn quickly and seem to talk to one another with whistles and clicks. Since ancient times, there has been a special friendship between humans and these playful animals. There are many stories of dolphins saving drowning sailors.

Large, cur[v]ed dorsal fin

Brain *Melon*

Built-in sonar
A dolphin uses sound to find its food and to work out where it is. The melon, a fatty organ in its head, concentrates a stream of clicks which bounce back when they hit something. These echoes tell dolphins where an object is.

Dolphins do not need to drink. They get all the water they need from the fish and squid they eat.

Sonar clicks

The shape of a dolphin's mouth makes it look as if it is always smiling.

Toothy grin
This bottlenose dolphin has more than 100 pointed teeth, which are about 0.3 inches (eight millimeters) long.

Hitching a ride
Just in front of a speeding ship there is a wave. Dolphins love to swim in this spot. Like surfers, if they catch the wave in the right way, it will push them through the sea.

Blowhole

Most dolphins have a long snout, called a beak.

104

Family life
Dolphins live in family groups called pods. Baby dolphins often stay with their mothers for many years. They learn how to catch fish, signal to each other, and escape from sharks by copying other members of their pod.

Dolphins, like all toothed whales, have only one blowhole. Baleen whales have two.

Bottlenose dolphins are very playful. They love to leap out of the water.

Just as you have your own personal name and voice, every dolphin has its own whistle, which other dolphins recognize.

Tail fluke

Types of dolphins

Harbor porpoise

Bottlenose dolphin

Striped dolphin

Common dolphin

Risso's dolphin

Killer whale (male)

The biggest dolphin
Killer whales are fierce dolphins which can grow to be 30 feet (nine meters) long. This one is trying to grab a sea lion to eat.

Seals

Seals are warm-blooded mammals, which means that they can make their own heat. Because they often swim in very cold water, they need to be able to keep this heat inside their bodies. Seals can't put on a winter coat like you to keep warm. Instead, they are covered in short hair or fur and have a layer of fat, called blubber. Sometimes, when seals swim in warmer water, they get too hot and have to fan their flippers in the air to cool down!

Ball of fluff
Baby seals, or pups, a born on land. For a f weeks, many of them have white, fluffy fur.

All seals have good hearing, but only sea lions and fur seals have ear flaps. All that can be seen of this harbor seal's ears are two tiny holes.

When a seal dives under wate it closes its nose, mouth, and e

These whiskers, which are 10 times thicker than your hair, can sense movement in the water. This helps the seal find fish, clams, squid, and octopus to eat.

Pile up!
When walruses climb up onto beaches, they often lie right on top of each other to keep warm.

Flip flop

Sea lions, fur seals, and walruses use their front flippers to sit up straight. Their back flippers can turn forward. This means that they can walk, and even run, on dry land. True seals can only slide around on their bellies when they leave the sea.

Types of seals

There are three different groups of seals.

Gray seal

True seals

Elephant seal

's smooth, streamlined ody helps the seal speed way from killer whales nd polar bears.

Blubber is between three to four inches (seven and 10 centimeters) thick.

Seal-eating seals

Leopard seals are fierce. They leap out of the sea and thump onto the ice to grab penguins and other seals.

This seal is less than 6.5 feet (two meters) long from nose to back flippers. An elephant seal can measure more than three times that!

Eared seals

Northern fur seal

California sea lion

Walrus

Male walruses fight each other with their big tusks.

Hair seals, like this harbor or common seal, speed through the sea by moving their back flippers up and down.

INSECTS AND SPIDERS

Hundreds of millions of years ago, long before dinosaurs arrived, there were insects on Earth. Today there are more than a million known types of insects, and scientists think there are many more waiting to be found.

All insects start as eggs and most go through a larval stage. Their bodies are divided into three parts—head, thorax, and abdomen. Adults have six legs, and most have wings.

Spiders are not insects—they are arachnids. In fact, spiders love to eat insects. Unlike an insect, a spider has eight legs, and its head and thorax are joined.

All insects and spiders are small animals that creep through undergrowth and live in gardens and forests. But occasionally, they come to stay in our homes.

Garden spider

Dragonfly

Honeybee

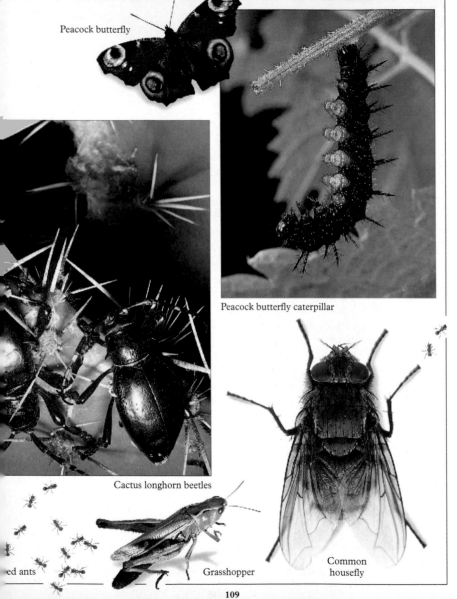

Peacock butterfly

Peacock butterfly caterpillar

Cactus longhorn beetles

ed ants

Grasshopper

Common
housefly

FLIES

You have probably seen a housefly zooming around your kitchen. Most people think of flies as pests—annoying little creatures that buzz around us, bite us, walk on our food, and spread disease. But in other ways, flies are a necessary and useful part of our world. They help to pollinate plants and are a source of food for a variety of other animals.

A hoverfly taking off

Sensitive flies
Flies have surprisingly strong senses. This means they have very good eyesight, and a keen sense of taste and smell.

Nice to see you!
Our eyes have just one rounded lens. A housefly has thousands of six-sided lenses. Each lens sees a part of a bigger picture. This creates an image of colored dots, like a pixelated picture from a digital camera.

Flies have two large compound eyes which see colors and shapes.

Many flies, like the housefly, have small antennae.

When the fly finds liquid food, it simply sucks it up. If it finds solid food, the fly first dissolves it with special juices.

At the end of a fly's mouth are two pads that look like lips.

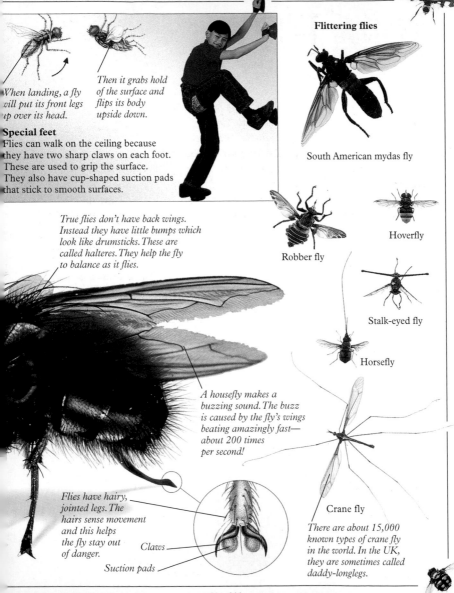

When landing, a fly will put its front legs up over its head.

Then it grabs hold of the surface and flips its body upside down.

Special feet
Flies can walk on the ceiling because they have two sharp claws on each foot. These are used to grip the surface. They also have cup-shaped suction pads that stick to smooth surfaces.

Flittering flies

South American mydas fly

Robber fly

Hoverfly

Stalk-eyed fly

Horsefly

True flies don't have back wings. Instead they have little bumps which look like drumsticks. These are called halteres. They help the fly to balance as it flies.

A housefly makes a buzzing sound. The buzz is caused by the fly's wings beating amazingly fast— about 200 times per second!

Flies have hairy, jointed legs. The hairs sense movement and this helps the fly stay out of danger.

Claws

Suction pads

Crane fly

There are about 15,000 known types of crane fly in the world. In the UK, they are sometimes called daddy-longlegs.

BEETLES

There are more species of beetles in the world than any other kind of animal. It is thought there are at least 300,000. Most are plant-eaters, but some battling beetles attack and eat other insects and are quite ferocious. Beetles can be pests because they eat valuable crops. But mostly they are helpful to us because they eat dead plants and animals and return them to the Earth as important nutrients.

Ready for battle
A beetle's hard outer casing acts like a protective armor.

Wing case

Take that!
These fighting beetles are stag beetles. They get their name because male stag beetles have large "horns." These are really large jaws that are used for fighting like the antlers of a real stag. Males fight to defend their territory.

The forewings are turned into tough wing cases that protect the delicate hind wings.

Hind wing

The beetle's claws help it to grip.

Garden visitor
Ladybugs are beetles, too. Not all beetles can fly but ladybugs can. They use their hind wings to fly.

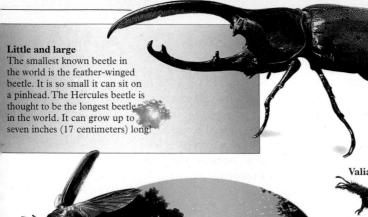

Little and large
The smallest known beetle in the world is the feather-winged beetle. It is so small it can sit on a pinhead. The Hercules beetle is thought to be the longest beetle in the world. It can grow up to seven inches (17 centimeters) long!

Valiant beetles

Rove beetle

...ting males ...ach other off ...ground. They do ... by grabbing their ...pponent around ... the middle.

Tortoise beetle

Night lights
Fireflies are not really flies, they are beetles. At night, the females put on a light show as they flash their tails to attract a mate. They are able to do this because they have a special chemical in their body.

Giraffe beetle

Hard, antlerlike jaws.

If it's attacked, it fires off a mixture of burning chemicals.

Bombardier beetle

...tles have ...ps to ... them ...e food.

Roll over
Dung beetles go to a lot of trouble to find a safe and nutritious home for their young. They collect animal dung and roll it into large balls. They roll the dung balls all the way to their underground homes. There they lay their eggs in the dung. When the beetle larvae hatch, they discover a tasty meal in front of them!

Beetle storing dung

CATERPILLARS

Caterpillars are like tiny eating machines. They spend most of their time chomping on leaves. Caterpillars are actually the young of butterflies and moths. They hatch from the eggs the adult female has laid on plants. With constant eating they get bigger and bigger, until they are ready to change into adult butterflies and moths.

A new skin
Caterpillar skin cannot stretch. So as it gets larger, the caterpillar breaks out of its skin. Underneath is a new, larger skin which will last until the caterpillar needs to molt again.

The front three pair of legs are called thoracic legs, and are used for walking and clasping.

Caterpillars produce silk from special glands and force it out through a spinneret under the head.

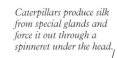

Caterpillars have twelve tiny, simple eyes, called ocelli, on their head.

Hatching out
The butterfly's eggs are laid on the underside of a leaf.

The caterpillar uses its jaws to bite its way out of the egg.

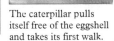

The caterpillar pulls itself free of the eggshell and takes its first walk.

The caterpillar's head is armed with a pair of stout jaws called mandibles.

Caterpillars test food and guide it to their mouth with mouthparts called maxillary palps.

The body is divided into 13 segments.

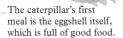

The caterpillar's first meal is the eggshell itself, which is full of good food.

...derful caterpillars

...rpillars can be hairy or spiny,
...have unusual shapes.

Tiger moth caterpillar

...age white caterpillar

Emperor moth
caterpillar

Puss moth caterpillar

...e most insects,
...erpillars breathe
...ough openings
...led spiracles.

*The five pairs of stumpy,
suckerlike legs are called
prolegs. The caterpillar
uses them for holding
onto plant stalks.*

Silkworms

Silk is produced by most moth caterpillars.
But the finest silk is produced by the silkmoth
caterpillar, often known as a silkworm.
After the caterpillars have spun themselves
into a silken cocoon, they are put into
boiling water. The silk
is removed and spun
into threads to create
material for clothes.

...asters of disguise

...o avoid being eaten, some
...aterpillars have developed
...afty disguises. The sphinx
...awk moth caterpillar looks
...ke a deadly snake, the lobster
...oth looks like a raised lobster's
...aw, and the common sailer
...oks like a shriveled leaf.

Sphinx
hawk moth

Lobster
moth

Common sailer

Excuse me, I'm changing

To become adult moths, most
moth caterpillars spin themselves
a cocoon using silk, which comes
out of their spinnerets. Inside, they
undergo astonishing
physical changes.

BUTTERFLIES

Butterflies are perhaps the most beautiful of all insects. It is amazing to think that a fat, leaf-eating caterpillar can become a brightly colored, fluttering creature of the air. The change happens in the butterfly chrysalis. The caterpillar's body is broken down and completely changed. After about four weeks, a fully formed butterfly emerges.

Time to wake up
The butterfly comes out of the chrysalis in three stages. During this time it is very open to attack by hungry birds or spiders.

1. No longer a caterpillar, a beautiful butterfly comes out of the chrysalis with its wings crumpled up.

Monarchs on the move
Most butterflies are born, live, and die in one place. But when winter comes to the eastern and western coasts of North America, thousands of monarchs fly south to the warmth of California and Mexico. When warm weather returns to their first home, they fly north again.

...py landings

...uded yellow butterfly comes
...land on a thistle. Butterfly
...t is more controlled than it
...s. The insect is able to
...ge course instantly and
...e sudden landings.

...terflies feed through a tube
...ed a proboscis. This is
...ed up when not in use.

*Butterflies
have clubbed
antennae.*

Wings open.

In the background

Some butterflies make a tasty meal for
birds. But if they are able to blend in with
their background, they may avoid being
eaten. The open wings of the Indian leaf
butterfly have a striking
orange pattern. But
when its wings are closed,
the butterfly looks exactly
like an old, dry leaf.

*Wings closed,
resting on leaf.*

2. The butterfly must stay
still for many hours, as blood
is pumped into the wing veins
to stretch the wings. Later it
holds its wings apart to
let them harden.

3. When its wings have
hardened, the butterfly
is ready to fly off to find
its first meal of nectar.

Brilliant butterflies

Wallace's golden birdwing

Glass swallowtail butterfly

88 butterfly

Scaly wings

The wings of both butterflies
and moths are covered with
tiny scales, which overlap like
the tiles on a roof. Bright
colors can either be used to
attract a mate, or to warn
predators that the butterfly,
or moth, is not good to eat.

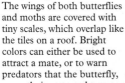

Cramer's blue morpho butterfly

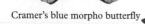

MOTHS

Most moths are night-fliers, and their strong senses of smell and hearing make them well suited to a nighttime existence. They can easily find their way through darkness and although attracted to light, they are dazed by it. Moths rest by day, and many are colored to look like tree bark or leaves so that they cannot be spotted by natural enemies such as birds and lizards.

Moths' antennae are straight or fernlike. They are used for smelling out nectar or other moths at night.

The South American ghost moth has one of the biggest wingspans of any moth. Wingtip to wingtip, it can measure up to 12 inches (30 centimeters).

Nymphalid butterfly

Wings at rest
One way to tell a moth from a butterfly is to see how the insect folds its wings. Most moths rest with their wings folded over their backs. But butterflies close their wings upright.

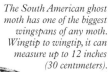

White ermine moth

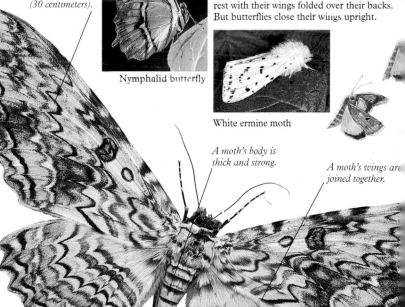

A moth's body is thick and strong.

A moth's wings are joined together.

Whooosss whooo?

To scare off enemies, like birds, the wing patterns of some moths mimic the appearance of fierce animals. The great peacock moth has big eyespots on its wings which look like an owl's eyes. With these staring back at them, birds think twice before attacking!

Day-flying moths

Colombian blue wing moth

Madagascan red-tailed moth

Verdant hawk moth

A real eyeful!

Pyraustinae moths have strange feeding habits. With their long proboscises, they drink the tears of animals such as cows and buffaloes. They are so gentle, that the animal's eye does not become irritated.

Sloan's urania moth

The veins of the moth's wings help warm or cool the insect.

Spot the moth!

This geometrid moth from the jungles of Borneo looks like lichen on a tree trunk. The secret of its camouflage is not just color, but also ragged outlines and broken patterns.

ANTS

Ants live together in nests that are like underground towns. There may be millions of ants living in one nest. Most of these are female and are called workers. Some workers build and repair the nest, while some are "soldiers" and guard the entrance. Others gather food for the larvae and the huge queen. Her life is spent laying millions of eggs, and the survival of the nest depends upon her well-being.

Weaving away
Weaver ants make their nests in trees. They sew leaves together using a sticky silk thread produced by their larvae. The queen lives inside the leaf envelope.

Some ants will spray a nasty chemical from their rear end if they sense danger!

Ants have powerful jaws, or mandibles, for chopping food. Their mouth is just below the mandibles.

When ants meet they "tap" antennae. The antennae contain chemical "messages" which can be passed on by touching.

Ants can run very fast because they have long legs.

Farming fungus
Leafcutter ants are the farmers of the ant world. They cut up bits of leaf and take them back to the nest. Fungus grows on the rotting leaf— and then the ants feed on the fungus!

Left, right!
Army ants from South America are very fierce insects. They are nomadic, which means they are always on the move. They march in columns through the forest, killing and eating everything in their path. Here they are raiding a wasp's nest.

Red ant

Black ant

Living pantries
ome honeypot ant
orkers spend their
hole lives feeding
on nectar. Their
domens swell and
en food is hard to
nd, other workers
use them as a
food supply.

Harvester ant

Wood ant

Dinoponera—
the largest ant

side an ant's nest
e success of an ant's nest relies on the
rdworking and organized inhabitants.

*The queen lays her eggs in
he royal chamber.*

*lier ant
rding
entrance.*

*Workers take care
of the ant larvae.*

*A network of tunnels
joins the chambers in
the ant's nest.*

GRASSHOPPERS

Grasshoppers are known for the "ticking" sounds they make and for their ability to leap high into the air. There are more than 20,000 different kinds of grasshoppers in the world. Grasshoppers are plant-eaters, feeding on leaves and stems. Normally, they live alone. But under special conditions, some species undergo a series of physical changes. They increase in size, become more brightly colored, and gather in the millions to become a swarm of hungry locusts.

The long back legs are good for leaping. A grasshopper can jump over three feet (one meter).

Its legs and feet have spikes which it uses to defend itself against enemies.

Grasshoppers have good eyesight and hearing.

Grasshoppers' c[ol...] help them to blend in [with] their backgro[und]

Name that tune
Grasshoppers are good fiddle players. They make music the same way a violin produces sound. The grasshopper's leg is its bow and the tough wing vein is the string. Crickets are also known for their musical ability. They use their wings to make sounds. One wing has a thick vein with bumps on it. This is called the file. The cricket rubs the file over a rough ridge on the other wing to make cricket music.

Cricket

Grasshopper

Chirping cousins
Crickets belong to the same insect group as grasshoppers, but crick[ets] have longer antennae a[nd] like eating other insect[s]

Growing up

Female locusts lay their eggs in the sand. The babies, called nymphs, hatch and dig their way out. When they appear, they are tiny versions of their parents. In order to become fully grown adults, the nymphs molt between three and five times. After each molt the nymphs are bigger than before. When they molt for the final time, they emerge with full-sized wings.

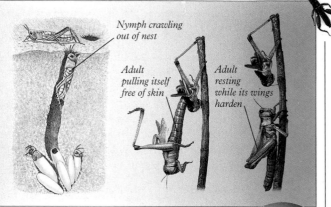

Nymph crawling out of nest

Adult pulling itself free of skin

Adult resting while its wings harden

The trouble with locusts

When heavy rains fall in hot, dry regions, lush plant life begins to grow. With lots of food, large numbers of grasshoppers get together to mate. After mating, they eat all the plant life around them and grow much larger. In search of more food, they take to the air in huge swarms, devouring fields of valuable crops.

Locust-infested areas

Extended family

All of these insects are related to grasshoppers but they have quite different features—and very clever disguises.

Leaf insect

Stick insect

Praying mantis

BEES

Bumblebee

You have probably heard the buzz of a honeybee as it flies from flower to flower. During the spring and summer months, bees spend their time collecting food. There are thousands of different types of bees and many of them live alone. But social bees, such as honeybees, live in large nests or hives. They gather nectar to be stored in the hive and turned into honey.

Nest-making
Wild honeybees often build their nests in trees, hanging the waxy honeycomb from branches.

Working hives
Man-made hives are specifically n to house thousan of bees. Farmers place these hives their orchards so bees will pollinat the trees.

As the honeybee moves from flower to flower, bright yellow pollen sticks to its body. The bee combs the pollen into pollen baskets on its back legs and carries it back to the hive, where it is turned into food.

This honeybee is feeding on nectar, a sweet liquid found in flowers. It sucks out the nectar with its lo tubelike mouthparts.

Bees help to pollinate flowers by carrying pollen from flower to flower.

The bee's sting is in its tail.

Buzzy bees

African killer bee

Orchid bee

Parasitic bee

weet drink
orker honeybees look
er the young and turn
ctar into another sweet
uid we call honey.

*A large hive
can hold up
to 50,000 bees.*

*Inside the hive, the bees store
honey in a comb, which is
made up of thousands of little
six-sided cells. The bees feed
on the honey during the cold
winter months.*

Shall we dance?
Worker bees scout for food.
When they find a good supply
they do a dance—in a figure-eight
pattern—to tell the other bees where
the food is. The bees in the hive then
know where the food is by the angle
of the "figure eight" and the
position of the sun in the sky.

Asian carpenter bee

een bee
ry hive needs a queen. The
en bee mates with the male, called
one. She then lays all the eggs.
v hives are formed in summer
n a young queen leads
of workers out of
old hive to
w one.

A feast fit for a queen
Royal jelly is actually bees' milk.
It is filled with good things like
sugar, protein, and vitamins. The
worker bee larvae do not get to
eat the royal food—they are fed
on pollen and honey. Only the
honeybee larvae that are destined
to become queens eat royal jelly.
Because it is so rich in vitamins
and proteins, people now use
it to make face creams, soap,
and vitamins.

Royal jelly
products

DRAGONFLIES

Many insects are good fliers, but dragonflies are truly the champions of flight. Millions of years ago, enormous dragonflies patrolled the skies. Even today's finger-length dragonflies are quite large compared to other insects. Once dragonflies have emerged from their water-based nymph stage, they take to the air, flying at speeds of up to 34 miles (54 kilometers) per hour.

Wing power
Dragonflies have stro[ng] muscles which contr[ol] the base of the wings. In flight, the wings l[ook] like a rapidly changin[g] X shape.

Mating dragonflies
Brightly colored male dragonflies cling to the necks of females with their tails.

Laying eggs
When the female is ready to lay her eggs, she dips her abdomen into the water. The eggs sink below the surface where they hatch as wingless nymphs that live underwater for up to four years.

Each pair of clear, veined wings can beat separately. This means that dragonflies can hover.

Dragonflies have excellent eyesight. They have two huge compound eyes. Each eye can have up to 30,000 lenses.

The bristles on the dragonfly's front legs help it to trap prey in the air.

Breaking out
When the nymph is fully developed, it climbs out of the water and clings to a plant stem where it undergoes a spectacular change. The nymph's skin cracks open at the back and an adult dragonfly slowly pulls itself free.

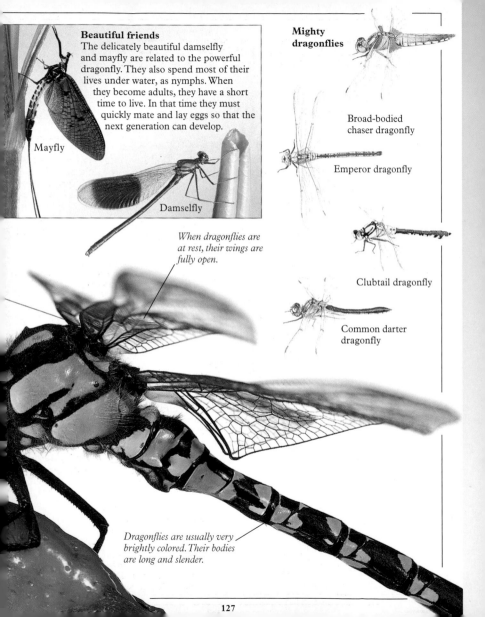

Beautiful friends
The delicately beautiful damselfly and mayfly are related to the powerful dragonfly. They also spend most of their lives under water, as nymphs. When they become adults, they have a short time to live. In that time they must quickly mate and lay eggs so that the next generation can develop.

Mayfly

Damselfly

When dragonflies are at rest, their wings are fully open.

Mighty dragonflies

Broad-bodied chaser dragonfly

Emperor dragonfly

Clubtail dragonfly

Common darter dragonfly

Dragonflies are usually very brightly colored. Their bodies are long and slender.

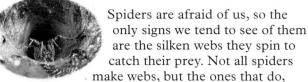

WEB SPIDERS

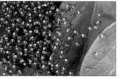

Spiders are afraid of us, so the only signs we tend to see of them are the silken webs they spin to catch their prey. Not all spiders make webs, but the ones that do, like this funnel-web spider, are good at recycling. When its web gets damaged, the spider eats it, digests the silk, then uses it to spin another one.

I'll eat you later
If a spider catches a tasty insect, but is not hungry, it poisons it but does not kill it. Then it wraps it in silk and keeps it for later.

Up, up and away
When baby spiders—called spiderlings—want to travel long distances they take to the air. They do not have wings but they are still able to fly. They produce a piece of silk and use it like a balloon.

Spiders do not have bones. Their head and thorax are covered by a hardened shield.

The spiderling suspends itself from a long line.

It makes a loop, which is slowly drawn up by the breeze.

When it's ready to take off, it cuts itself free.

Silk is produced through the spinnerets on the end of the spider's abdomen. Spiders use their legs to pull out the silk.

The saclike abdomen contains the heart, lungs, silk glands, and the reproductive parts.

Fatal fascination
Scientists think that insects are attracted to spiderwebs because patterns in the webs reflect ultraviolet light. Unlike us, insects see ultraviolet light and use it to find food.

Ready to attack

This Australian funnel-web spider is one of the world's deadliest. Here it is poised, ready to attack! When spiders catch their prey, usually insects, they use their fangs to poison and kill them. The funnel-web spider, like most spiders, uses its strong digestive juices to dissolve the insect's insides so the spider can suck it dry.

Spiders and webs

The net-casting spider lives in trees, mostly in jungle areas. To catch prey, it spins a sticky net and throws it over passing insects.

Most web spiders have eight simple eyes, called ocelli. But even so, they cannot see very well.

Making a web
Making a web takes time and special care. Spiders only spin new webs when the old ones become messy or damaged.

Spiders have a pair of small, leglike appendages, called palps, on each side of their mouthparts. They help spiders smell, taste, and detect prey.

Spiders have eight legs.

Even though spiders do not have ears, they can "listen" to the world around them through their webs. The webs are very sensitive to vibrations in the air.

The water spider spins a web in the shape of a bell under the water. It fills the bell with a bubble of air and moves in.

The web of an orb-web spider looks like a target. It takes about an hour to spin a complete web.

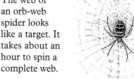

The female purse web spider lives in a silken pouch. When an unsuspecting insect lands on top, the spider bites through the pouch and grabs it.

HUNTING SPIDERS

Many spiders catch their prey without the use of silk. They are called hunting spiders. Some patrol their territory looking for insects to pounce on. Others crouch in burrows and wait for prey to wander by. Unlike web spiders, many hunting spiders have strong jumping legs and sharp eyesight so that they can easily spot their victims.

This jumping spider is an active hunter, so it doesn't need a web to catch its prey. Instead, these spiders go out to find their prey and pounce on it.

The hairs on the spider's body are very sensitive to vibrations made by moving prey.

All spiders have eight eyes on the front of their heads, but they can come in different sizes and arrangements depending on the type of spider. The eyes of this spider are in rows with two big eyes in the middle of the front row which help them to hunt.

Hide and seek
Some spiders ambush prey instead of trapping or chasing after it. Tree-bark trapdoor spiders, for example, use their powerful jaws to make a burrow with a trapdoor at the entrance. Unseen, they lie in wait behind the trapdoor, ready to leap upon any unsuspecting insects that might crawl by.

Long jumpers
Hunting spiders need good eyesight because they have to see and chase after their next meal. Many can measure exactly the leap they must make onto their victim, as they run along after it.

Happy hunters

Brazilian wandering spider

Crab spider

Raft spider

Full speed ahead
Wolf spiders hunt during the day. This Australian wolf spider lurks at the entrance of its silk-lined tunnel, ready to race full-speed after prey.

Woodlouse spider

These spiders live anywhere from deserts to forests, or even swamps.

Ready, aim, fire!
Spitting spiders spit when they are hungry. When they spot an insect, they spit streams of sticky gum from each fang. This glues the insect to the ground until the spider can arrive to eat it.

DINOSAURS

Few animals hold such fascination as dinosaurs. The last of these incredible creatures died about 66 million years ago, long before the first humans appeared. Fossilized skeletons and lifelike models can help us imagine what they were like. We know that dinosaurs hatched out of eggs and grew up in just a few years. Scientists believe that some lived like we do, in families where the adults took care of their young. Most dinosaurs had tiny brains, but some may have been smart enough to hunt in packs.

Tyrannosaurus rex head

Dinosaurs were the most successful big land animals of all time, and some of their relatives live around us today. We call them birds!

Maiasaura growing up

Camarasaurus sk

Maiasaura family

Barosaurus

Triceratops

...inonychus's
...ot bones

133

DIFFERENT DINOSAURS

The word "dinosaur" was first used nearly 200 years ago. There has been an explosion of excitement about them ever since. The huge number of different dinosaur species makes the study of dinosaurs fascinating for everyone. Thousands of bones belonging to hundreds of different dinosaurs have now been discovered. Today, dinosaurs are big business, with millions of dinosaur books and toys on sale in stores.

First and last
Herrerasaurus was one of the first dinosaurs. It lived about 251 million years ago. *Tyrannosaurus* was one of the last dinosaur and became extinct abo 67 million years ago. Today, we are closer in time to *Tyrannosaurus* than *Tyrannosaurus* was to *Herrerasaurus*!

Dinosaur ancestor
Scientists think that over millions of years, the dinosaurs may have developed from small, agile reptiles like *Marasuchus*. The hips and long legs of this primitive reptile are similar to those of the earliest dinosaurs.

Classic Jurassic
The middle part of the dinosaur a is called the Jurassic period. It star about 200 million years ago and lasted 55 million years.

The age of the dinosaurs
Dinosaurs didn't all live at the same time. When one species died out, another came along to take its place. The dinosaur age is split into the Triassic, Jurassic, and Cretaceous periods. The first dinosaurs appeared during the Triassic period, about 251 million years ago.

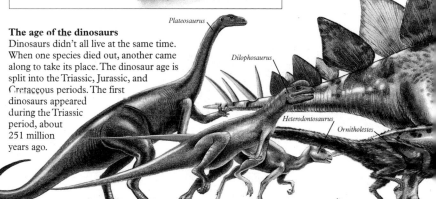

Plateosaurus

Dilophosaurus

Heterodontosaurus

Ornitholestes

Theropod

This group of dinosaurs walked on two legs and had three-toed limbs. They were almost always meateaters, and some were huge and powerful hunters.

Tyrannosaurus rex

Triceratops

Marginocephalian

Their name means "fringed heads." This group included the horned and herbivorous *Triceratops*, as well as *Pachycephalosaurus*.

Leaellynasaura

Ornithopod

These beaked dinosaurs were plant-eaters; *Iguanodon* was one of the largest to be identified.

Vulcanodon

Euoplocephalus

Sauropod

These huge, long-necked plant-eaters walked on four legs and included the *Diplodocus*.

Thyreophoran

This group of armored herbivores included *Euoplocephalus*.

Cretaceous creatures

The last part of the dinosaur age is called the Cretaceous period. This stage lasted for about 79 million years. The fiercest ever meat-eaters lived during this time, alongside their heavily armored prey.

...osaurus

Ceratosaurus

Tyrannosaurus rex

Saltasaurus

Torosaurus

...mpsognathus

Euoplocephalus

DIGGING UP A DINOSAUR

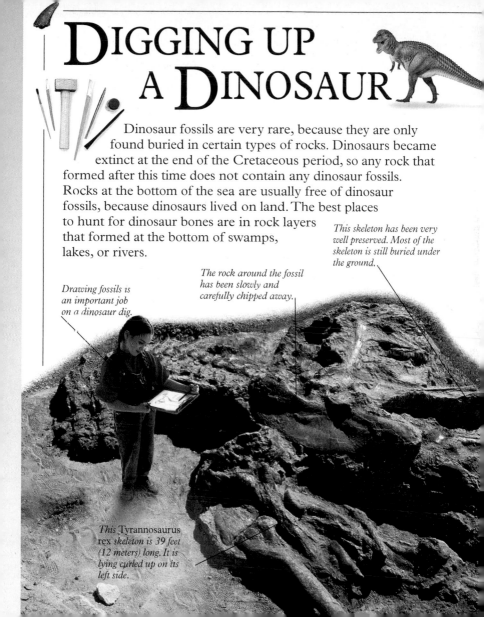

Dinosaur fossils are very rare, because they are only found buried in certain types of rocks. Dinosaurs became extinct at the end of the Cretaceous period, so any rock that formed after this time does not contain any dinosaur fossils. Rocks at the bottom of the sea are usually free of dinosaur fossils, because dinosaurs lived on land. The best places to hunt for dinosaur bones are in rock layers that formed at the bottom of swamps, lakes, or rivers.

This skeleton has been very well preserved. Most of the skeleton is still buried under the ground.

The rock around the fossil has been slowly and carefully chipped away.

Drawing fossils is an important job on a dinosaur dig.

This Tyrannosaurus rex skeleton is 39 feet (12 meters) long. It is lying curled up on its left side.

Old bones, new technology
Modern technology, like this ground-penetrating radar, can be used to find bones below the rock surface. In the 1980s, a dinosaur named *Seismosaurus* was found in this way, in New Mexico.

Dinosaur trap
The Dinosaur National Monument in America is one of the world's richest dinosaur treasure troves. It was once a sandy riverbed, which trapped many dying dinosaurs and preserved their bones.

Handle with care
Although dinosaurs were strong when they were alive, their fossils are very fragile now. Digging up a dinosaur is a slow and very delicate process.

1. The thick layers of rock above the dinosaur are often cleared away with mechanical diggers, and sometimes blasted away with explosives.

2. The last 8 inches (20 centimeters) or so of rock above the dinosaur are removed very carefully with tools.

3. The exact positions of the bones are then mapped out and recorded with drawings and photographs.

Fossil collection
Dinosaur bones are not the only kind of fossils found at dinosaur sites.

Footprints

Skin

Stomach stones

Eggs

Droppings

Teeth

4. The fragile bones must be covered with plaster for protection, before they can be moved away from the site.

5. Finally the strengthened bones are loaded up in a van and driven to a laboratory for further study.

REBUILDING A DINOSAUR

Thick bones in the neck held up the heavy weight of the Tyrannosaurus's head.

Jigsaw puzzles can be tricky, especially if some pieces are missing and pieces from different puzzles are mixed in. People who rebuild dinosaur skeletons are faced with a similar puzzle. Fossil bones must be put together in the right order to form a skeleton. Bones belonging to different dinosaurs may have found their way into the collection by mistake. Missing bones are modeled by looking at the bones of similar dinosaurs. Broken bones must be cleaned and repaired before they can be assembled.

Back at the lab

Dinosaur bones are taken from the fossil site to a laboratory. Experts clean and repair them before they are rebuilt into a skeleton. Sometimes, fossils may be prepared for study, but are never displayed in museums.

Bellyache

Early last century, scientists argued over how to rebuild the skeleton of a *Diplodocus*. Some believed *Diplodocus* was built like a lizard, with long legs sprawling out from its body. This was an impossible pose. *Diplodocus* would have needed to drag its belly through a ditch to walk!

1. First, the hard, protective plaster must be removed from the bone with special tools.

2. Next, the bones must be carefully cleaned. This stage can take a very long time.

3. The bones are then treated with resin to make them stronger. They must also be repaired, if necessary.

4. Finally, copies are made of the bones using a light material, like fiberglass. The copies, called casts, can be put together to make a museum display.

Super skull
Some fossils are almost perfectly preserved. After millions of years buried under rock, this *Tyrannosaurus* skull did not need much patching up in the fossil laboratory!

Model making
This model of a *Maiasaura* nest was sculpted by a scientific artist.

1. The basic *Maiasaura* shapes are made with wood and wire.

2. The nest site is built around the models. The wire skeletons are covered with paper and clay.

3. The clay models are carefully painted a sandy color. In life, *Maiasaura* was probably well camouflaged.

Building *Tyrannosaurus rex*
This skeleton of *Tyrannosaurus rex* has been on display in an American museum since 1915. Today, scientists think that a big mistake was made in the way the skeleton was put together. They now think the *Tyrannosaurus* held its tail up high above the ground.

trong ribcage ected its heart, liver, nach and lungs.

Massive leg bones supported the dinosaur's weight.

s of steel nderneath bone, fitting y into the s shape.

etal work rting the on is called mature.

A strong metal pillar holds up the metal strips, supporting the full weight of the skeleton.

The tail bones were an extension of the Tyrannosaurus's spine.

LOOKING CLOSER

Staring up at the towering skeletons of dinosaurs can make you feel tiny. But bones alone do not give the whole picture of a living, breathing dinosaur. What color was the dinosaur when it was alive? How strong were its muscles, and how big were its heart and lungs? Looking closely at animals alive today gives us useful clues about features, such as the skin color of dinosaurs. We can even imagine what their insides may have looked like!

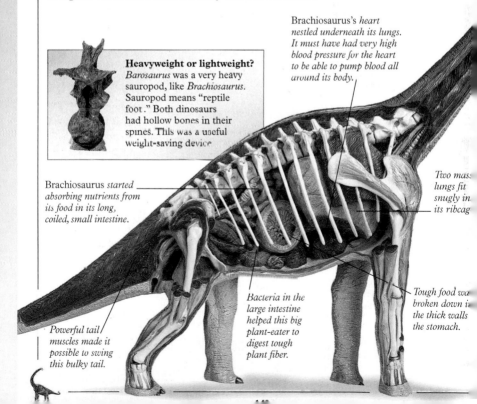

Heavyweight or lightweight?
Barosaurus was a very heavy sauropod, like *Brachiosaurus*. Sauropod means "reptile foot." Both dinosaurs had hollow bones in their spines. This was a useful weight-saving device.

Brachiosaurus's *heart nestled underneath its lungs. It must have had very high blood pressure for the heart to be able to pump blood all around its body.*

Brachiosaurus *started absorbing nutrients from its food in its long, coiled, small intestine.*

Two mass lungs fit snugly in its ribcag

Bacteria in the large intestine helped this big plant-eater to digest tough plant fiber.

Tough food wa broken down i the thick walls the stomach.

Powerful tail muscles made it possible to swing this bulky tail.

ng neck
cles held up
ong neck.

Cunning colors
We can't tell the color of a dinosaur by looking at fossils. But we can follow clues given by the colors of modern animals.

Chameleons hide from their enemies among the leaves. *Hypsilophodon* may have been brown, to blend in with its dry surroundings.

Hadrosaur skin

This brightly colored cockatoo can recognize others of its own kind. *Corythosaurus* may have had a striking crest for the same reason.

In recent years it has been discovered that some dinosaurs had feathers and were more closely related to birds than once thought. One of these is the *Velociraptor*.

Scolosaurus skin

Sauropod skin

n and bones
big model of *Brachiosaurus* was
le by building muscles onto
skeleton. Then, a layer
kin was wrapped
the model
give a lifelike
earance.

BIG HERBIVORES

Plant-eating dinosaurs were some of the biggest animals that ever roamed the Earth. Imagine stepping into the footprint of a *Barosaurus*—it would be big enough to have a bath in! The big vegetarian dinosaurs called sauropods were peaceful creatures. They grew to their huge sizes on a diet of plants alone.

Gentle giants
Sauropods had small heads, bulky bodies, and long necks and tails.

Brachiosaurus

A long tail could come in handy for whacking an enemy, but most of the time it was used to help Barosaurus *balance.*

Weedy teeth
Many big vegetarian sauropods had weak teeth. This meant they did not chew plants, but often swallowed them whole.

Teeth

Camarasaurus

Mamenchisaurus

Apatosaurus

Its feet were and padded, like an eleph

Long?
e reason why
ropods had
h long necks
't certain. There
two theories.

While
osaurus stayed
ne spot, its neck stretched out
food on land or in the water.

. Did *Barosaurus* use its
neck as an underwater
orkel, breathing through
the nostrils on top of its
head? Probably not, as
ter pressure on its body
would have meant it
couldn't breathe at all.

Plant binge
No plant was safe from
a sauropod unless it
was more than 50 feet
(15 meters) above ground!

*Conifers are plants with
cones.* Barosaurus *and
many other vegetarian
dinosaurs ate conifers.*

*Ferns varied in height,
from small to tree-sized
plants. No fern was too
tall for* Barosaurus*!*

Barosaurus *ate
cycads. These
plants still grow
in hot climates.*

*Huge legs supported
the crushing weight
of the* Barosaurus.

FEEDING ON PLANTS

The huge, treetop-munching dinosaurs were not the only plant-eaters of their time. There were many smaller, beaked dinosaurs that also fed on plants, relying more on their teeth to mash the leaves to a pulp and make them easier to digest. *Iguanodon* was well adapted to chewing and chomping. Its jaws were packed with rows of ridged teeth. These grinders pounded away at leaves the *Iguanodon* nipped off with a sharp, beaky snout.

Chewy chops
Your cheeks keep food inside your mouth as you chew. Unlike the big sauropods, *Iguanodon* had cheeks to hold in plant food while it chewed with its teeth.

Big, fleshy cheeks kept food in the Iguanodon's *mouth as it ate.*

A sharp beak nipped off the leaves, and strong teeth at the back of its mouth chewed them into a pulp.

Iguanodon *ate plant but no meat, like all t beaked dinosaurs.*

Iguanodon *browsed on ferns and horsetails.*

Snatch a snack
Iguanodon's bendy finge grasped plants tightly. I sharp thumb claw was a defensive weapon.

...uth shapes

...e mouths of these dinosaurs
...re well adapted for eating plants.
...erodontosaurus ate meat and
...nts, and had three types of teeth,
... cutting, puncturing, and
...nding. *Edmontosaurus* had
...road snout for big mouthfuls.
...psilophodon had a bony beak,
...h short teeth farther back in its
...uth for chopping up its food.

Heterodontosaurus   *Edmontosaurus*   *Hypsilophodon*

Edmontosaurus

*Rows of teeth for
grinding down plants*

Jaw bone of *Edmontosaurus*

Chomp

The jaws of *Edmontosaurus* had hundreds of
teeth that were constantly renewed by new
teeth replacing the old. The teeth were tightly
packed together for grinding and pulping
plants. Scientists think they are some of the
most efficient chewing teeth ever.

Fighting back

Dinosaurs were the biggest plant-eaters of
all time. Plants had to find ways of fighting
back to survive. Some were so successful, they
outlived the dinosaurs, and are still around.

*The spikes of a
monkey puzzle
tree put off most
dinosaurs. Today,
no animal will
touch them.*

Battle of the flowers

The first flowering plants bloomed
about 100 million years ago. They
were successful because they could
spread their seeds and reproduce
more quickly than the plant-eaters
could gobble them up.

*Waxy pine needles taste as bad today
as they did in the dinosaur age.*

HUNTING IN PACKS

Not all dinosaurs were plant-eaters. Packs of hungry meat-eating dinosaurs roamed around, looking for their next meal. *Deinonychus* was a small dinosaur that might have hunted in a pack. It could outrun its prey and pounce to kill with frightening accuracy. Dinosaurs much bigger than *Deinonychus* probably lived in fear of this speedy hunter. *Deinonychus* was named after its most deadly weapon—its name means "terrible claw."

Running reptiles
Deinonychus was in a family of feathered meat-eating dinosaurs called the dromaeosaurids, which means "running reptiles."

Compsognathus

Compsognathus fossil

Lizard lunch
Many pack-hunting dinosaurs chased other dinosaurs, but the smaller hunters enjoyed a diet of lizards or shrewlike mammals. This fossil of the hen-sized *Compsognathus* has the bones of its last meal inside its stomach. It was a Bavarisaurus lizard.

Sharp eyesight was very useful for spotting prey.

Sinornithosaurus

Velociraptor

Utahraptor

Deadly claw
Deinonychus had a claw on the tip of each of its toes, but one claw was much bigger than the rest. This huge, sharp talon could swipe around in a semicircle, slashing a deadly wound into the flesh of the dinosaur's prey.

The claw was five inches (13 cm) long.

Savage hunter
Despite their large skulls, *Deinonychus* probably weren't smart enough to communicate with each other to use complicated hunting tactics when attacking their prey. It's likely that the pack hunt was more of a free-for-all, with each dino fighting for its own meal.

Why hunt in packs?
One wolf cannot attack a deer on its own, but a pack of wolves can easily pull one down, just as small, meat-eating dinosaurs joined together to overpower much bigger dinosaurs. However, wolves are more intelligent than *Deinonychus* were, and use more complicated hunting techniques.

The body of Deinonychus *was light and fast. This was ideal for chasing after prey. Often just a quarter of the size of its prey,* Deinonychus *was about 10 feet (3 meters) long and 6 feet (1.8 meters) tall.*

Sharp, jagged teeth pointed backward for a strong, tearing bite.

is plant-eating nontosaurus bled death from the hes made by the inonychus pack.

ENORMOUS CARNIVORES

Like tigers today, *Tyrannosaurus rex* may have hunted alone, terrorizing its prey with surprise attacks. This fierce dinosaur was a carnivore, which means it lived on a diet of meat. The biggest meat-eater ever to walk on this planet, *Tyrannosaurus rex* was heavier than an elephant and as tall as a two-story building. Its name means "king of the tyrant reptiles."

Hunters need good eyesight and a strong sense of smell. Large parts of Tyrannosaurus *brain controlled its sense of sight and smell.*

Tyrannosaurus *had a massive skull. It took the shock of crashing into p at speeds of up to 12 miles (19 km) per h*

Tyrannosaurus *may have charged with op jaws, ready to sink its deadly teeth into its p Big chunks of flesh we swallowed whole.*

Its short "arms" weren't long enough to reach its mouth, but they may have been used to grip and kill prey.

Duck-billed dinner
Tyrannosaurus probably hunted duck-billed dinosaurs, called *hadrosaurs*. It may have hidden among the trees, waiting for the right moment to charge at a peaceful herd of grazing duckbil

Life-sized tooth
A *Tyrannosaurus* tooth grew up to seven inches (18 centimeters) long.

Stretch those legs
Tyrannosaurus's short "arms" may also have been used to help the dinosaur up after a rest on the ground.

1. Small front arms hold its body steady, as *Tyrannosaurus* begins to move.

A Tyrannosaurus *tooth was covered with tough enamel.*

2. *Tyrannosaurus* then lifts its head and body backward, stretching out its long back legs.

The teeth of a Tyrannosaurus *were massive— built for biting straight though the bones of its victims.*

3. *Tyrannosaurus* stands up straight. The weight of its tail balances its big head.

Not a cannibal
When this *Coelophysis* skeleton was found, scientists thought that there were tiny bones of a baby *Coelophysis* inside its stomach. It's now thought that this baby's bones were just underneath the adult's, and were never actually inside its stomach at all.

Look how small a human tooth is!

t the family
se big, meat-eating dinosaurs shown w are all theropods like *Tyrannosaurus* Theropod means "beast-footed."

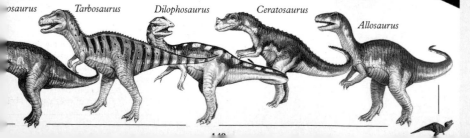

osaurus   *Tarbosaurus*   *Dilophosaurus*   *Ceratosaurus*   *Allosaurus*

DEATH OF THE DINOSAURS

We can tell how old dinosaur fossils are by looking at the age of the rock they were found in. From this, we know that the last of the giant dinosaurs died out about 66 million years ago. Perhaps a huge disaster wiped them all out in one shot.

Rock-solid proof
Many rocks on the Earth's surface are formed in layers. The deeper the layer, the older the rock. No fossil of a big dinosaur has been found above the layer that formed 66 million years ago. This proves they died out this long ago.

From outer space
An enormous asteroid crashed into Earth 66 million years ago. It hit what is now part of Mexico, and the huge impact of the asteroid could have caused catastrophic climate change that made life impossible for the giant dinosaurs.

North America

South America

Yucatán

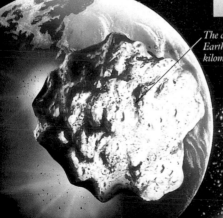

The asteroid may have hurtled toward Earth at about 40,000 miles (64,000 kilometers) per hour.

ⱳw change
e big, spectacular dinosaurs may
t have disappeared overnight.
e world's climate could have
ᵽled over millions of years, slowly
ing them off. New plants grew
ᴡhis colder climate. The warm
ᵷles that covered most of the
ᵼosaurs' world slowly turned
ᴑ cooler forests.

Wild guesses
Many theories try to explain the
death of the dinosaurs. Some of the
most unlikely include the idea that
hungry mammals ate their eggs.

Or that dinosaurs were poisoned
by new, nasty plants. But no
single theory can explain what
really happened.

*Shocked
quartz*

Finding proof
The asteroid crushed rock in the
Earth's surface as it hit Yucatán.
Shocked quartz has been found at
the crater site. Iridium is a rare metal,
found in asteroids. There are high
levels of iridium in the rock that
contains dinosaur fossils.

Iridium

The survivors
Despite the disaster,
a few animals survived.
They included birds,
mammals, reptiles,
and amphibians that
became the ancestors
of animals that live
around us today.

Bird

Mammal

Reptile

Amphibian

What a hole
The asteroid impact
formed a gigantic crater
115 miles (185 kilometers)
wide in Yucatán, Central
America. This photo shows
a similar crater in Arizona
that was made by a more
recent asteroid impact.

*The disaster would have set off a chain
reaction. 440 trillion tons of rock and
dust blocked out the sun's light and the
temperature dropped to -14°F (-10°C).
Acid rain fell on the dinosaurs.*

BIRDS

Any animal that grows feathers is a bird. Some are bigger than people; others are almost as small as bees. Birds hatch out of eggs, which are kept in a nest. All birds have feathers and wings, even the ones that do not fly.

Blue-tit nest

Because they have no teeth, birds cannot chew. Instead, they grind food in a gizzard. Some food stays in a storage bag called a crop so it can be coughed up later for chicks to eat! Birds are like us in the way they breathe oxygen into their lungs. However, they appeared long before humans. Birds are descended from small, feathered, meat-eating dinosaurs with long arms that could be used as wings. This means that all 10,000 different types of birds that live here with us on Earth are actually living dinosaurs!

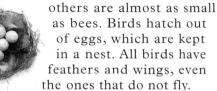

Parrot feathers

Budgerigar feathers

Owl feather

Green-winged parrot skeleton

Wood duck

Kestrel

Flock of starlings in flight

Blue-tit egg

Magpie egg

American robin egg

Guillemot egg

Crop

Gizzard

Senegal parrot

FEATHERS AND FLYING

Feathers are made of keratin, like your hair and nails!

Three types of animals can fly—birds, bats, and insects. Birds are excellent fliers thanks to their coats of feathers. Long, light feathers or small, soft feathers cover almost every part of a bird's body. Usually, only a bird's beak, eyes, legs, and feet are bare. Feathers do much more than cover a bird's naked body: they keep birds warm and dry, and enable them to stay up in the air.

Ducks fly in a straight line.

Flapping *Resting* *Scarlet tanagers bob up and down as they flap, then rest, then flap again.*

Flight patterns
Flying can be hard work. Not all birds flap their wings all the time. Some birds save energy by resting between short bursts of flapping.

Wind power
If you blow hard across the top of a piece of paper, the air on top moves faster than the air underneath. This difference in air speed creates lift and the paper rises. In a similar way, the air moving over the top of a bird's wing moves faster than the air going underneath it. This lifts the bird up in the sky.

rproof body
rs keep the
ry.

Underneath its body feathers, the bird wears a warm vest of fluffy down feathers.

Flapping flight
As this pigeon flaps its wings down, its feathers close so that they can push against the air. On the way up, the feathers open to let the air slip through.

This rosella has about 4,000 feathers.

Adult birds lose old feathers and grow new ones. This is called molting.

Primary feathers can twist like propellers to power the bird through the air.

Vane

Barbule

These secondary flight feathers help lift the bird up in the air.

Hooked up
Each flight feather has thousands of fine strands, called barbules. These hook around each other and hold the feather in shape, even in very windy weather.

Barb

Strong shaft

Wash and brush
Birds keep their feathers clean and tidy by preening. They nibble each feather to zip the barbules back together and to get rid of insects. Most birds also waterproof their feathers by rubbing oil into them. This oil comes from a preen gland which is just above their tail.

Tail feathers are used for steering and stopping.

Quill

SETTING UP HOME

A nest is a cradle in which eggs and baby birds are kept safe from enemies such as snakes and rats. Nests can be holes in trees, mounds of earth, or piles of branches. Greenfinches tuck their cup-shaped nests into bushes where they cannot be seen, whereas eagles' lofty nests are easy to see but hard to reach. Each species tries to give its chicks the best chance of survival.

Courting
Before starting a family, many birds have to attract a mate. Peacocks do this by showing off!

Nesting material
Birds, just like people, build their homes out of all sorts of things. Most nests are made with twigs and leaves, but a few use much stranger ingredients, such as string.

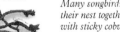
Cattle hair

Seeds

String

Tinfoil

Many songbirds glue their nest together with sticky cobwebs!

Birds may make thousands of trips to collect all their nesting material.

Building a nursery
In many species of birds, both parents build the nest. These long-legged great blue herons are trampling on twigs to make a huge, cup-shaped nest.

Spot the eggs
Ringed plovers don't build a nest. They lay their pebblelike eggs on the beach.

No teacher needed

Weavers are brilliant builders, but they don't have lessons or copy other birds. They just know how to weave their nest. This "knowing without learning" is called instinct.

Knitted nest

The weaver uses his beak and feet to tie the grass into knots!

p-shaped nests have lls to stop eggs from ing out.

Baby birds don't need pillows—they have soft feathers to lie on.

Grass is sewn into the nest to form a ring.

After weaving the walls, roof, and door, he hangs upside down from his home and invites a female to move in.

Nests in trees and bushes are kept dry by the leaves— they form little umbrellas!

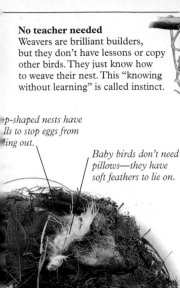

Lichen is used to camouflage the nest.

Dried moss helps to keep the eggs warm.

s cup-nest was built by ishing! The greenfinch sed the material into e with its breast as it n round in a circle.

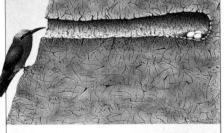

Burrowing bee-eater

Carmine bee-eaters nest underground! The male chooses a sandy riverbank and pecks at the earth. When the dent is big enough to cling to, he starts to dig with his beak and feet. The female moves in when all the work is done!

157

FAMILY LIFE

Family life for most birds is brief, but busy. After the female bird has mated, she lays her eggs, usually in a nest. The baby birds, or chicks, do not grow inside her because this would make her too heavy to fly. When they hatch, the chicks eat a lot, grow bigger and bigger, and then, as soon as they can fly, they leave home forever.

Baby sitting
Eggs must be incubated, or kept warm, otherwise the baby birds inside will die. The parents do this by sitting on them.

What's inside an egg?
All bird eggs have the same things inside them: a growing baby bird which feeds on a yellow yolk, and a watery egg white that cushions the chick from knocks. Woodpeckers and warblers are ready to hatch in 11 days, but Royal albatrosses take more than 11 weeks!

Ostrich eggs are the largest.

Hummingbird eggs are the smallest.

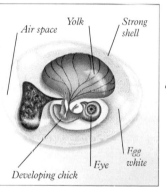

Air space

Yolk

Strong shell

Egg white

Eye

Developing chick

Peck, peck, peck . . .
Getting out of an egg is called hatching. The chick taps at the tough shell until it is free. This can take hours or even days!

The blunt end of the egg is pecked off by the chick with a horny spike called an egg tooth.

First crack

The chick cheeps to tell its parents it is hatching.

Empty shell

Nearly grown up

After baby birds have left home they are called fledglings. Many are eaten by cats and hawks, but some from each nest survive and have families of their own.

Feed me!

Most nestlings are helpless when they hatch; they are blind and naked. All they can do is eat and grow.

The parents push food into their chicks' bright, begging beaks.

Fast food

Blue tits bring back more than 1,000 juicy caterpillars and aphids to the nest each day for their hungry chicks.

Caterpillar

Ducks' eyes are open when they are born.

The wet, sticky stuff, or down, soon dries out.

After the chick has pushed itself head-first out of the egg, it is very tired.

Follow the leader

Baby ducks follow the first big, moving thing that they see— usually one of their parents. This instinct is called imprinting.

Like most waterbirds, just one hour after hatching this duckling can walk, see, swim, and feed itself.

This egg tooth falls off after a few days.

159

THE FROZEN NORTH

The North Pole lies in the middle of a frozen ocean, which is surrounded by a cold, flat, treeless, snowy wasteland, called the tundra. Few birds can survive the long, dark winters of the tundra. But in the summer, when the sun never sets, millions of birds arrive to raise their families. Flowers bloom and the air is full of buzzing insects, but in just a few short weeks the summer vacation is over, and they all fly south again.

The big melt
During the summer, the ice melts. But this water can't sink into the frozen ground, so it forms lots of lakes–ideal for ducks!

Bird's-eye view
Hunting birds have eyes on the front of their head, so that the sight from both eyes overlaps and they can see exactly how far away their victims are. Birds which are eaten by other animals have eyes on the sides of their head, so they can look around for danger.

Blind area

Snowy owl

Ptarmigan

Both eyes can see this dark area.

Only one eye can see this light area.

Tundra residents

Snowy owl

Snow bunting

Gyr falcon

Raven

160

Tough ptarmigans survive the winter by eating dwarf willow twigs.

Birds have a third eyelid that is see-through and helps keep their eyes moist.

Ptarmigans shiver to keep warm.

Snow-colored feathers camouflage ptarmigans.

Causing a stir

Red phalaropes reach the insects that live at the bottom of lakes by swimming in circles! This stirs up the water and makes the insects float upward. You can try this too—put some buttons in a bowl of water, stir it up, and watch!

Duck down

Eider ducks pluck soft feathers, called down, from their breast to line their nest. People collect this down to make soft pillows.

Eider down

Summer coat

Willow ptarmigans don't need thick, white coats in the warm summer, so they molt and grow dark red feathers.

Just like big, woolly socks, these feathers keep the ptarmigan's legs, feet, and toes warm.

Willow ptarmigans are about 17 inches (43 centimeters) in length and live in the Arctic.

mmer visitors

Ruff

Red phalarope

Red-breasted goose

King eider

COLD FORESTS

One-tenth of the land on Earth, especially in the cold north, is covered in conifers. These tall trees, such as pines and firs, have needles instead of broad leaves and woody cones instead of flowers. They form forests that are home to many birds, from seed-eating siskins to big birds of prey.

The siskin's tail spreads out and acts as a brake.

This Japanese waxwing has a bunch of little feathers, called a crest, on its head

These feathers are called the alula—they are joined to the bird's thumb.

The feet are stretched out to grab the branch.

Sleeping safely
When birds bend their legs to sit down, or perch, muscles in their legs make their toes curl. Now the bird can't fall off its perch, even if it falls asleep!

Waxwings are named after these red dots—which look like drops of wax.

Ant antics
A Steller's jay gets rid of mites or feather lice by making ants crawl all over its body. The ants get annoyed and squirt out formic acid, which kills the tiny pests!

Angry an

Cone-opener

Crossbills' beaks can snip open cones a bit like a can opener. Red crossbills eat spruce seeds, but bigger species can open up large pine cones.

Larch cone

Crossed beak

Spruce cone

This greenish-brown bird is a female red crossbill—only the males are red!

Inside a cone

Pine cone

Woody scale

Tasty seed

...rved out

...ry few years, winter is even colder ...n usual. When this happens, the ...sbills and waxwings leave the cold ...st to feed in warmer woods.

...pening up ...athers, the ...n can reduce ...eed.

...uchdown

...ds have to slow down to land, but, ...t like planes, if they go too slowly ...y can stall and fall out of the sky. ...sticking out their alula, they can ...nge the flow of the wind over ...ir body and avoid crash-landings!

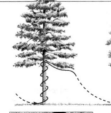

Up and over

Like a little feathered mouse, the treecreeper creeps up tree trunks looking for spiders and earwigs to eat. It starts at the bottom of the tree, spirals its way up the trunk, walks along the first big branch, and then drops down to the bottom of the next tree.

IN THE WOODS

Large parts of America and Europe were once covered by trees. Most of these maple, beech, and oak woods have been cut down to make room for farms and cities. But if you go into the woods that are left, you may still find some of the beautiful birds that live there. Even if you cannot spot them through all the leaves, you will hear them. Male songbirds, such as nightingales, sing flutelike songs to defend their territory.

First-class flier
Woodland birds, such as this sassy blue tit, have short wings. This allows them to twist and turn between the trees.

Woodpeckers' feet have two toes that point forward and two that point backward to get a good grip on tree bark.

Pied flycatcher chasing flies

Tough beak

Tawny owls sleep during the day. This one is being woken up by birds who think it is roosting too near their nests.

This greater spotted woodpecker has a "shock absorber" around its brain to stop it from getting hurt when the bird hammers.

Who's there?
Knock, knock—this is the sound a woodpecker makes when it hammers its beak onto a tree to dig out insects!

By placing their long, stiff tail feathers against the tree trunk, woodpeckers are able to stay steady while they feed.

Song thrushes open up snails by hitting them against rocks.

Robins sing to claim their territory.

All fall down

Most woodland trees are deciduous—they lose all their leaves in winter. Before they drop their leaves, a few, like this rowan, grow juicy berries that many woodland birds love to eat.

Big baby

Cuckoos are lazy. They lay their eggs in other birds' nests, and let them do all the hard work.

A cuckoo has laid its big egg in this dunnock's nest.

As soon as the baby cuckoo hatches, it pushes all the other eggs out of the nest.

The tiny dunnock keeps feeding the cuckoo chick, even when it grows very big!

Crow's nest

Chaffinch eating a caterpillar

This hungry, crafty magpie is waiting for a chance to steal the wood pigeon's eggs.

Wood pigeon

This sparrow hawk is plucking feathers from a hawfinch it has just caught.

Nuthatch   *Woodcock*

Hawfinch eating seeds

SWAMPS AND MARSHES

Pied avocet

Half water, half land, swamps and marshes are strange places to live. But to thousands of birds, the shallow water and soggy soil is an ideal home—it is full of food. Birds that live these tree-filled swamps or murky marshes either walk through the water or swim. Those that walk are called waders. Wading birds have long, thin legs, sometimes thinner than a pencil!

To keep their eggs and chicks dry, reed warblers build their nests high up in the reeds, well above the water.

Young scarlet ibises have gray feathers. They only grow red feathers when they are several years old.

Black tip to the long, red wing

This is not a knee, but an ankle!

Scarlet ibises are about 18 inches (46 centimeters) tall and live in swamps in South America.

Highly strung
Foxes and other egg-thieves can't walk on marshy ground. So, to keep their family safe, reed warblers build their homes in tall marsh plants, called reeds. The nest is tied tightly onto the reeds and won't fall down, even on a windy day.

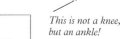

Up in the air
Walking on stilts makes your legs longer. Now you can splash through puddles and your clothes still won't get wet. A little wading bird, called the black-winged stilt, likes to keep its feathers dry, so it has very, very long legs, which work like stilts.

Fitting the bill
Storks stab, shoebills dig, flamingos sieve, and spoonbills trap—these amazing beaks, or bills, are all shaped to catch food.

Spoonbill

Nostril

Saddle-billed stork

All birds' legs are covered in small scales.

These big feet stop the ibis from sinking into the mud by spreading its weight over a larger area.

This long, curved beak can poke deep down into the sticky mud and water at the bottom of the swamp to find frogs and fish.

Shoebill

Greater flamingo

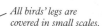

A shady bird
Sunlight shining on water makes it hard to see the fish below. Black herons solve this problem by shading the water with their wings.

LAKES AND RIVERS

Still lakes and flowing rivers provide a well-stocked pantry for flocks of ducks, geese, swans, and many more unusual birds. Wherever you live in the world, you can spot these wonderful waterbirds bobbing around on the surface or paddling in the shallows, for they are not shy of people and live on lakes and rivers in cities, too.

Flipper feet
Waterbirds have webbed feet. They use these webs of s[...] like flippers, to pus[...] through the water.

Splash!
The brilliant blue kingfisher plunges into rivers to catch minnows that are half the length of its body. With its wings folded and its eyes and nostrils tightly shut, the kingfisher flies into the water. It has to struggle to free itself from the pull of the water, but it soon succeeds and flies away with its fish.

Treading water
These western grebes are dancing. When th[...] birds have paired up, they dance across the lake together. Often, a male bird will try to steal another's partne[...]

Water skiing *Gathering speed* *Liftoff*
Touchdown

Water-runways
Heavy waterbirds can[...] land or take off on the[...] spot. Like airplanes, they need runways!

168

inding food

ifferent ducks feed in different ways. Some dabble—they p their beaks into the water to sieve out tiny plants and nimals. Others dive several yards under water to reach eeds, mussels, and insects on the bottom of the lake.

Broad beaks are best for dabbling.

Dabbling ducks never put their whole body under water.

Some diving ducks have notched beaks to hold onto fish.

Shoveler

Teal

Smew

ards are about hes (40 cm) tall e all over rld.

It is easy to tell male and female mallards apart—males have green heads.

Water drips off a duck's back because its feathers are waterproof.

Male mallard

e rds can louder nales.

Female mallard

Ducks molt their flight feathers all at once, so for a few weeks each year they can't fly.

s trapped en the ard duck's 0 tightly d feathers p it float.

These wild mallards may live for up to 29 years, but most only survive for 5-10 years.

Webbed foot

Waterbirds

Black swan

Slavonian grebe

Jacana

Ruddy duck

SEABIRDS

Playful puffins and graceful gannets, like most seabirds, feed, preen, and sleep out on the sea for most of the year. But each summer they come ashore to lay their eggs. Most nest in huge groups, called colonies. Their families are safer with thousands of pairs of eyes watching for danger. Some seabirds choose to crowd onto steep cliffs, well out of the reach of many egg thieves.

Herring gull chicks peck this red spot to make the parents cough up food.

These long wings catch the breeze and lift the herring gull up in the air like a kite.

Some seabirds spend most of their lives in the air, so they don't often use their legs

Waterproof feathers

Webbed feet

Seabirds do not tired on long trip because they can glide for hours on end without flap, their wings.

Dive, dive, dive!
When a gannet spots a shoal of fish, it folds up its wings and hurtles into the water. Less than 10 seconds later, having swallowed the fish under water, it is flying again.

A bony flap covers each nostril.

Gannets dive from up to 150 feet (45 meters) into the sea and reach speeds of 60 mph (100 km/h).

The hard skull protects the gannet like a crash helmet!

This spear-sh bill is ideal for catching fish.

Floating on air
When the wind hits a cliff,
it shoots up toward the sky.
By stretching out their wings,
seabirds, such as puffins, can
use this breeze to lift them up
to their lofty nests.

Beaky bird
A puffin's big, bright
beak is hinged so
that it can snap up
fish and still keep
a grip on those it
has already caught.

Puffin

Herring gull

Gannet

Guillemot

Spinning eggs
Guillemots do not build
nests. Their eggs are pointed
at one end, so if they are
moved, they just roll in a
circle and not off the cliff.

Going up!
A cliff is like a high-rise
apartment building.
Shags nest on the ground
floor, in caves near to
the bottom of the cliff.

Pebbles that move
Ringed plovers live on the beach.
They are camouflaged so well
that they are hard to see.

Shag

TROPICAL FORESTS

Giant trees, which seem to stretch to the sky, form a huge umbrella over the top of a tropical forest. In the shade beneath this green canopy live thousands of weird and wonderful birds. The hot, wet jungles are home to over half of the world's 10,000 species of birds. Noisy parrots gather fruit and nuts, colorful sunbirds sip the juice out of flowers, and harpy eagles swoop down on chattering monkeys.

When a toucan goes to sleep, it rests its big, brightly colored beak on its back.

Toco toucans
are about 14 inches (35 cm) tall and live in South America.

This beak is not as heavy as it looks. It is hollow, and has thin rods of bone inside for strength and support.

The toucan uses the jagged edge of its beak like a saw to cut through large fruit.

Big stretch
With its long, clumsy-looking beak, the toucan can reach fruit and berries that are farther away. It picks them up and tosses them into its throat.

With their strong, hooked beaks, parrots can crack open tough nuts.

Parrots come in all colors. But even bright green ones are hard to spot among tropical fruit and flowers.

...fronted parrots
...out 10 inches
...) tall and live
...ica.

Parrots hold their food with their claws. Some use their right foot and others their left!

This hummingbird's beak is just the right shape to reach to the bottom of the flower.

Hummingbirds are the only birds that can fly backward!

Fancy feathers

King of Saxony bird of paradise

Hovering hummingbird
By flapping their wings very fast, hummingbirds can hover near a flower. They then suck out the flower's juice, or nectar.

Magnificent bird of paradise

...ck-a-doodle-doo!
...ickens have been bred from
...pical birds, called jungle
...wl. These wild birds look
...d sound a lot like chickens,
...t they don't lay as many eggs.

King bird of paradise

White-plumed bird of paradise

GRASSLANDS

Grass grows in the vast spaces between wet forests and dry deserts. These rolling seas of grass have several names: the tropical African plains are known as savanna, while the colder grasslands are called prairies, pampas, or steppes. These green lands are important to people because they make good farmland. To birds, they are a perfect place to live. There are tall grasses to hide in, and seeds, grasshoppers, beetles, and worms just waiting to be eaten.

Crowned crane

Two for dinner
Honeyguides love beeswax but they can't open a bees' nest. Th have to find a big-clawed badg to rip open the nest for them.

The honeyguide leads the way.

The badger leaves p for the patient bird.

Bees

If an oxpecker sees a lion, it calls very loudly and warns the buffalo of danger.

Oxpeckers have strong, sharp claws for clinging to thick skin.

Oxpeckers
are about 5 inches (12 cm) tall and live in Africa.

The buffalo ignores the oxpecker, unless it pecks inside its ears!

Doctor oxpecker!
Oxpeckers peck bloodsucking pests, called ticks, out of the skin of buffalo and zebras. This "surgery" helps to keep the animals healthy.

assland birds

Western meadowlark

Vulturine guinea fowl

Budgerigar

Gouldian finch

Save the chicken!
Every year there are fewer and fewer prairie chickens living on the American prairies. This is because the grass is being plowed up and turned into gigantic fields of corn.

assland parrots
Igerigars are small, green Australian rots. In rainy years, there are more "budgies" Australia than any other species of bird.

litching a ride
Kori bustards kick up thousands of insects as hey stride through tall grass. Bee-eaters use the ustard as a perch to catch these swarming flies.

The bustard's back is sed as a takeoff and anding strip!

Kori bustards weigh about 42 pounds (19 kilograms)!

White throat

Bee-watching bird
Dainty, white-throated bee-eaters eat most insects but like bees best. When they spot one, they grab it, kill it, and swallow it up!

After killing the bee by thumping it against a branch, the bee-eater closes its beak around the bee and squeezes out the stinger.

DRY LANDS

At midday, hot, dusty, dry lands are quiet and appear to be empty. Only at sunrise and sunset, when the air and ground are cooler, do birds come out of the shade to feed and find water. Elf owls are lucky—they eat juicy meat and do not need to drink. Sandgrouse eat dry seeds and have to fly up to 75 miles (120 kilometers) every day to get a drink of water.

Sandgrouse suck
Most birds have to tip their heads back to make water trickle down their throats. Sandgrouse are unusual—like you, they can suck.

Shaggy crest

Roadrunners run, but they can also fly.

In cartoons, roadrunners say "beep beep!" In real life, they rattle their bills to make a "clack."

Takeout water
Male sandgrouse sit in puddles! Their belly feathers soak up water like sponges. When they return to their nests, the chicks drink from the soggy coat.

After the cold desert night, roadrunners warm up by standing with their backs to the sun and sunbathing.

Roadrunners are about 12 inches (30 cm) tall and live in Mexico and North America.

Roadrunners swallow rattlesnakes that are up to 24 inches (60 centimeters) long.

Like most ground-feeding birds, roadrunners have long legs and toes.

Roadrunners can run as fast as an Olympic sprinter!

Roadrunners use their tail to balance as they zigzag across the desert.

Building a sand castle!
A mallee bird doesn't build a nest, it makes a massive mound. It piles leaves into a pit and covers them with sand. The rotting leaves give off heat and incubate the eggs.

The chicks will dig their way out.

Sand is scraped away if the eggs overheat.

This little elf owl is taking shelter from the scorching sun in a hole made by a gila woodpecker.

Tiny verdin hang upside down from cactus branches to look for insects.

Cactus wrens have scaly legs and tough feathers to protect them from the cactus spines.

...ndy birds
...le-colored feathers reflect the sun's ...at and are good desert camouflage.

Gila woodpeckers peck away dead bits of cactus as they hunt for insects.

...is Western ...ebird is ...ping cool in ...hady bush.

Gambel's quail search under stones for seeds and scorpions.

THE FROZEN SOUTH

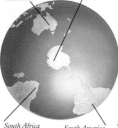

Australia
Antarctica
South Africa
South America

Chinstrap penguin

Antarctica, the land that surrounds the South Pole, is almost empty. The layer of ice 1.2 miles (two kilometers) thick, howling winds, and freezing temperatures stop plants and land-living animals from surviving. Yet the ocean around this frozen land is full of fish and krill, so the coasts are home to millions of birds. Penguins are the best-known residents of the snowy south, but there are also seabirds such as skuas, petrels, and terns.

Belly flop

The quickest way to get around on slippery ice is to slide. Penguins can't use a sled like you, so they scoot along on their big bellies!

They push themselves along with their strong feet and wings.

These Adélie penguins may have to slip and slide up to 60 miles (100 kilometers) from their nesting colonies to the sea.

Egg thief

Skuas rarely go hungry because there are plenty of penguin eggs and chicks for them to steal. While one sku distracts the parent penguins, the other one grabs a mea

They can't fly, but penguins are excellent swimmers.

Adélies eat small animals called krill.

e longest night
ce the Antarctic winter
sets, it is dark for
re than six months.

e and female penguins
h up food from their
achs to feed their chicks.

eror penguins
e biggest
n Antarctica.
can be 4 feet
neters) tall.

penguins keep
n by sitting on
parents' feet!

This feathery
coat keeps
warm air
in and cold
water out.

On ice
Female emperor penguins lay
an egg at the start of winter. For
the next 62-67 cold, dark days
and nights, the male incubates
this egg by standing still and
balancing it on his feet.

Safety in numbers
When their parents are fishing,
the fat, fluffy chicks form groups
called crèches. This helps keep them
warm and protects them from skuas.

Thick fat, called blubber,
keeps penguins warm.

uins come to
urface to gulp
air about
2-3 minutes.

Adélie penguins
can swim at
up to 20 miles
(32 km) per hour.

By building up speed,
they can shoot themselves
out of the sea.

Leopard seals
eat penguins.

179

BIRDS OF PREY

Eagles, hawks, and falcons are birds of prey, or raptors. These strong, fast, fearless birds kill and eat other birds and animals—their prey. Whether they are the size of a sparrow or have a wingspan of 10 feet (three meters), like the condor, they all have three things in common: hooked beaks, sharp claws, and "eagle" eyes that can spot rabbits more than three miles (five kilometers) away!

Dressed for dinner
Vultures poke their hea
into dead animals to e
Their heads are bare—
feathers would get mes

Steep stoop
Peregrines have been timed diving at speeds of more than 185 miles (300 kilometers) per hour. At the last moment, they thrust out their feet and stab their victim with their claws.

Wings are swept back, and the tail closes like a fan.

The wings are stron enough to lift the fal into the air even if i carrying a dead duc

Its pointed wings help the peregrine falcon fly faster than any other bird.

The pigeon dies and falls to the ground

The tail is used for steering.

The biggest nest in the world
Golden eagles' nests, often called aeries, can be over 13 feet (four meters) wide—bigger than some cars! They do not build a new nest every year but fly back to an old nest and just add new twigs. Some nests are hundreds of years old.

Peregrine falcons are about 13 inches (32 centimeters) tall and live all over the world.

Bendy legs!
African harrier hawks have long legs which they use to reach eggs, chicks, and bats inside holes in trees. To make it easier to snatch a meal, they can bend their legs backward, forward, and even sideways.

Working together
Raptors do not hurt humans, and for many hundreds of years, they have been trained to hunt with people. In the Middle Ages, this lanner falcon would have been flown by a squire, a boy who worked for a knight.

The glove stops the bird's claws from scratching you.

Birds of prey have excellent color vision.

Nostril

This powerful, hooked beak is used to pull apart animals that are too big to be swallowed whole.

Like all birds of prey, peregrines spend most of the day resting or preening, not hunting.

Many birds of prey have bare legs, but others wear feathered "pants."

This needle-sharp claw, or talon, is used to grab prey.

Meat-eating birds

American kestrel

Goshawk

Harpy eagle

All-American eagle
This US army badge has a bald eagle on it because it is the national bird of the United States.

FLIGHTLESS BIRDS

Emu

Kagu

Flying is hard work—it takes a lot of energy to flap wings and lift off the ground. For most birds it is wort the effort because it helps them escape from danger o search for things to eat. But some birds, such as kiwis and kagus, live on islands where there are no enemies. and others run or swim after food instead of flying.

Over millions of years, birds such as ostriches, emu and penguins have gradually lost the ability to fly.

Eye-to-eye
Ostriches' round eyes are nearly as big as tennis balls!

The shell is about 0.08 inches (two millimeters) thick.

Super egg
Ostriches lay bigger eggs than any other bird: they are 24 times bigger than a chicken's egg! The shell is incredibly strong.

Its tiny wings ai hidden under br furlike feathers.

The kiu nostrils on the t of its lo beak.

Sniff sniff
The national bird of New Zealand, the kiwi, is one of only a few birds to have a good sense of smell. It sniffs out worms that are in the soil.

Ready, set, go!
Ostriches live on the African grasslands. They cannot fly away from lions and hyenas, but they can run very fast. They sprint at speeds of 45 miles (70 kilometers) per hour—much faster than a galloping horse.

King penguin

Kakapo

Rhea

Takahe

Cassowary

Brown kiwi

Rheas peck the ground with their big, flat beaks to snap up grass, seeds, and leaves.

These frilly feathers keep the rhea warm at night.

By spreading its wings out like a sail, the rhea can catch the wind and run even faster.

...are five feet
...eters) tall, weigh
...han 45 pounds
...ograms), and live
...th America.

Males wave their skinny, bare necks from side to side to attract a female.

...me to daddy

...as are unusual. The males, not the
...les, incubate the eggs and look after
... big babies for up to five months.

...ary

Ostrich
foot

Running birds have massive, muscular legs.

The bones inside their legs are solid. Rheas don't fly, so they do not need lightweight bones.

Rheas look shaggy because the barbules on their feathers do not "zip together." Flightless birds do not need neat feathers.

Three front-facing toes.

...ning "shoes"

...ostrich is the only bird to have
...oes; most birds have four.

183

NIGHT BIRDS

As the sun sets, most birds settle down to sleep, but some are just waking up. Owls and other birds that feed and fly in the dark are called nocturnal birds. They come out at night to find animals to eat and also because many of their enemies are asleep! Owls hoot loudly to one another in the dead of night—they are often heard but rarely seen.

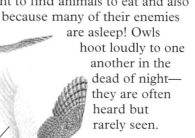

Owls can fly without making a noise because special fringed feathers slow down the air as it rushes over their wings.

Night fishing
Waders, like this black-crowned night heron, feed in shallow water. So if the tide is out in the middle of the night that is when they fish.

Slow, silent swoop
In the dark, barn owls use their ears, not their eyes, to find food. They can even hear a tiny mouse munching on a seed.

Did you spot this nightjar?

Short tail

Spot the bird
During the day, nightjars sleep on the ground. Their feathers are the color of leaves, so if they don't move, foxes and falcons won't find them.

▪oden actor
▪ frogmouth sees you, it will
▪nt its head up at the sky and
▪tend to be a broken branch. It
▪ves one eye slightly open though,
▪t in case you're not fooled.

*▪ls cannot move
▪r eyes, but they
▪ turn their necks all
▪way around to
▪ backward.*

*Owls see 35-100
times better than
you in the dark!*

*Like all birds, the ears
are small slits hidden
under the feathers.*

*Boobook owls are
often called
"morepork" owls—
this is what
they shout!*

Boobook owls are
about eight inches
(20 centimeters) tall
and live in Australia
and New Zealand.

*Soft
feathers*

*This curved
claw kills rats,
mice, lizards,
and spiders.*

Face to face

Long-eared owl

Elf owl

Barn owl

Eagle owl

Cough it up
Owls don't have teeth,
so they can't chew their
food—mice and birds
are swallowed whole!
Bones, feathers, and fur
cannot be digested, so
they are made into
pellets and coughed up.

Vole rib

*Mouse
leg bone*

Vole fur

Skull   Hip bones   Jaw   Leg bones   Shoulder blades

185

Mammals

Mammals are amazing animals. Some climb trees, others race across the ground, burrow, or even fly. Seals and otters are examples of mammals that live in the water. Mammals come in many shapes and sizes—a giraffe is tall, a mouse is small, and a platypus looks like an otter with a duck's beak. So what makes them all mammals? They are hairy, they breathe air into lungs, and they feed their babies milk.

Mammals are warm-blooded, which means their temperature is controlled by their bodies. Most are born live, not hatched from eggs, although platypuses lay eggs. Marsupials are a special kind of mammal because they give birth to babies that are only half formed. These tiny creatures grow into adults nestled in a warm safe pouch on their mother's body. Many mammals eat only plants, while others eat meat or insects. You are a mammal, too.

Pale kangaroo mouse

Giant panda

Black-tailed jack rabbit

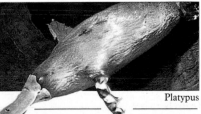

Platypus

Golden mice

Ge

Snow leopard cub

Little brown bats

Giraffe

Asian elephant

Tiger

Koala

Giant otter   Royal antelope

Desert hedgehog

MARSUPIALS

A marsupial is an animal that has a pocket, called a pouch, on its tummy for carrying its babies. Inside this nursery the baby is safe and has milk to drink. Today, the widest variety of marsupials live in Australia, but 50 million years ago many more lived in the Americas and the Antarctic. Most of the American ones died out when more modern mammals, such as horses, cats, and rats, developed. Marsupials survived in Australia because the "new" mammals could not reach this island. Kangaroos are the most famous marsupials, but there are also marsupial "mice" and "dogs."

Australia

Like deer, kangaroos have long faces to make room for their big, flat, grass-grinding teeth.

Kangaroos can't walk backward!

Female red kangaroos are three feet (one meter) tall. Males are twice as big. They live in Australia.

Female red kangaroos are called blue fliers because they have blue-gray fur and bound faster than the red males.

The tail helps it to balance as it bounds along.

Kangaroos lick a bald spot on their arms to cool down! As the saliva dries it takes heat away.

Only females have pouches—males don't need them because they don't have babies!

The baby, or joey, hops into the pouch if it sees an eagle or dingo.

Jump to it!
A kangaroo's back legs are so big that it would fall over if it ran. But they are good for jumping—a red kangaroo can bounce along at 30 miles (50 kilometers) per hour.

Huge leg muscles

188

Missing marsupial
The last Tasmanian tiger is thought to have died in a zoo in 1936. It was striped like a tiger and had a thick tail like a kangaroo. Farmers shot them all because they ate sheep.

Jumping bean?
A newborn wallaby looks like a red bean! It is less than one inch (two cm) long and has no legs, hair, or eyes. Like all marsupials, it continues to grow in a pouch, not inside the mother's body.

Birth

The "bean" squirms through the forest of hair by waving its stumpy arms.

Three minutes later it reaches the pouch.

It hooks onto a nipple and starts to suck milk.

Acting star
Opossums are the only living American marsupials. When a Virginia opossum is attacked, it sticks out its tongue, lies very still, and pretends to be dead—it plays possum!

Hold on tight
This baby koala is too big to fit inside its mother's pouch, so it clings to her fur as she climbs through the eucalyptus leaves!

Mammals with pouches

oney possum

Numbat

Ring-tailed rock wallaby

Tasmanian devil

INSECTIVORES

Insectivores are sharp-toothed, long-nosed animals that eat insects and juicy worms, slugs, and snails! Their busy little bodies lose heat easily, so they need to eat frequently. The food they eat produces the energy needed to keep them warm. But how do insectivores survive winters, when there are fewer insects to eat? Shrews search through rotting leaves and most manage to find enough food. Moles stay underground, and hedgehogs spend cold winters in a deep sleep, called hibernation.

A bite for lunch
The water shrew is one of the few venomous mammals. Its saliva can kill frogs, but not peopl

How hungry?
Imagine having to eat a pile of food that weighs twice as much you— shrews have to do this every day!

The tiny eyes are covered by fur A mole can barely tell the difference between light and dark.

Little bumps on its tail and its nose help this European mole sense where it is going.

A mole's wide front foot are shaped like spades— ideal for digging.

Molehill

The grass nest is the size of a footb

Worms burrow into the tunne and are caugh by the mole.

Moles turn around by do forward rolls. If the tunnel i too narrow, th run backwards

Moles eat mo than 50 worm a day! Live ones are store in a pantry.

Moles live alone. This worm thief will soon be chased away.

~~edy guts~~

~~ews~~ often eat animals that are bigger ~~1~~ themselves. This long, juicy worm ~~fill~~ its tummy for two or three hours!

Worms in a week
Streaked tenrecs grow up faster than any other mammals. They stop drinking milk and start to eat worms when they are only six days old.

A hedgehog can stay rolled up for hours.

~~Roll~~ up, roll up!

~~Fearless~~ hedgehogs don't run away ~~from~~ danger—they stick out their ~~spines~~ and roll into a ball. No one ~~wants~~ to eat a mouthful of needles!

Head

Some foxes and badgers have learned to push hedgehogs into puddles to make them unroll!

The hedgehog's skin is larger than its body. When it curls up, it can pull its prickly skin over its head!

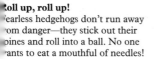

Spines are just stiff, hollow hairs.

~~dult~~ European ~~dgehogs~~ have more than ~~000~~ needle-sharp spines.

One-week-old baby shrews hold onto one another so that they don't get lost.

Insect eaters

Golden mole

Desman

Star-nosed mole

Solenodon

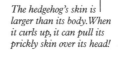

White-tailed shrews

CATS

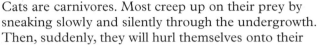

Cats are carnivores. Most creep up on their prey by sneaking slowly and silently through the undergrowth. Then, suddenly, they will hurl themselves onto their surprised victim. The sharp canine teeth quickly deal the deadly blow. The biggest cat of all, the striped tiger, can eat 55 pounds (25 kilograms) of meat in a meal! Its appetite is almost matched by the majestic lion, the biggest cat and most powerful hunter in Africa.

A cheetah can acceler as quickly as a Ferra

Tigers

Bright eyes
When light shines on a cat's eyes, they glow like the reflectors on the back of a bike. This happens because the light bounces back off a special layer in the cat's eyes. This layer collects light. It helps cats see six times better than you in dim light.

Aerial ambush
All cats climb trees. This spotted jaguar is waiting to drop down on a passing peccary or tapir. It will even tackle alligators.

Grassland queens
Lions are the odd-cat because they live in g called prides. Male li are often called the "I of the Jungle," but the do not live in jungles, the females, or liones do most of the huntir

Speedy cat
Cheetahs are the only cats that run down their meals. They can sprint at 60 miles (100 km) per hour and are the fastest mammals.

A cheetah can only sprint for 20 seconds because it gets tired.

...dy
...kbone

Play fight
Baby cats, or kittens, are playful. They chase one another, jump into the air, and chew twitching tails! This is the way they learn to hunt.

Sensitive whiskers

The rough tongue can rub meat off bones!

...ards are
...24 inches
...n) tall.
...live in
... and
...ern Asia.

...pards sleep 16
...urs a day, usually
...short "cat naps."

Big cats roar; they can't purr.

Really wild cat
There are more than 300 million pet cats in the world. They are believed to have been bred from wildcats over 12,000 years ago. This Scottish wildcat is much fiercer than a tame tabby!

Black leopards, or panthers, can be born to "yellow" parents.

Panthers are spotted, but their spots are hard to see!

Leopards live and hunt on their own. Groups of lions often gang up on them and steal their food.

Cats comb and clean their fur coat with their tongue.

Soft pads let cats creep quietly.

Put your claws in!
Little muscles pull most cats' daggerlike claws into special pockets, to stop them from becoming dull.

DOGS

On its own, a dog can only trap animals that are smaller than itself, but 20 African hunting dogs working together can easily catch and kill a zebra. Many dogs have learned this lesson and prefer to live and hunt in family groups, called packs. The 39 types of wild dogs have often been treated as enemies, not loved like pet dogs. Wolves have been wiped out in many places. Foxes only survive because they are smaller and more cunning.

All pet dogs ha
been bred from
or timber, wolv
The first dogs z
tamed more tho
12,000 years a

Hooooowl!
In the dead of night, the wolves in a pack get together, throw back their heads, and howl. This warns other wolves to keep out of their territory.

A wolf can hear a watch ticking more than 30 feet (10 meters) away.

Gray wolves are about three feet (one meter) tall. They live in Canada, the US, Europe, and northern Asia.

Dogs cool down by panting.

Pointed canine teeth stab the prey. Cheek teeth slice the meat into pieces that are small enough to swallow.

Gray wolves trot more than 40 miles (60 kilometers) each day when they are hunting a moose or an ox.

Team effort
Female African hunting dogs can have as many as 16 puppies. They are looked after by the whole pack, not just the mother. They are even suckled by other females.

This pup is eight weeks old. It already eats meat but will not go hunting with the pack until it is six months old.

New neighbor
Red foxes used to live in the woods, but many have moved into cities. They roam the streets at night, searching for fruit and mice or garbage cans to raid!

Cleaning up
The African dogs called jackals love leftover lion food—lions hardly ever finish their dinners! Meat eaters that do not kill their own food are called scavengers.

A fox's tail is called a brush.

A gray wolf's thick coat can be any color, from white to black!

Bushy tail

Win by a nose
When you smell a flower, you can often tell what sort of flower it is without opening your eyes. Dogs can do even better than this—they can smell who touched the flower the day before!

Dog "talk"
Every dog has to know its place in the pack—they can't all be the leader! Dogs can't talk, so they use body language instead to let one another know whether they make or take orders.

Dogs wag their tails when they are happy.

Dogs are marathon runners, not sprinters. A wolf can only run 28 miles (45 kilometers) per hour—much slower than a lion.

The pack leader holds its tail upright and snarls.

Ankle

This Indian wild dog, called a dhole, does not want to fight, so it rolls on its back.

gs walk their toes.

The claws stay out all the time.

BEARS

Bears are big and usually have thick, shaggy coats. Brown bears are the most common, but giant pandas are more famous. People have argued for years about whether giant pandas are bears or not. Scientists now think, as any child can see, that they are black-and-white bears! Bears look cuddly, but they are fierce. People have shot so many of these big beasts that today bears only survive in hilly hideaways.

The big sleep
Bears that live in cold places spend the winter inside warm caves. The females give birth to their tiny cubs, usually twins, while they are asleep.

Polar bear pawprint

Honey and nuts for dinner?
Most bears eat all sorts of things—they are omnivores. These are a few of their favorite foods.

Honey

Hazelnuts

Berries

Masters of disguise
Polar bears live in the icy Arctic and are the only completely carnivorous bears. Seal skin is their favorite food.

The polar bear hides its black nose with its white paw.

Open wide!
A grizzly bear has a simple way of fishing. It stands in a river and waits for fish to jump right into its mouth.

It sneaks up on the seal by pretending to be an iceberg!

The cunning bear springs out of the icy water to knock the surprised seal with a swipe of its huge paw.

Half-webbed toes

Ringed seal

wprints

...ike cats and dogs, bears ...e flat feet. Their heels ...ch the ground when ... walk.

A special pad on a panda's paw is used as a sort of thumb—useful for grabbing bamboo shoots.

This big brown bear is more than twice the size of a tiger!

All bears have small, round ears.

...ear's face always ...ks the same—you ...'t tell whether it is ...ry or happy!

Save the giant panda!
There are less than 2,000 giant pandas left. It is not going to be easy to save them—females are only fertile for three days a year. They also need to eat 30 pounds (14 kilograms) of one special type of bamboo a day.

Grizzly bears are a type of brown bear. They are called grizzly bears because the tips of their brown hairs are gray, or grizzled.

With their big, strong arms, bears can hug a person to death!

Grizzly bears stand up to 10 feet (3 meters) tall. They live in Canada and the US.

The front paws can be used as clubs to hit other large animals.

APES

Playful

Begging for fo

There are four sorts of apes: chimpanzees, orangutans, gibbons, and gorillas. They all live for many years, have big brains and no tails, and can walk upright. Apes are the closest relatives of people.

Orangutan (male)

Gorillas are the biggest and strongest apes, but they are gentle giants. Chattering chimps are sassy and cute, but much more dangerous—they even kill deer and monkeys to eat! Family life is important to all of these intelligent animals; chimps cuddle and shake hands when they meet.

Playtime
Baby chimps take a long time to grow up. Their mothers feed them milk for five or six years—so they have plenty of time to play.

Brainy beast
Chimps are one of the few animals to use tools. They use leaves as sponges! First they soften handfuls of leaves by chewing them, and then they use them to soak up water.

Go bananas
Gorillas really do eat bananas. They also like nettles, giant cele and banana leave

*Apes walk o
their knuckle*

Walk like an ape
All apes can stand on just two feet, but they usually walk on all fours like this.

Frightened

Angry

Not a word
The chimp is one of the few mammals that can make faces to show its feelings.

Holding hands
You can pick up things because you are able to fold your thumb across your hand. Apes and monkeys have these useful, "opposable" thumbs, too.

Like you, apes have sensitive hands.

Male gorillas stand up to 6.5 feet (two meters) tall. They live in Africa.

An orangutan's big toes can grip things, too!

Gorillas have about the same number of hairs as you. They look hairier because their hair is long and thick.

Big brain

Gorillas can climb trees, but they spend most of the day relaxing on the ground.

Is it a bird?
Every night, orangs build a cozy nest to sleep in. It takes just five minutes to build a mattress of branches and a blanket of leaves.

Apes see things in color—just like you.

Baby gorillas learn to crawl at nine weeks, climb at six or seven months, and walk at eight months. They may live to be forty.

All apes can sit and stand up straight.

MONKEYS

Monkeys are primates. It is easy to tell them apart from the smarter primates, people, and apes, because they have tails. Some, such as mandrills, live on the ground, but most monkeys are light enough to jump or swing through the trees. They always look before they leap, though, because there is danger all around. Large eagles may swoop down from above and leopards lurk below. If they miss their footing, monkeys may plunge up to 200 feet (60 meters) to the ground!

Squirrel monkey

Built to balance
If you start to lose your balance, you can use your arms to steady yourself. Monkeys use their instead—leaving t arms free for clim

Keep it clean!
These rhesus monkeys are lining up to have insects and dirt picked out of their fur. They even pick one another's teeth clean! This grooming helps to keep them tidy and also good friends.

Groups of monkeys are called troops.

Face to face

Telltale tail
Ring-tailed lemurs are primitive primates and live in troops like monkeys. They keep together in tall grass by pointing their tails upward.

This lemur is looking for a tail to follow!

Mandrill (male)

Proboscis monkey (

Bald uakari

Cotton-top tamar

A gripping tail
Many South American monkeys have three "arms"— their tails are prehensile, so they can hold on to things. A spider monkey can hang by its strong tail, leaving both hands free for feeding.

Both eyes face forward to spot safe landing places!

All primates, including you, see in color.

Narrow chest

Mane of soft, silky hair.

Monkeys are not fussy eaters. They eat fruit, flowers, lizards, butterflies, and even frogs' legs!

Monkeys' legs are shorter than their arms.

...is tamarin weighs only ... ounces (600 grams), ... it is light enough to ...mper across small ...anches without ...aking them.

People have chopped down so many of the trees that golden lion tamarins live in that there are only about 1,000 of these monkeys left in the wild.

Hairy tail

Golden lion tamarins are 13–15 inches (32–37 centimeters) tall. They live in Brazil.

Bath time
These Japanese snow monkeys relax and warm up in winter by sitting in pools of hot water that bubble up from beneath the icy ground.

BATS

Bats are furry, flying mammals. Their wings are made of thin, leathery skin, which is stretched across their fingers like material over the spokes of an umbrella. Bats live all over the world, but you will not often see them flying. Most bats hang upside down and sleep during the day. They hunt at night. Most small bats eat moths and flies. Larger, vegetarian bats, often called flying foxes because they have foxlike faces, feed on bananas and nectar.

The ears of this long-ea bat are almost as big as body. It tucks them unde its wings when it sleeps

Bats hear better than all other mammals.

Acrobatic bats swoop through the sky at up to 40 miles (64 kilometers) per hour—fast enough to escape from owls.

Mouselike, furry body

Wrist

This bat has caught a night-flying moth, which it found by listening for it in the dark.

Moth

Fruity bat
Jungles might not exist without bats! Fruit-eating bats pollinate plants, and the seeds they spit out or leave in their droppings can grow into trees.

The bat cave
Nearly all bats are awake at night—they are nocturnal. Sleep days are spent inside caves or holes trees. As the sun sets, millions of ba stream out of their caves to go hun

Camping bats

Imagine having to build a new house every night—tent bats do! These small, white bats nibble through the middle rib of a palm leaf until it droops down to form a tiny tent. The bats hang underneath, out of the wind and rain.

The smallest mammal

The bumblebee bat can fit in the palm of your hand. Its body is one inch (three cm) long and its wingspan is just 5 inches (13 cm). It weighs less than a grape.

This is a thumb. Bats use their thumbs as combs to groom their fur and as hooks to hold onto things.

The wing can be used as a scoop to catch flying insects.

Long finger

Long-eared bats

have a wingspan of 9–10 inches (22–25 centimeters). They live in northern Europe.

Fangs for dinner!

Vampire bats love the taste of blood. This one has sliced open the foot of a sleeping chicken with its sharp teeth. It will lap up about one tablespoonful of blood.

Sounds tasty

Many bats can't see well enough to fly in the dark, so they use their voice and ears instead! American fishing bats make clicking noises as they fly over ponds. When these sounds bounce back off ripples, they know that a fish is near to the surface.

The bat hears the tiny echo and swiftly swoops down to grab the fish.

SMALL RODENTS

These newborn, rubbery, wriggling mice can only squeak, sleep, and suckle.

A rodent is an animal that gnaws with sharp, chisel-shaped teeth. Most are mouselike and vegetarian: they nibble plant stems, seeds, and roots. Forty percent of all mammals are rodents. They live all over the world, from African jungles where crested rats clamber up trees, to scorching deserts where jerboas hop across the sand. House mice have even hitched rides on ships to reach huts in Antarctica.

Dormouse

Moving house
Every three or four years, thousands of lemmings run from their overcrowded homes. Many die in the frantic search for new places to live and feed.

A plague of rats
Every year, millions of nibbling rats wreck one fifth of the world's crops!

The greasy fur leaves dirty marks on things it touches.

Many brown rats live in sewers. They use their feet as paddles when they swim and can tread water for three days!

Flat teeth in back of a rat's mouth grind grass and gr...

Scaly tail

After walking thr... dirt, rats may wa... food and spread ...

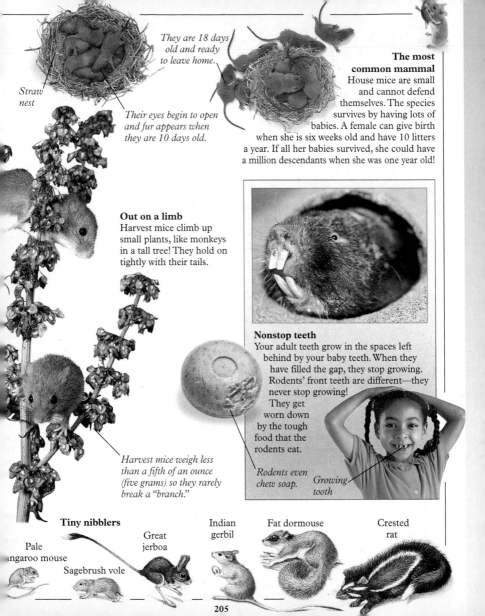

Straw nest

They are 18 days old and ready to leave home.

Their eyes begin to open and fur appears when they are 10 days old.

The most common mammal

House mice are small and cannot defend themselves. The species survives by having lots of babies. A female can give birth when she is six weeks old and have 10 litters a year. If all her babies survived, she could have a million descendants when she was one year old!

Out on a limb

Harvest mice climb up small plants, like monkeys in a tall tree! They hold on tightly with their tails.

Nonstop teeth

Your adult teeth grow in the spaces left behind by your baby teeth. When they have filled the gap, they stop growing. Rodents' front teeth are different—they never stop growing! They get worn down by the tough food that the rodents eat.

Harvest mice weigh less than a fifth of an ounce (five grams) so they rarely break a "branch."

Rodents even chew soap.

Growing tooth

Tiny nibblers

Pale ngaroo mouse

Sagebrush vole

Great jerboa

Indian gerbil

Fat dormouse

Crested rat

LARGE RODENTS

Most rodents are small and look like mice, but some are much bigger. There are two sorts of large rodents—those that look like squirrels and those, such as porcupines, that look like pigs. Rodents' teeth get worn down by gnawing, and all rodents have front teeth that keep growing throughout their lives.

Chipmunks

Size of a sheep!
The capybara is the largest rodent in the world. It is a relative of the guinea pig.

The lion lost
A porcupine will run backward and stick its quills into an attacker's face!

Hollow, striped quill

A porcupine can hear fruit drop to the ground several yards away.

Porcupines chew old bones to keep their teeth sharp.

The n... or drey, is abo... the size of a footb...

Angry African porcupines stam... their back feet to rattle their qui... This tells other animals to go a...

Busy nibblers

The sharp quills only stick up when the porcupine is attacked.

European red squirrel

Chinchilla

Rock cavy

Springhare

Woodchuck

nting trees
irrels bury nuts
at later. Those that
can't find again
grow into trees.

A squirrel's strong jaws can crack open acorns.

Digging "dogs"
Prairie dogs live in underground towns! These towns usually have a population of about 1,000, but one in Texas had more than 400 million prairie dogs in it.

The "garden" is weeded.

Watch "dog".

Prairie dogs touch teeth when they meet.

Warm, leafy lining

When it sleeps, the squirrel wraps its bushy tail around itself like a blanket.

Tufted squirrel
European red squirrels don't scamper through gardens and parks like their gray American cousins. They are shy and hide from people in forests.

Grey squirrels race through trees at up to 24 km (15 miles) per hour.

A gray squirrel can leap more than six meters (20 feet) from one tree to another.

Squirrels can walk up and down the sides of trees to reach their nests.

A hole in the roof lets in air.

The house, or lodge, is the size of a large tent.

The underwater entrance keeps out enemies.

Food storage

nber!
vers are excellent builders. They bite
ough trees with their teeth and then
up the logs in a river. Behind this
a, a pond soon forms where they
build their home.

Dam

THE HORSE FAMILY

Almost all the horses in the world are tame. The only wild species left is the Przewalski's horse. It survives in zoos. The most common wild member of the horse family today is not a horse, but a zebra.

Fast, striped zebras are herbivores—they chew grass with their flat back teeth. Horses, zebras, and asses walk on the tips of their toes, which are hidden inside hard "shoes," called hooves.

Przewalski's horse

Desert "donkeys"
Wild asses are shy and rare. They live in the dr_ North African deserts.

A zebra's mane stands up straight.

The ears twist around to listen for danger

Plains zebras are up to 5 feet (1.5 meters) tall at the shoulder. They live in Africa.

Best friends
Zebras and wildebeest like to live together. The zebras keep watch, while wildebeest sniff the air for lions.

Wildebeest eat the short grass left by the zebras.

The hoof is just a large toenail!

Foals can walk when they are a few minutes old.

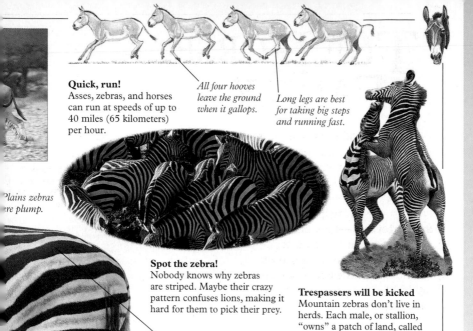

Quick, run!
Asses, zebras, and horses can run at speeds of up to 40 miles (65 kilometers) per hour.

All four hooves leave the ground when it gallops.

Long legs are best for taking big steps and running fast.

Plains zebras are plump.

Spot the zebra!
Nobody knows why zebras are striped. Maybe their crazy pattern confuses lions, making it hard for them to pick their prey.

A zebra scratches its back by rolling on the ground.

thigh muscles over plains zebras across African islands.

The swishing tail swats annoying, buzzing flies.

Females, foals, and stallions live together in the same herd.

Trespassers will be kicked
Mountain zebras don't live in herds. Each male, or stallion, "owns" a patch of land, called a territory. He will chase off any male zebra that enters his home.

Make your mark
Your fingerprints are different from everyone else's. So are a zebra's stripes—each zebra has a different-patterned coat! Some even have thin, white stripes on a black background.

re is only one toe de this hard hoof.

Born free
Some of the 75 million tame horses have escaped and learned to live in the wild. The ancestors of these American "wild" horses, called mustangs, belonged to cowboys.

HIPPOS, PIGS, AND PECCARIES

Hippo is short for hippopotamus, which means "river horse." They are called river horses because they live in rivers and lakes, and eat grass. Pigs and peccaries do not live in rivers, but they enjoy wallowing in mud as much as their huge relatives. Although these water-loving mammals are not carnivores, they are all able to protect themselves. Wild pigs can stab and kill tigers with their tusks, peccaries fight jaguars, and a heavy hippo will tussle with a crocodile or smash into a boat!

Very important pig
Farmyard pigs have all been bred from wild boars.

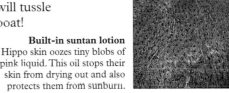

Built-in suntan lotion
Hippo skin oozes tiny blobs of pink liquid. This oil stops their skin from drying out and also protects them from sunburn.

Open wide
You yawn when you are tired or bored, but male hippos yawn when they are angry! Smaller males are frightened off by the big teeth and swim away without starting a fight.

The eyes and nostrils are high up on a hippo's head. This means it can stick just the top of its head out of the water and still see and breathe.

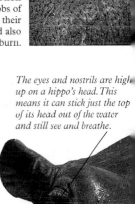

Smooth, almost hairless, skin.

The 1.5 feet-long (half meter) tusks are sometimes used to stab crocodiles.

Hippos are 5 feet (1.5 meters) tall. They live in Africa.

This big male hippo weighs as much as 120 eight-year-old children!

Lumbering lawn mowers

Every night, hippos leave the water and spend five or six hours grazing. They march back into the water, down well-worn paths, long before the scorching sun rises.

Plucky peccary

If a mountain lion attacks a group of peccaries, one brave animal may charge the lion with its sharp tusks while the others escape, but it will be lucky to survive.

Pigs on parade

Bush pig

Collared peccary

Underwater ballet

Hippos can hold their breath for more than five minutes. This is plenty of time to dive down and tiptoe gracefully across the bottom of the lake.

Hippo

To keep cool and moist, hippos spend 16 hours a day up to their necks in water.

The hippo shuts its ears and nostrils when it is under water.

There are four toes on each foot.

Thick skin protects the hippo from snapping crocodiles.

Hippos do eat water lilies, but prefer grass.

Pygmy hippo

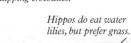

THE CAMEL FAMILY

Camels and their smaller South American relatives, vicuñas and guanacos, are found on sandy deserts, rocky plains, and bare mountains. They survive in some of the harshest places on Earth.

The fat inside a camel's hump is an energy store so it can survive a long time without food.

Vicuñas can breathe thin mountain air and camels can cope with freezing nights and scorching desert days. People have made good use of these animals' amazing survival skills—most are domesticated and work for a living. There are few wild members of the camel family left.

Domestic dromedary
Desert people could not survive without their one humped camels. They are ridden, milked, and eaten. Camel skin is made into shoes, hair is woven into clothes, and dry droppings are used as fuel!

Food is brought back up from the rumen to be rechewed.

The rumen is the large part of the stomach where chewed food goes first to be partly digested.

Second stomach

Third stomach

Swallow that!
Camels can go for months without water, then drink up to 29 gallons (130 liters) of water in 13 minutes.

Twice as tasty
To get all the goodness out of grass, some mammals, such as camels, deer, and cattle, have more than one stomach and chew their food twice!

ears and
rils can be
sed flat to
out sand.

*Two rows of eyelashes
keep out sand and stop
their eyes from freezing
on cold desert nights.*

*A camel doesn't waste water.
Liquid from its runny nose drips
down the split lip into its mouth!*

How many humps?

Bactrian camels are
7 feet (2.2 meters) tall.
They live in the Gobi
desert in Asia.

Dromedary

*Camels spit at things
that annoy them.*

*Tough lips can grip
thorny desert plants.*

*Camels hardly
ever sweat. This
saves water.*

Bactrian camel

King of the castle
While the females graze, the male
vicuña stands on a rock. If it spots
a mountain lion, it whistles and
the fleecy females flee.

Guanaco

*Camels roll
from side to
side when they walk
because they lift both legs
on one side at the same time.*

Vicuña

*The two toes spread
out to stop the
camel from sinking
into soft sand.*

Hardworking mammals
Llamas and alpacas have
been bred by people from
wild guanacos. Llamas are
milked and used to carry
heavy loads. Alpacas are
kept for their fine wool.

Alpaca

Llama

CATTLE AND ANTELOPES

Roundup
Musk oxen form a ring around their babies to protect them from hungry wolves—who can't get through the circle of h...

Cattle, antelopes, and their relatives goats and sheep, are all bovids. This means that they have horns attached to the tops of their heads. Horns have a bony core and an outer layer made of the same stuff as your fingernails. Gerenuk antelopes eat leaves, but bison prefer to graze on grass. Like all bovids, they make the most of their poor-quality food by coughing up partly digested food and chewing it a second time. This is called chewing the cud.

Gerenuk (male)

All cattle have four stomachs!

These horns are about half as tall as you!

This rare Arabian oryx antelope chews the cud as it walks across the desert.

Arabian oryx

On the march
At the beginning of the dry season, huge herds of wildebeest walk more than 990 miles (1,600 km) to wetter, greener pastures. When the wet season begins, they come back. These long, yearly journeys are called migrations.

Like cattle, b... have s... hoov...

It sniffs the air for rain and then walks to where the grass is growing.

Built-in radiator
The Tibetan yak lives near the top of the world in the Himalayan Mountains. It does not get cold because it has its own central heating system—the moss being digested in its stomach is hot and keeps it warm.

Heads with horns

African buffalo (male)

This thick, winter coat falls off in big clumps during the spring.

A dark coat soaks up the sun's heat. This helps to keep the bison warm in cold weather.

Male bison fight for females by putting their heads together and pushing. The winner is the one who pushes the other backward.

Blackbuck (male)

Horns are different than antlers. They never form branches or stop growing, and they are not replaced each year.

Male bison weigh more than a small car!

Wild goat (male)

American bison are 6.5 feet (two meters) tall. They live in Canada and the US.

Herds of bison spend most of the day eating grass and most of the night chewing!

Bighorn sheep (male)

ELEPHANTS

Matriarch

Elephants have enormous ears, long noses, tusks—and weigh more than six cars. They are the biggest land mammals. Herds of elephants shape the land they live in by treading paths that are wide enough to stop bush fires, by digging wells in dry riverbeds, by fertilizing the ground with dung, and by trampling grass for zebras to eat. They also open up forests by pushing over trees!

A family of females
The leader of a herd of elephants is an old female called a matriarch. She is followed by all her female relatives and their babies.

Wrinkles trap water to help to keep them cool.

Ivory towers
Many elephants are killed for their valuable ivory tusks. People have burned huge piles of old tusks to show that they want this cruelty to stop.

Elephants never stop growing.

It's all relative
The elephant's closest relative, the hyrax, looks like a guinea pig! Millions of years ago they were huge. All that elephants and hyraxes have in common now are tusks and nails instead of hooves.

Tusks are teeth. They grow about 7 inches (17 centimeters) a year and can be as long as a car!

Who's who?
There are two sorts of elephants.

Humped back *Smaller ears* *Longer tusks* *Bigger, rounder ears* *Taller*

Elephants eat grass, bark, and leaves for up to 16 hours a day.

This toenail is bigger than your whole hand!

Asian   African

Males leave their families when they are about fourteen.

Young females act as nannies.

African elephant's ears are almost as big as sheets for a single bed!

Stay cool
Elephants have lots of ways of cooling their big bodies. They can wallow in mud or throw water and dust over their skin. Sometimes they flap their ears like giant fans!

The elephant spreads out its ears to make itself look bigger and more dangerous.

This is one of the first four teeth.

The sixth, and last, set of teeth are bigger than bricks!

Elephants keep in touch by making deep, rumbling noises in their tummies!

The bendy trunk is formed from the nose and the upper lip. It is used for breathing, smelling, touching, and picking up things.

What's inside?
Elephants may look like they have flat feet, but they really walk on their tiptoes!

Toe

The heel rests on a fatty cushion.

Always teething!
Other than tusks, elephants have only four teeth. These molars are replaced every few years. Bigger teeth appear at the back of the mouth and push out the old, worn teeth—like a conveyor belt of teeth!

THE HUMAN BODY

Your body is one of the most amazing machines in the world. It is made up of thousands of parts all working together. Each group of parts is called a system. The body is so complicated that it is easier to imagine the different systems separately. But your digestive system, nervous system, skeleton, blood or circulatory system, and muscles all work together. You need all of them to stay alive.

When you are born, all you can do is sleep, eat, and cry. It takes time to discover how the parts of your body move and how to get them to work together. As you grow, you learn to do more difficult things, like crawling, walking, and riding a bicycle.

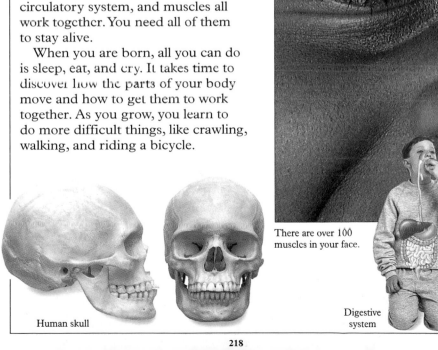

There are over 100 muscles in your face.

Human skull

Digestive system

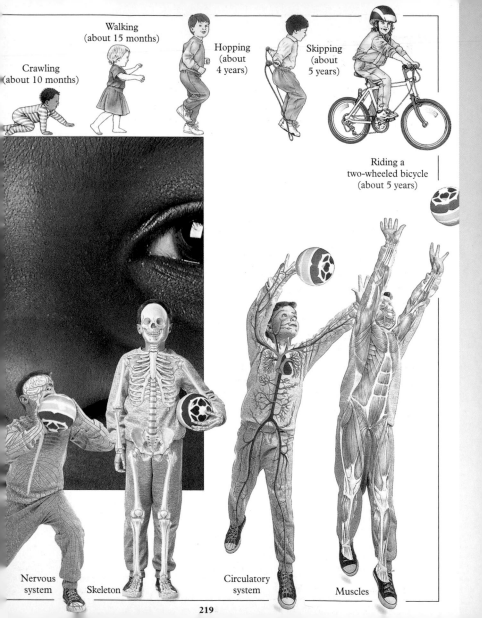

Crawling
(about 10 months)

Walking
(about 15 months)

Hopping
(about
4 years)

Skipping
(about
5 years)

Riding a
two-wheeled bicycle
(about 5 years)

Nervous
system

Skeleton

Circulatory
system

Muscles

HEARING

"Canaphone"
A piece of string threaded through two empty cans works kind of like a telephone. If you speak into one can, the vibrations travel along the string to the other can—allowing your voice to be heard.

Hearing is one of your five senses. Your ears are important and delicate: they pick up sounds and send messages to your brain. Sounds travel through the air in waves. Your outer ears, the shell-shaped flaps on the side of your head, catch sound waves and funnel them inside. These waves hit the eardrum and make it vibrate. The middle ear and the inner ear change the vibrations into electrical signals, which are sorted out and recognized by your brain.

The outer ear collects the sounds and funnels them along the ear canal.

Kneel

Hunger

Crash!
The loudness of sound is measured in decibels. Quiet whispering is less than 25 decibels, the clash of cymbals about 90, and a jet plane taking off can measure more than 130 decibels. Noises over 120 decibels can cause pain and may damage your ears.

Hope

Talking in signs
If deaf people have never heard speech, they may not have learned to talk. To help them to communicate, many learn a special language called signing. There are many different forms of sign language used in different countries and regions. Deaf people also learn to spell using their hands, and to read lips by watching the shape of people's mouths as they speak.

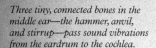

Three tiny, connected bones in the middle ear—the hammer, anvil, and stirrup—pass sound vibrations from the eardrum to the cochlea.

The semicircular canals help you balance.

Nerves

Hello . . . hello!

If you shout in a large, empty space, the sound waves from your voice bounce off the nearest surface, back to your ears. This is called an echo. The farther a sound has to travel before it is reflected, the longer you must wait for the echo.

Nerve cells in the cochlea send messages about sounds to the brain.

The inner ear is made up of the cochlea and the semicircular canals. It is filled with liquid.

Visible and invisible ears

Not all animals hear the same way you do. Some do not have any ears on the outside of their body.

Elephants have huge ear flaps and good hearing.

The eardrum is a thin sheet of skin that vibrates when sound waves hit it—just like the skin on a drum.

Birds and lizards have good hearing but no ear flaps on the sides of their heads.

A rabbit can turn its ears to hear sounds all around it.

SEEING

Sight is perhaps the most important of your five sense
Your eyes work together with your brain to help you
to see. The cornea, at the front of your eye, bends ligh
This light is then focused by the lens, to form an image
of what you are looking at on the retina at the back o
your eye. But the image is upside down! Nerve cells in
the retina send messages to your brain, which sorts ou
the messages so that you see things the right way.

Tear-full
Tears help to keep your eyes moist and clean. When too many are made, they cannot all drain away down your nose, so tears come out of your eyes.

Tricky eyes
Sometimes your eyes play tricks on you, called optical illusions. Try these:

Which of these two girls is the taller?

Which red circle is bigger: the left one or the right one?

Which line is longer?

Double vision?
Because they are set apart, each of your eyes sees a slig different picture. Your brain puts the two pictures togeth This is called stereoscopic o binocular vision, and it mea you can judge depth and distances. Try this: close on eye, point to something, and keep your finger still. Now through the other eye. Are still pointing to the same p

Eye spy
You can have your eyes tested by an optician to make sure they are working properly. Glasses or contact lenses will help if you cannot see clearly. Your eyes are very important, so have them checked regularly!

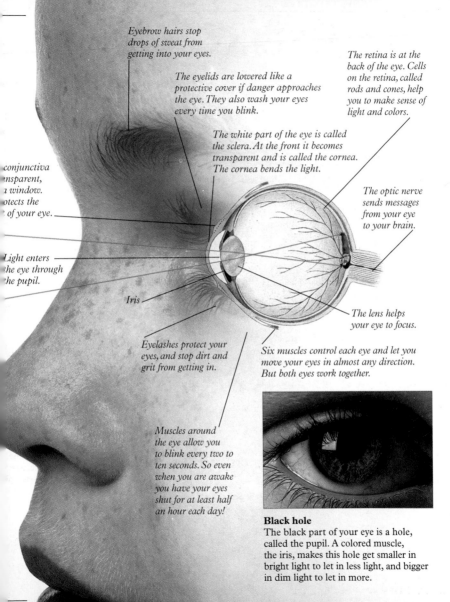

Eyebrow hairs stop drops of sweat from getting into your eyes.

The eyelids are lowered like a protective cover if danger approaches the eye. They also wash your eyes every time you blink.

The retina is at the back of the eye. Cells on the retina, called rods and cones, help you to make sense of light and colors.

The white part of the eye is called the sclera. At the front it becomes transparent and is called the cornea. The cornea bends the light.

conjunctiva
nsparent,
a window.
otects the
of your eye.

The optic nerve sends messages from your eye to your brain.

Light enters the eye through the pupil.

Iris

The lens helps your eye to focus.

Eyelashes protect your eyes, and stop dirt and grit from getting in.

Six muscles control each eye and let you move your eyes in almost any direction. But both eyes work together.

Muscles around the eye allow you to blink every two to ten seconds. So even when you are awake you have your eyes shut for at least half an hour each day!

Black hole
The black part of your eye is a hole, called the pupil. A colored muscle, the iris, makes this hole get smaller in bright light to let in less light, and bigger in dim light to let in more.

BRAIN

Inside your head, protected by a bony skull, is your brain. It looks crinkled like a walnut and is the control center for your entire body. Your heart pumps oxygen-filled blood into it through a mass of tubes, called arteries. After only four minutes without oxygen, brain cells will die and they cannot be replaced. Your brain is very complex and is divided into many parts that have different functions. The largest and uppermost part in the human brain is called the cerebrum. It has two halves, called hemispheres. The outermost layer of the cerebrum also contains sections known as lobes, which control different activities and make sense of the information from your five senses.

Brain protection
To stop you from injuring your brain, you should wear a helmet whenever you take part in a sport that might make you hit your head.

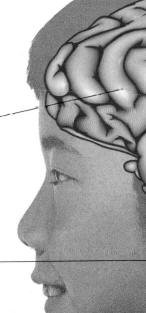

The frontal lobe is the part of the brain where you do your big thinking. You use it when you make a decision or solve a problem. It also allows you to communicate with other people and express your own unique personality.

Brain control
Your brain is the most important part of your body. It is your control center, but is only a little bigger than your two fists!

Each part of your brain has a different job to do. Some parts send out signals to your body and some parts make sense of signals that come in.

The brain stem controls many of your automatic actions, such as your heartbeat and breathing.

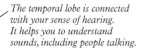

Kim's game

When we are learning, we depend on our memory to help us. Test your memory with this game. Set out a number of objects and look at them for a few moments. Ask a friend to remove an object, then try to tell what is missing.

Different brains

Animals have brains of various shapes and sizes, suited to the things they do.

Fish

Bird

Cat

Human

The parietal lobe has many functions, such as processing signals associated with taste and touch.

The temporal lobe is connected with your sense of hearing. It helps you to understand sounds, including people talking.

The occipital lobe is connected with your sense of sight. It helps control eye movement, makes sense of what you see, and allows you to remember things that you've seen before.

The cerebellum is a structure at the base of your brain. It controls many of your voluntary muscle movements, such as balancing, walking, writing, and speaking.

Brain relay

When you want to touch something, a signal is passed from your brain to other parts of your body like a baton in a relay race. It goes first to the spinal nerves then to the motor nerves, which tell muscles to move.

Brain   Spinal nerves   Motor nerves

NERVES

Nerves are like telephone wires carrying information between the brain and all parts of the body. One set of nerves—the sensory nerves—carries signals to your brain from your senses, telling your brain what is happening around you. When your brain has decided what to do, it sends signals along another set of nerves—the motor nerves—to make your muscles work.

Nerve network

Speedy reflex
If someone claps their hands by your face, your brain thinks something is flying toward your eyes and they blink. This blink is a reflex action to protect them.

With your eyes covered, can you tell it is a teddy bear?

What's on the "feely table?"
The sense of touch is very important. It is one of your five senses. Receptor cells under your skin send messages, through sensory nerves, to your brain about what your fingers are feeling.

A bottle feels hard and smooth.

Reading by touch
Blind people cannot see to read, so they learn a special alphabet of raised dots, called braille. They feel these dots with their fingertips.

Get the message?
Messages about how objects feel are sent through the sensory nerves and the spinal nerves to the brain to be understood.

Sensory nerves   Spinal nerves   Brain

If you touch some honey, your fingers will feel that it is sticky.

Ice is cold and slippery. When it starts to melt it feels wet.

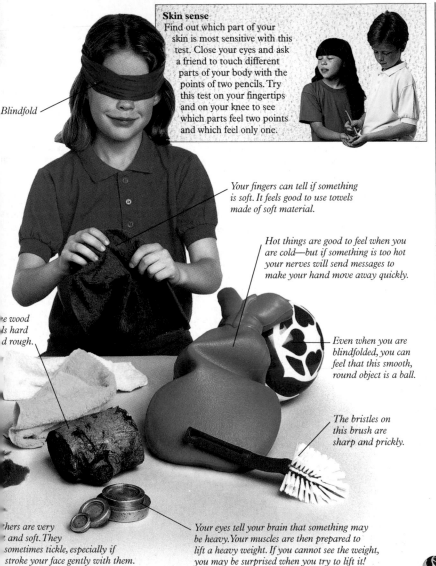

Blindfold

Your fingers can tell if something is soft. It feels good to use towels made of soft material.

Hot things are good to feel when you are cold—but if something is too hot your nerves will send messages to make your hand move away quickly.

...e wood ...ls hard ...d rough.

Even when you are blindfolded, you can feel that this smooth, round object is a ball.

The bristles on this brush are sharp and prickly.

...hers are very ...t and soft. They ...sometimes tickle, especially if ...stroke your face gently with them.

Your eyes tell your brain that something may be heavy. Your muscles are then prepared to lift a heavy weight. If you cannot see the weight, you may be surprised when you try to lift it!

227

SKIN

If you could unwrap your skin, you might be surprised at how much you have—enough to cover a large towel. It goes over all your bumps and curves, and into every crease of your body. Your skin grows with you, so that when you are an adult it will cover an area of about 5.6 square feet (1.7 square meters). It is waterproof and protective, and can heal itself if it gets damaged.

New skin grows all the time to replace old skin that rubs off. Most house dust is really old, dead skin.

The thinnest skin is on your eyelids.

Personal prints

Fingerprints are patterns of lines and swirls on your fingers. Try printing yours using paint or ink! Everyone has different fingerprints, so they are used to identify people. There are three basic patterns.

Arch

Loop

Whorl

Hairs grow on every part of your skin except for your lips, the palms of your hands, and the soles of your feet.

A fingernail takes about six months to grow from base to tip. It grows about 0.02 inches (half a millimeter) a week.

Nails are made of dead cells which contain a protein called keratin.

The cuticle is the fold of skin overlapping the nail bed from where the nail grows.

The half moon at the base of your nail looks white because this part is not firmly attached to the skin below.

Shades

All skin contains a coloring substance called melanin. Dark skin contains more melanin than fair skin. As a protection from burning by the sun, the skin produces more melanin, which tans the skin a darker color.

The roots of your hair are alive and grow about 0.08 inches (two millimeters) a week. When the hairs reach the surface of your skin they die— having your hair cut does not hurt!

Growing old

Your skin is elastic. If you pinch the back of your hand and then release it, the skin goes back to its original place. As people get older their skin becomes less elastic and often gets wrinkled. Some people's hair turns gray because it stops making melanin.

Dead or alive?

Your skin has two layers. The dead, outer layer, called the epidermis, protects the living dermis underneath.

Hair

A pore is the opening of a sweat gland.

Epidermis

Dermis

Nerve ending

Oil glands stop skin from drying out.

Hair follicle

Sweat glands open to let moisture out of your skin to help keep you cool.

Blood vessels bring food and oxygen to the skin.

Hair styles

How straight or curly a hair is depends upon the shape of the pocket, or follicle, it grows from. The color of your hair depends upon the amount of black or red melanin there is inside these pockets.

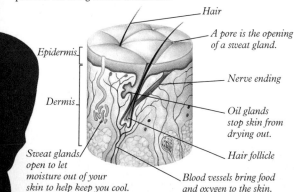

BLOOD

Blood is pumped all around your body by your heart. It travels in long tubes called blood vessels. Before it begins this journey, it is pushed to your lungs to collect oxygen. Then it returns to your heart to be pumped around your body. Blood also carries nutrients from your food to the cells.

There . . .
Blood vessels th[ ]
take blood away
from your heart
are called arteri[ ]

Power pump
Your heart is made of strong muscle. In just one minute, it can pump a drop of blood all the way down to your toes and back to your heart again.

The heart is divided into four spaces called chambers, two at the top and two at the bottom. There is a wall of muscle down the middle.

Blood enters the top right chamber through the vena cava. It passes down to the bottom right chamber. Then it is pushed out to your lungs.

Blood, filled with oxygen from the lungs, comes into the top left chamber. It passes down to the bottom left chamber. Then it is pumped around your body.

After going around your body, the blood returns to the right side of your heart, to start the journey again.

Aorta

Flaps, ca[ ] valves, stop b[ ] from flowing wrong way. It is[ ] "lub-dub" soun[ ] these doors clo[ ] that you hear w[ ] your heart b[ ]

le Vein

Vena cava
(largest vein)

. and back
ose that take blood
ck to your heart are
led veins.

Feeling the pressure
You can feel the beat of your
heart as it pumps blood, at high
pressure, through your arteries.
This beat is called the pulse.
Put the fingers of one hand on the inside
of your other wrist, in line with your thumb.
You can feel your pulse beating there.
You can only hear
a heartbeat by using
a stethoscope or
by putting your ear
to a friend's chest.

Heart work
When you skip, or do any
kind of exercise, your muscles
need extra oxygen and food
from your blood. To provide this,
your heart has to pump faster.

Side view of a
red blood cell

*You have nearly one gallon (about four
liters) of blood in your body. An adult has
more and a baby has less.*

*A drop of blood goes around your body
more than a thousand times a day.
Every five minutes all your blood passes
through your kidneys to be cleaned.*

Super cells
In one tiny drop of blood
there are red cells, white
cells, and platelets, all floating
in a liquid called plasma.
The blood in your arteries is
carrying more oxygen, which
makes it a brighter red color
than the blood
in your veins.

*Red cells carry oxygen
around the body. They are
made in the bone marrow.*

*White blood
cells defend the
body against germs.*

*If you cut yourself, platelets
rush to the broken blood
vessel and stick themselves
together to plug the cut.*

BREATHING

You must breathe all the time to stay alive. If you try to hold your breath for more than about a minute, your body will force you to start breathing again. The air that you breathe is made up of many different gases mixed together, but your body only needs one of them, oxygen, to keep you alive. If you ran out of oxygen, even for a very short time, you would die. The air you breathe goes into two soft, moist sponges, called lungs. You have one on each side of your chest.

Lung capacity
Breathe in deeply. Blow into a balloon until you run out of breath. Tie a knot in the balloon. Now you can see just how much air your lungs are able to hold.

Bad breath!
The air that you breathe can contain things that are bad for you. This woman is wearing a mask to protect herself from car fumes.

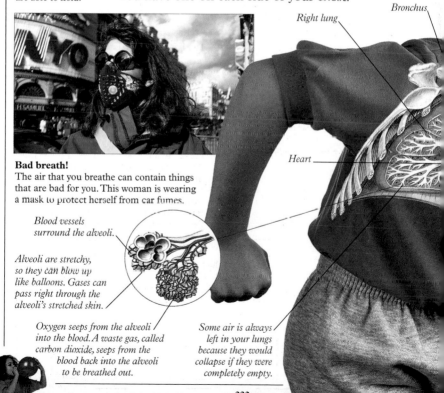

Right lung

Bronchus

Heart

Blood vessels surround the alveoli.

Alveoli are stretchy, so they can blow up like balloons. Gases can pass right through the alveoli's stretched skin.

Oxygen seeps from the alveoli into the blood. A waste gas, called carbon dioxide, seeps from the blood back into the alveoli to be breathed out.

Some air is always left in your lungs because they would collapse if they were completely empty.

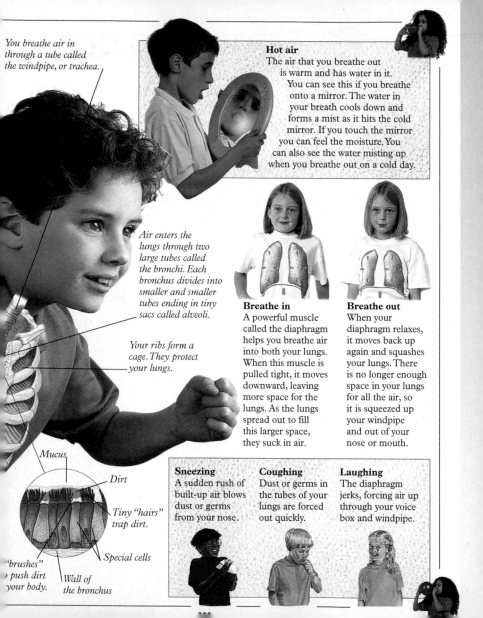

You breathe air in through a tube called the windpipe, or trachea.

Hot air
The air that you breathe out is warm and has water in it. You can see this if you breathe onto a mirror. The water in your breath cools down and forms a mist as it hits the cold mirror. If you touch the mirror you can feel the moisture. You can also see the water misting up when you breathe out on a cold day.

Air enters the lungs through two large tubes called the bronchi. Each bronchus divides into smaller and smaller tubes ending in tiny sacs called alveoli.

Your ribs form a cage. They protect your lungs.

Breathe in
A powerful muscle called the diaphragm helps you breathe air into both your lungs. When this muscle is pulled tight, it moves downward, leaving more space for the lungs. As the lungs spread out to fill this larger space, they suck in air.

Breathe out
When your diaphragm relaxes, it moves back up again and squashes your lungs. There is no longer enough space in your lungs for all the air, so it is squeezed up your windpipe and out of your nose or mouth.

Mucus

Dirt

Tiny "hairs" trap dirt.

"brushes" push dirt your body.

Special cells

Wall of the bronchus

Sneezing
A sudden rush of built-up air blows dust or germs from your nose.

Coughing
Dust or germs in the tubes of your lungs are forced out quickly.

Laughing
The diaphragm jerks, forcing air up through your voice box and windpipe.

TASTE AND SMELL

Your senses of taste and smell are very closely linked. They depend on each other. Tiny dimples on your tongue, and hairs at the top of the inside of your nose, detect chemicals that cause tastes and smells. Special sensory cells then send messages through to your brain to be recognized. Your sense of smell is twenty thousand times stronger than your sense of taste! Often what you think you are tasting you are really just smelling.

When you want to smell something, you have to suck air right up to the top of your nose to reach your smell sense cells.

The smell of tasty f[o] automatically mak[e] you produce saliva.

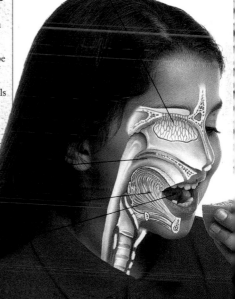

Nice and not so nice
You are able to distinguish several thousand different smells. The clean smell of the countryside can be lovely, but the smell of milk that has spoiled is horrible. Bad smells can warn you not to drink or eat things that are not fresh.

The roof of your mouth, the back of your throat, and your tongue are covered in small dimples called taste buds.

As the food is pushed around your mouth by your tongue, your taste buds pick up its taste.

Taste buds can only detect the flavors of food that has been dissolved in saliva.

Trick your taste buds
When you eat something, your sense of smell helps you to get the flavor. Block your nose and taste carrot and cucumber. It is hard to tell the difference between them. If you hold a piece of onion under someone's nose and give them mashed apple to eat, they think they are eating onion. This is why you cannot taste your food properly when you have a cold.

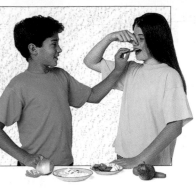

Coffee grains are bitter.

Still hungry?
The look of food is important as well as its taste and smell—pink sweetcorn still tastes like sweetcorn, but would you want to eat it?

Lemon is sour.

Kippers are salty.

...ey ...eet.

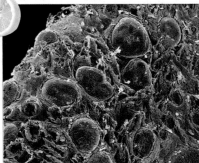

Five tastes
You have around 20,000 taste buds on your tongue, which pick up five different types of taste: salty, sweet, bitter, sour, and umami (savory).

Busy buds
If you look at a tongue through a strong magnifying glass you can see lots of bumps. Around the base of these bumps there are taste buds. Inside them there are special cells that sense taste.

TEETH

You use your teeth to break food into pieces that are small enough to swallow. Some teeth are shaped for biting and others for chewing. You have two sets of teeth. The first set are called baby teeth, and there are 20 of them. At the age of about six, you start to lose your baby teeth. One by one, the second set, the 32 adult teeth, grow in their place. Teeth are strong and keep working for many years.

Gappy grin
Children are left with gaps where their baby teeth have fallen out and they are waiting for their adult teeth to come through.

Healthy gums are j[ust] as important as hea[lthy] teeth—they help to [hold] your teeth in place.

Cases for braces
Sometimes teeth grow crookedly or become overcrowded in the mouth. Often this can be corrected by wearing braces.

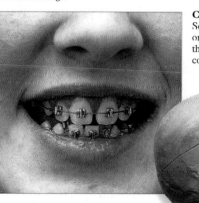

Still rooted
This skull shows how teeth are rooted firmly i[n] the strong bone of the upper and lower jaws.

Complete set
A full set of adult teeth has eight incisors, four canines, eight premolars, and twelve molars. Four of the molars are called wisdom teeth.

Jawbone

Incisors	Canine	Premolar	Molars

ide story
ur teeth are alive.
e part that sticks out
n your gum is the
wn. The part under
gum is the root.

Enamel is the hardest substance your body makes. A thin layer of it covers all your teeth.

Nerve

Gum

Jnder the ̇namel there ̇ a layer of hard, onelike material alled dentine.

Jawbone

The soft, middle part of the tooth is called the pulp. It contains nerves and blood vessels.

Brushing up
If you don't keep your teeth clean, bacteria build up to form a layer called plaque. If plaque builds up on your teeth, it can cause them to decay and even fall out. Brushing your teeth and gums after meals and before going to bed helps to remove the sugary foods that the bacteria use to grow.

Your bumpy back teeth are called molars. They crush and grind food when you chew.

The sharp, chisel-shaped teeth at the front of your mouth are incisors. They can cut and bite tough food.

Sometimes people have extra teeth.

At about the age of eighteen, wisdom teeth may come through at the back of your mouth—but they don't make you wise!

There are molars on the bottom, too.

Premolars have two edges, or cusps. They tear and grind up your food.

̇anine teeth are ̇arp and pointed. ̇hey are used for ̇aring food.

EATING

Food is the fuel that provides energy for your body. The energy is measured in units called calories. Before your body can use the food you eat, it has to be broken down into tiny bits that are small enough to pass into your blood. This digestion takes about 24 hours, as the food flows through a long tube winding all the way from your mouth to your bottom.

In and out
The inside wall of the small intestine has a very bumpy surface.

1. *Food starts being digested in your mout*
Your spit, or saliva, a digestive juice which starts to break down the food.

Your liver *a "chem* *factory* *also s* *vita*

Windpipe

2. *The food travels down a food pipe called the gullet.*

3. *Your stomach is a thick bag. Food is churned up inside it and mixed with strong stomach juices to make a kind of soup.*

4. *After leaving your stomach, your food flows down your small intestine. Goodness from the food seeps through the thin walls into your blood.*

Large intesti

Small intestine

Fats

Vitamins and minerals

Protei

Get into groups!
Foods can be put into groups. Fats and carbohydrates provide you with energy. Vitamins and minerals keep you healthy. Proteins build cells and help your body to grow and repair itself.

5. *Your large intestine takes back the water from digested food. Later it is passed out of your body through your anus.*

6. *Your bladder sto urine. When it fills you need to go to th bathroom to empty*

238

A lump in the throat

You can swallow even if you are standing on your head! This is because your food does not slide down through you—it is squeezed along by muscles in your digestive tube. This is called peristalsis and it happens all the time, without you having to think about it.

The muscles of a snake can squeeze an egg through its body in the same way.

Walking uses about 240 calories an hour

Sleeping uses about 65 calories an hour

Drawing uses about 85 calories an hour

Basketball and other vigorous sports use about 550 calories an hour

Fuel burning

If a car travels very fast, it uses up more fuel than if it goes slowly. The same is true of your body. When you exercise you use up more calories than when you are asleep.

You have two kidneys. Each one is about the size of your clenched fist.

Narrow tubes, called ureters, take urine from the kidneys to the bladder.

Carbohydrates

Any water your body does not need is turned into urine by your kidneys.

How long?

If you could stretch your whole digestive system out in a straight line, it would be about 33 feet (10 meters) long!

MUSCLES

Try to sit as still as you can. Is anything moving? Even when you think you are completely still, many parts of your body are moving.

Your heart is beating and your intestines and lungs are working. All these movements are made by muscles. You have more than 600 muscles spread throughout your body. Every bend, stretch, twist, and turn you make depends on them. You use about 200 muscles each time you take a step, and many more when you jump.

Your brain sends messages to your muscles and makes them move.

The largest m in your body gluteus maxi muscle in you thigh and bo

If you stand on tiptoe, you can your calf muscl the back of you

Muscle food
To keep your muscles working properly you need a diet that includes protein. Foods that are full of protein include meat, eggs, cheese, and dried beans.

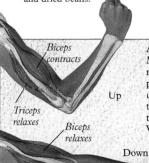

Biceps contracts

Triceps relaxes

Biceps relaxes

Up

Down

Triceps contracts

Arm bend
Muscles are attached to bones and make them move. But they can only pull; they cannot push—which is why they always work in pairs. In your arm, the biceps and triceps muscles work together to move it up and down. When the biceps pulls, or contracts, it gets shorter and fatter and bends the arm. As the biceps pulls, the triceps muscle relaxes.

Before you begin to make any strenuous movements, you should always warm up your muscles by a gentle warm-up and stretching exercises.

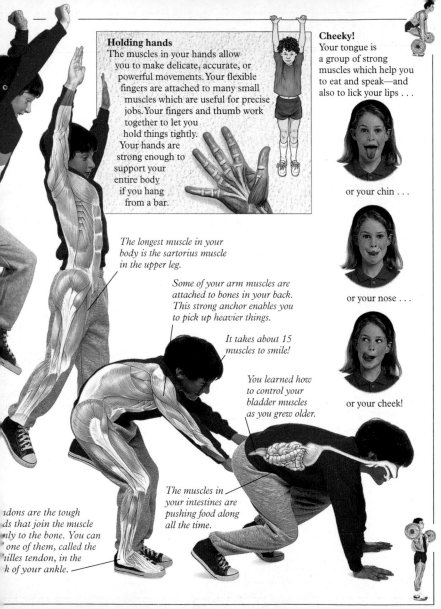

Holding hands

The muscles in your hands allow you to make delicate, accurate, or powerful movements. Your flexible fingers are attached to many small muscles which are useful for precise jobs. Your fingers and thumb work together to let you hold things tightly. Your hands are strong enough to support your entire body if you hang from a bar.

Cheeky!

Your tongue is a group of strong muscles which help you to eat and speak—and also to lick your lips . . .

or your chin . . .

or your nose . . .

or your cheek!

The longest muscle in your body is the sartorius muscle in the upper leg.

Some of your arm muscles are attached to bones in your back. This strong anchor enables you to pick up heavier things.

It takes about 15 muscles to smile!

You learned how to control your bladder muscles as you grew older.

The muscles in your intestines are pushing food along all the time.

ndons are the tough ds that join the muscle nly to the bone. You can one of them, called the illes tendon, in the k of your ankle.

SKELETON

Without a frame to support your body you would collapse, lose your shape, and be unable to move. Your body's frame is called a skeleton. It gives your body strength and it protects the soft parts inside. Your skeleton is made up of more than 200 bones. They are light enough to allow you to move around easily, and they have joints so that you can bend your body to do many things.

You have twelve pairs of ribs. They are all joined to a row of bones in your back called your spine.

From the side, your spine looks curved, like the letter S. It helps you to stand up straight.

Ulna

Femur

A tall order
Your bones keep growing until you are in your early 20s. You cannot change your height—it is decided in your genes and passed on from your parents. But you are about half an inch (one centimeter) shorter in the evening than you are in the morning! This is because the pads of cartilage in your spine get squashed as you walk around all day.

Yes and no bo
The bones of your spine called vertebrae. The top vertebrae, the atlas and a fit together to al your head to and to move f side to s

Atlas

Axis

Your nose is made of bone b rubbery mat called carti If you loo a skeleton will not nose bone, a nose

Radius

Fibula

Tibia

Your ankle joint. It is m up of bones the foot and ends of the l bones, the ti and fibula.

oft center

ome animals, such as this crab,
o not have a skeleton inside
em. Instead, they have a hard
uter covering, called
n exoskeleton.

Inside information

Your bones are all hidden
inside your body. So if
doctors want to look at
them, they have to take
special photographs, called
X-rays. The X-ray camera
can see straight through your
skin and show what the bones
look like. On this X-ray of
a hand, you can see that
the bone connected to the
little finger is broken.

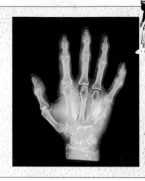

*Bones give muscles a place to hang on
to, but without these muscles, the bones
would not be able to move. Muscle power
is transferred to the bones along strong
bands called tendons.*

*ur hip joint is where the end of the
gh bone, or femur, fits into a socket
your pelvis. This joint helps you to
nd your body almost in half.*

*Your basin-shaped pelvis supports
the upper half of your body and
also protects soft parts, such
as your bladder.*

*Your spine can only curve gently. If it bent
any further it would damage your spinal
cord—the nerve cable that carries
messages to and from your brain.*

Skull

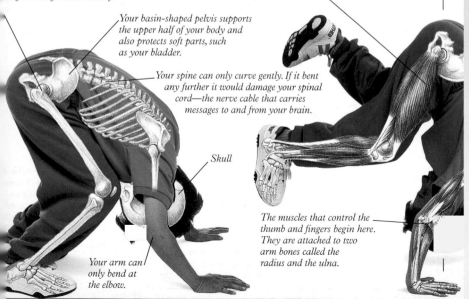

*The muscles that control the
thumb and fingers begin here.
They are attached to two
arm bones called the
radius and the ulna.*

*Your arm can
only bend at
the elbow.*

BONES

Your bones are hard and strong. They are not solid though, so they are not as heavy as you would think. In fact, they only make up 14 percent of your total body weight—they are lighter than your muscles. Bones are not dead and dry. They are living, and can repair themselves if they break. Your body is made up of lots of bones all working together and linked by joints. If you had no knee joints, you would have to walk with stiff legs.

What's inside a bone?
The outer part of all your bones is hard and tough, but the inside of many of them is spongy. These lightweight, soft centers are crisscrossed by small struts which make your bones strong, but not too heavy. This idea of strength without weight is copied in buildings such as the Eiffel Tower.

Crisscross struts

The spongy inner bone looks like a honeycomb.

Blood vessels take oxygen and food to bone cells.

Some bones are filled with jellylike marrow. Platelets and red and white blood cells are made in the bone marrow.

Your two feet contain one qua of the bones in y whole body!

Your neck is much shorter than a giraffe's, but it has the same number of vertebrae!

The tiny tailbones at the end of your spine, called the coccyx, help to support your body when you sit down.

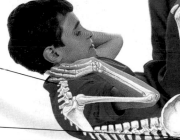

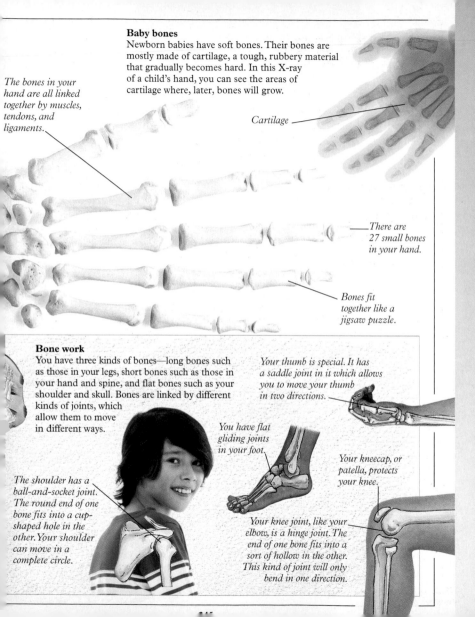

Baby bones

Newborn babies have soft bones. Their bones are mostly made of cartilage, a tough, rubbery material that gradually becomes hard. In this X-ray of a child's hand, you can see the areas of cartilage where, later, bones will grow.

The bones in your hand are all linked together by muscles, tendons, and ligaments.

Cartilage

There are 27 small bones in your hand.

Bones fit together like a jigsaw puzzle.

Bone work

You have three kinds of bones—long bones such as those in your legs, short bones such as those in your hand and spine, and flat bones such as your shoulder and skull. Bones are linked by different kinds of joints, which allow them to move in different ways.

Your thumb is special. It has a saddle joint in it which allows you to move your thumb in two directions.

You have flat gliding joints in your foot.

Your kneecap, or patella, protects your knee.

The shoulder has a ball-and-socket joint. The round end of one bone fits into a cup-shaped hole in the other. Your shoulder can move in a complete circle.

Your knee joint, like your elbow, is a hinge joint. The end of one bone fits into a sort of hollow in the other. This kind of joint will only bend in one direction.

WHERE DO I COME FROM?

You began your life as an egg, which was only about the size of this period. This tiny fertilized egg grew for about nine months inside your mother before you were born. While a baby is growing, it relies on the mother for everything, and although a baby cannot do very much when it is first born, already it is a complete and very special person.

The beginning

Everyone is made up of billions of living units, called cells. A baby starts when an egg cell from a woman and a sperm cell from a man join together to make one new cell. For the egg and sperm to meet, the man and woman must have sexual intercourse. This is sometimes called making love because the man and woman treat each other lovingly. The man's penis gets firm and he puts it into the woman's vagina. The penis releases a mixture called semen, which has sperm in it, to join the egg.

Egg tube

Egg

Ovary

Uterus

Vagina

Bladder — Penis

Testes make sperm

The fertilized egg grows and divides into two.

It divides into four, eight, sixteen, and so on . . .

Sperm are like tiny tadpoles with long tails. They swim to the tube to find the egg. One sperm may then fertilize the egg.

While it is dividing, it is traveling to the womb, or uterus.

After nine days the egg attaches itself to the wall of the uterus.

After about eight weeks, the group of cells starts to look more like a baby.

The finge toes, and are forme

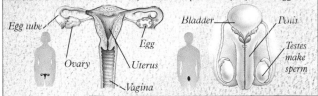

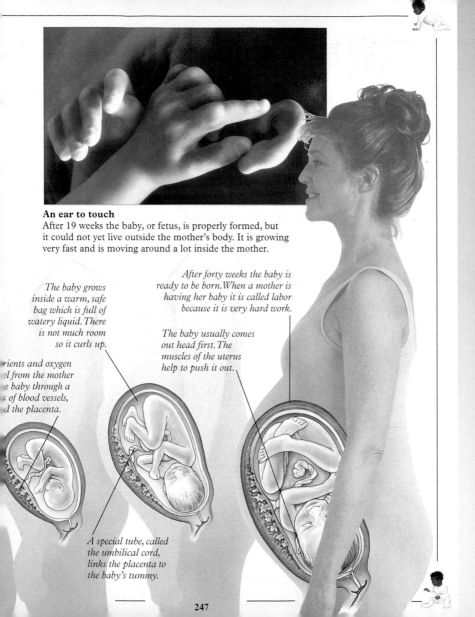

An ear to touch

After 19 weeks the baby, or fetus, is properly formed, but it could not yet live outside the mother's body. It is growing very fast and is moving around a lot inside the mother.

The baby grows inside a warm, safe bag which is full of watery liquid. There is not much room so it curls up.

After forty weeks the baby is ready to be born. When a mother is having her baby it is called labor because it is very hard work.

...rients and oxygen ...l from the mother ...e baby through a ...s of blood vessels, ...d the placenta.

The baby usually comes out head first. The muscles of the uterus help to push it out.

A special tube, called the umbilical cord, links the placenta to the baby's tummy.

247

CHAPTER 3

OUR WORLD

Early people hunted animals and gathered wild plants for food. Later, they learned to farm, growing crops and keeping animals so they had a more regular supply of food. Today, most of the food in stores and supermarkets still comes from farms—meat and dairy products, grains and rice, fruit and vegetables. However, machines now do most of the work, and special chemicals kill pests and help crops to grow.

As their lives became more settled, our ancestors gathered into communities and their forms of entertainment changed. Singing, dancing, and drawing branched out over time into plays, and, much later, films, and television.

Today, whether they live on high mountains, in dry deserts, or in swampy marshlands, all men and women have to feed, clothe, and house themselves. But from country to country, people do these things in an enormous variety of ways.

People in the Past
Arts and Entertainment
Food and Farming
People and Places

PEOPLE IN THE PAST

The lives of men and women who lived a long time ago were very different from ours. The first people made their homes in caves and had to kill their food or find it growing wild. For a long time, no one could read or write, so information and stories had to be learned by heart so they could be passed on.

Changes in the way people lived came gradually, when travelers—traders, or soldiers who went to war in foreign lands—took new ways of doing things, new foods, or new materials from one place to another. Sometimes, changes were particularly important, like the invention of the wheel or the printing press. These changes tended to spread quickly, and completely altered everyday life.

Viking warrior

18th-century gold doubloons

Ancient
Peruvian pot

Pottery bea
c. 2200 B

250

19th-century Russian cossack pistol

17th-century samurai sword

Arapaho chief's headdress

Illuminated manuscript

Egyptian wall painting c. 1400 BCE

Ancient Egyptian reed pens

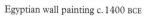

Beaded Blackfoot moccasins

HUNTERS AND GATHERERS

Horse

The earliest people lived by hunting and gathering to find their food—meat, fish, vegetables, and fruit. They moved with the seasons, taking shelter in caves or tents. The animals they hunted gave them food to eat, fat to fuel lamps, skins to make tents and clothes, and bones to make weapons, tent supports, jewelry, and toys.

Some European hunter-gatherers, who lived 35,000 years ago, painted animal pictures in caves. We don't know exactly why they did this, but cave painting may have been part of a ritual or a kind of magic.

Making flint tools

Flint was a stone that was easy to work and could be given a sharp edge. Hunter-gatherers used it to make tools and weapons. A pebble or bone hammer was used to strike long flakes of flint from the main stone. The flakes were shaped and then the edges were chipped to make them razor sharp.

The mammoth was like a modern-day elephant, but covered in fur. It was hunted for its meat, skin, bones, and tusks.

An ax with a flint blade

A spear with a bone tip

Animal magic

Beautiful pictures of the animals hunted by these people were painted on the walls and ceilings of caves in southwest France and in parts of northern Spain.

Bison

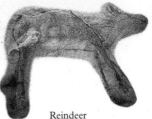

Reindeer

The hunters hurled heavy stones at their prey.

The spears used for hunting were often made from a flint or bone arrowhead tied onto a wooden shaft.

Unusual decoration

Teeth and bones from animals were made into pieces of jewelry, such as this necklace.

The hunters wore clothes made from animal skins.

First fashion

Animal skins were used to make clothes. First the skins were pegged down and then scraped to clean them and make them soft. Next the skins were cut to shape. The pieces were sewn together using needles made from animal bone and long, thin strips of hide.

A thong made from animal hide

Skin scrapers

A knife used to cut animal hide

THE EARLY FARMERS

Bullock

Goat

Sheep

About 12,000 years ago, there was an important change in the way people lived. People in parts of western Asia began to settle in one place and farm the land. They learned how to grow crops for food, and how to tame wild animals so they had a regular supply of meat. This new way of life was so successful that it soon spread far and wide.

As the people no longer moved around, they built houses to live in. They learned to spin and weave cloth and also to make pottery.

Taming animals
Young wild animals were caught by hunters and raised on the farms so they became used to being around people.

Bringing in the harvest
When the crop was ripe, it was cut down with a sickle. This was made of a sharp flint blade set in a wooden handle.

First crops
This is emmer wheat. Emmer was developed from the seeds of wild grasses become an important food source.

Before it is ground, this ear of corn will be beaten to separate the grains from the husk.

Coiling clay
This girl is making a pot by coiling long, thin rolls of clay on top of a flat clay base. She is making a pot in the same way the first potters did, 9,000 years ago.

The flour would be mixed with water and made into round, flat loaves.

...rain was ground between two ...stones and made into flour.

...om farm to town
...arms attracted ...ople. As they grew ...ger, villages and ...wns were formed. ...e first known town, ...atal Hüyük, was ...ilt in Turkey about ...000 years ago.

The walls of the houses were made of mud. They only had a few windows.

...e roofs were ...ade of branches, ...ds, and straw ...vered in mud.

...e houses ...uched each ...her and there ...re no streets.

People got into their houses by climbing a ladder and going through a hole in the roof.

THE SUMERIANS

About 9,000 years ago, farmers began to move into an area of land between the Tigris and Euphrates rivers. This fertile land was called Mesopotamia, in what is now Iraq. In the south of Mesopotamia was the land of Sumer. The Sumerians were very inventive. They developed the first form of writing and recording numbers, and invented the wheel and the plow.

The Sumerians grew bumper crops of cereals, which they traded for things they needed: wood, building stone, or metals. Wheeled carts, and their skills in writing and using numbers, helped them develop long-distance trade.

A merchant ma[kes] a record of the [goods] he has sold.

How writing began
The Sumerians drew pictures on soft clay with a pointed reed. The pictures were drawn downward in lines, from the right-hand side.

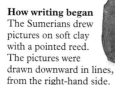

Later, they started to write across the tablet, from left to right. The reed tip made wedge-shaped marks.

Fish
Bird
Barley
Ox

The signs were then joined together to create words and sentences.

In time, the picture signs changed so much that the original objects were hard to recognize. This writing is called cuneiform, which means "wedge-shaped."

's a deal
nstead of writing their
ames, the Sumerian
aders used a seal to
gn their contracts.

Flooded fields
Mesopotamia was watered
by the Tigris and Euphrates,
which flooded in the spring.
The farmers dug
out basins and
canals so the river
water could be stored
and used to water fields away
from the river. Because of this,
land was very fertile and harvests
were good.

*Wood was imported
from Syria and
the Lebanon.*

*Wheeled carts were
able to carry heavy
objects over long
distances.*

*s were
d to store
in and oil.*

Crosspiece

Spokes

Tilling the soil
The first plows were
made of wood. Later, the
blade was made of bronze.
Despite the flooding from the
rivers, the ground in Sumer
was baked hard in hot weather.
The plow made it possible to
break up the hard-to-work soil.

volutionary invention
e first wheels were made
planks of solid wood held
ether with crosspieces.

They were clumsy and heavy.
In time, lighter wheels were
made. These had many spokes.

THE EGYPTIANS

The Egyptians believed that when they died they went on to another, everlasting, life. To live happily in the afterlife, they needed their earthly bodies and great care was taken to ensure that they arrived in style. The dead bodies were preserved in a special way called mummification.

To mummify a body took a long time, as much as 70 days. First, inner organs were taken out and put in tightly sealed jars. Next, the body was dried out by covering it with natron, a white powder like salt. It was left for 40 days, rubbed with sweet-smelling oils, and then covered in molten resin. Finally, the body was wrapped in linen to make a neat package.

Well kept
This is how the mummy of King Seti I loo[ked] underneath all his bandages. He was buried [at] Thebes over 3,[000] years ago. Desp[ite] his age, you ca[n] still see his fac[e] very clearly.

A picture of the dead person is painted on the mummy case, or coffin.

On this coffin, the arms are shown crossed over the chest.

The coffin is made to follow the shape of the body inside.

These little drawings are called hieroglyphs. Each picture means a word or sound in the ancient Egyptian language.

Royal tombs
Egyptian kings, called pharaohs, were buried in tombs known as pyramids.

Creatures great and small

The Egyptians believed in many different gods and goddesses, some of which took the form of animals. They mummified animals as offerings to these gods. When mummified, the creatures made some odd shapes.

Mummified crocodile

Mummified cow

Mummified cat

The lid of the coffin is decorated with symbols of the gods. These are the wings of the sky goddess, Nut.

This coffin is made of wood. Early ones were made of clay or woven out of reeds like a basket.

All wrapped up

All mummies were wrapped up tightly in lots of material. As much as 4,000 sq feet (375 sq meters) of linen might be needed to wrap up a single mummy.

The hieroglyphs were spells to help the priestess on her journey to the next life.

Brightly colored figures and symbols are painted on the inside of the coffin.

This mummy case may have been one of a nest of coffins, each fitting inside the next like a set of Russian dolls.

242

GREEK GAMES

All over Ancient Greece festivals were held in honor of the Greek gods. They included competitions in sports, music, and drama. The most famous of the festivals was the Olympic Games, an event first held in 776 BCE. There were no team races and the male athletes competed as individuals. Their prize was a simple wreath of olive leaves, but if you won you became a hero.

The discus was made of stone or bronze.

The athletes competed barefoot and wore no clothes.

Liftoff!
The long jump was the only jumping event included in Greek athletics.

Fighting fit
Athletics training kept men fit for war. The connection between sports and war is shown in the race-in-armor event.

The pentathlon

The decoration on this vase shows athletes training for the pentathlon. The contest included wrestling, throwing the javelin and discus, running, and the long jump.

Handing over

Relay races were included in some festivals, but not the Olympic Games. The runners used a torch as a baton.

ooden
n had
l tip.

Before they exercised, the athletes rubbed olive oil into their skin, perhaps to protect them from the sun.

Equal opportunities

Only men and boys were allowed to compete in the Olympic Games, but in Sparta girls were expected to go through the same tough athletic training as the boys. This little bronze statue of a girl runner from Sparta shows her barefoot and wearing a short tunic.

Inspiration from the past

The idea for today's Olympics came from the Ancient Greek games of more than 2,000 years ago. The interlocking Olympic rings represent the five competing continents.

ROMAN LIFE

The Romans planned their towns to include magnificent public buildings such as temples, the town hall, baths, and places of entertainment. There were also grand houses for wealthy families. But side by side with these were the tumbledown dwellings where most people lived—overcrowded apartments built over shops and workshops. The poor had no kitchens, so they lived on bread or bought hot food from stalls. Since the Romans lived, traded, and ate in the streets, their towns were noisy places. Traffic was bad, too, with carts and wagons bringing country goods through the busy streets.

In the kitc
This scene sh
what a typ
Roman kitchen
like. You would h
found it in the t
house or vill
a rich fan

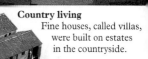

Country living
Fine houses, called villas, were built on estates in the countryside.

Building being built of bricks

Wharf

Fishing nets drying

A wooden bridge over the river

drying over the stove. Romans liked their food flavored. Herbs and also helped make food fresh longer.

Bread was an important part of Roman diet, and the basic food of the poor.

A saucepan made of bronze

Storage jars, called amphorae, were used to hold wine.

Slaves did the housework for wealthy Romans.

Jugs for serving wine

ng boat cargo he port.

Cats were kept as pets for children and to chase away mice and rats!

This floor is decorated with a mosaic, a picture made from tiny tiles.

All mod cons
Unlike the poor in their cramped dwellings, wealthy Romans lived in well-planned houses with lots of home comforts. There was running water, a toilet and bathroom, a kitchen, and even central heating. This worked by sending warmed air through pipes laid under the floor.

Raiders from the Sea

Late in the eighth century a seafaring people from the countries now known as Denmark, Norway, and Sweden began to sail abroad in search of wealth. They were called Vikings. In their amazingly fast and adaptable longships, Vikings were the best sailors in Europe. They began by raiding foreign lands, and went on to conquer and settle there. They were also great sea traders. Many of the Vikings became Christians. It was the Vikings who founded the cities of Dublin in Ireland and Kiev in Ukraine. The Normans were descended from Viking settlers in northern France.

The mast supported a big square sail. This was used when the longship was out at sea and there was plenty of wind to fill the sail.

Longships were called "Serpents of the Sea." They were decorated with scary animal carvings called figureheads.

As Vikings prepare to land on a foreign shore, warriors stand at the front of the longship, with settlers in the middle.

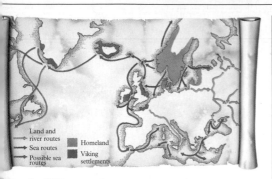

Land and river routes
Sea routes
Possible sea routes

Homeland
Viking settlements

Where the Vikings went

The Vikings roamed great distances. Merchants sailed across the rivers of Russia and around the Mediterranean Sea. They traded such northern objects as furs and walrus tusks for southern objects such as silk and silver. Explorers sailed to Iceland, Greenland, and to Newfoundland in North America. They called this Vinland.

Strange stones

The Vikings set up stones, called runestones. They were carved with many beautiful patterns and with letters developed by the Vikings called runes.

Runes

Fascinating tales

Storytelling was very popular. These stories, or sagas, were long poems describing brave deeds, journeys to strange lands, and victories in battle. Before the Vikings learned to write, they remembered stories by learning them by heart.

Longships were made of overlapping planks of wood. They were very light and could be carried overland for short distances to get from one river to another.

THE CRUSADES

The city of Jerusalem and the Holy Land of Palestine (now including Israel and Jordan) are special to people of three faiths—Jews, Muslims, and Christians. Nine hundred years ago, the first of a series of wars broke out over control of Jerusalem. In 1095, European Christians set out to take the city, then ruled by Muslims. The Europeans were called crusaders from the French word *croisade*, meaning "carrying a cross."

In 1099, after four years of struggle, the crusaders captured Jerusalem and held it for nearly one hundred years. Then it was recaptured by a great Muslim leader called Saladin. More crusades followed, but none was successful. However, the returning crusaders brought many new objects and ideas back to Europe.

Over his armor, the knight is wearing a cross—the sign of a crusader.

Stronghold
The crusaders built strong castles in the Arab style to defend the land they had captured. This is Krak des Chevaliers in Syria.

Body beautiful

The crusaders took back to Europe new customs that they learned in the Middle East. Cosmetics such as rouge to redden the cheeks and henna to color hair became common for women. Glass mirrors replaced polished metal discs. Perfumes to scent clothes and the body were used. Being clean became popular!

Roman numerals
I   II   III   IV   V   VI   VII   VIII   IX
Arabic numerals
0 1 2 3 4 5 6 7 8 9

One, two, three . . .

The Muslims used a series of numbers, called Arabic numerals, which were much easier to use than those of the old Roman system. They are used today throughout the world.

Bookworms

Arab learning was more advanced than that of the crusaders. They had lots of books and libraries at a time when there were very few in Europe. The crusaders took many books back with them.

Healing arts

Muslim doctors were very good surgeons and were skilled in using plants and herbs to make medicines. They used opium and myrrh to ease pain when people were having operations.

A Muslim foot soldier usually carried a round shield for protection. It may have been made of wood or of layers of hardened leather sewn together.

Musical instruments

The Muslims invented a musical instrument called the oud, which was called the lute in Europe. The modern guitar was developed from this instrument.

Boots made of leather or felt were the most common footwear for a Muslim soldier.

Great inventors

The Muslims made fine scientific instruments like this astrolabe. It used the positions of the stars and planets to show travelers which way to go in the empty deserts.

MARCO POLO

In 1271 a merchant named Marco Polo and his family set off from Venice on an extraordinary journey to China. They traveled along the Silk Road, an important trading route between Europe and the Far East. Merchants had been using the route for more than 1,700 years before the Polos, but they were the first Europeans to travel its whole length. In an age when there were no planes, trains, coaches, or cars, they crossed thousands of miles of mountains, deserts, and plains on foot, horseback, and even on camels. Their journey to China took them more than three years. The Silk Road could be very dangerous and the traders were sometimes attacked by bandits. Because of this threat, they traveled together in groups.

Making a trade
The Venetian merchants exchan jewels, silver, and gold for goods from the East that were highly valued in Europe. These included spices, si porcelain or "chin and fine carpets.

Wealthy traders
Venice was the most important port in Europe. Its merchants traveled by sea and land to bring back goods from the East to sell to other towns in Europe.

Camels were used by merchants when crossing the desert regions of central Asia. Unlike horses, they were able to travel long distances without needing water.

Besides the barren deserts, merchants traveling on the Silk Road had to climb ove extreme mountain ranges and cross flooded rivers.

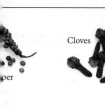

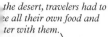

Pepper

Cloves

Cinnamon

Mace

Nutmeg

Silk tunic

In the desert, travelers had to take all their own food and water with them.

A large group of people traveling with camels was called a caravan.

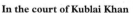

Persian carpet

Porcelain jar

In the court of Kublai Khan

When the Polos arrived in China they found it under the control of the Mongol emperor Kublai Khan. Marco Polo stayed at the Mongol court for 17 years and became a trusted advisor to Kublai Khan.

The camel driver is covered from head to toe in heavy clothing to protect him from the harsh winds of the desert.

THE RENAISSANCE

In the 15th century, Europe was bursting with new ideas about art, learning, and religion. Many of the people who could read and write began to ask questions, and to do experiments for themselves rather than follow what their rulers and priests told them to think. They rediscovered many of the ideas that the Greeks and Romans had about life and the world. As a result this period became known as the "Renaissance," a French word meaning rebirth. The Renaissance started in the cities of northern and central Italy but gradually spread all over Europe.

Before the Renaissance, most paintings showed mythical scenes or Bible charac[ters] and everything in them looked perfect. For the first time, Renaissance artis[ts] used live models [and] made them look li[ke] ordinary hum[an] beings.

A letter of type used in the printing press

The printed word
Before the printing press was invented by Johannes Gutenberg, books had to be copied by hand. Only the rich could afford them.

Artists began to make realistic paintings of everyday objects.

The apprentice is grind[ing] colors to make paints f[or] his master. He will mix the powder with oil to produce oil paints.

The Gutenberg Bible
These pages come from one of the three books that made up the Gutenberg Bible. It was printed in the 1450s and was admired for its quality.

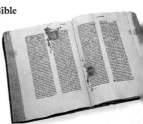

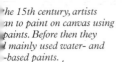

he 15th century, artists
an to paint on canvas using
paints. Before then they
l mainly used water- and
-based paints.

sts were no longer
nown craftsmen,
their names became
us throughout
pe during
Renaissance.

The quest for knowledge

During the Renaissance, scholars and
scientists began doing experiments
and inventing things to find out more
about the world they lived in.

With the invention
of the telescope,
faraway planets
could be seen
in detail for
the first time.

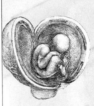

The artist Leonardo da Vinci
was interested in the workings
of the human body. This is
one of his drawings.

This model was made from
a design by Leonardo,
showing an early
form of a tank.

Leonardo's creative
imagination led him
to produce designs
for a flying machine.

Food from the New World

From 1492 onward, European explorers
sailed across the Atlantic to what they
called the New World of North, Central,
and South America. There they discovered
a treasure trove of gold and silver. But they
found other treasures, too. These were foods
that grew only in the New World, such as
sweet corn and potatoes, and plants that
could be made into medicines. In fact, you
may be surprised to find out how many of
the foods you eat come from the New World.
Every time you eat a tomato, or mashed
potatoes, or have chocolate for a treat,
just think, you owe them to the people
of the Americas.

Sunflower

Coco

A world of golden treasure
The Native Americans had vast quantities
of gold which they used to make into
jewelry. The Europeans plundered
most of this treasure.

*Corn was
eaten boiled or roasted,
or ground into flour.
The explorer Christopher
Columbus took it back to
Europe when he returned
from his voyages.*

*This is cornmeal, made
out of ground corn.
It was used to make
breadlike foods.*

Peanut

ative American plants
ese include cocoa (for
ocolate), sunflowers
give us oil to cook
h), and peanuts.

Healing plants
When the explorers reached the Americas, they found skilled healers among the people living there. These healers used thousands of plants to make medicines. Their remedies were used to cure many illnesses, including stomach pains, headaches, coughs, and fevers. Many of these plants are still used today to make medicines.

Cinchona leaf

Quinine is used to prevent an illness called malaria. It is made from the bark of the cinchona tree.

Cinchona bark

Quinine tablets

neapples were one of
e new fruits found
the explorers. They
re given this name
cause they looked
e pine cones.

ck
ns

Lots of different beans came from Mexico. These are red beans.

These small, hot peppers are chillies. They were used to flavor the bowls of corn porridge that the Mexicans ate for breakfast.

Sweet potatoes

Tomatoes, first grown in South America, spread to Mexico, where the Spanish came across them. The first ones they brought to Europe were small and yellow.

Potatoes were first grown in the Andes Mountains. They were loaded aboard the treasure ships as food for the sailors.

cados look like pears with
h, tough skins. They were
grown in Central America.

THE LIFE OF THE SAMURAI

For about seven hundred years the Samurai were the honored knights of Japan. Fierce fighters, they had a tough training, becoming experts in fencing, wrestling, archery, and acrobatics, and they had a special code of behavior. The word samurai means "one who serves," and any Samurai worthy of the name was absolutely loyal to his lord, ready to obey any command without question.

However, although the Samurai were professional fighters, away from battle they were not violent men. The Samurai believed in Zen Buddhism, a religion that taught respect for all living things. The Samurai were also taught to love art and learning, taking pride in their skill at painting, writing poetry, and even flower-arranging.

The large, horned helmet was meant to terrify enemies as much as to protect its wearer.

Western merchants
When the Portuguese arrived in Japan in 1543, they brought guns with them. The guns changed the nature of warfare in the country completely.

Women and ladies

Just as the Samurai obeyed his lord, the women of his own family had to obey him. Graceful, musical, and artistic, these Samurai ladies were expected to make homes for their lords and masters. By contrast, the peasant women who labored in the fields had to work as hard as beasts of burden.

Knowing their place

Life in Samurai Japan was strictly organized. From birth, everybody had a fixed place in society. Samurai families belonged to the upper classes.

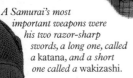

The godlike Emperor was the official ruler, but the Shogun, his chief general, was really the most powerful person in Japan.

Shogun

A Samurai's most important weapons were his two razor-sharp swords, a long one, called a katana, *and a short one called a* wakizashi.

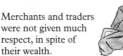

Daimyo

The Daimyo were the nobles of Japan, and they were supported by Samurai warriors. They preferred to have nothing to do with money or the buying and selling of goods.

A Samurai's armor consisted of six main pieces: the helmet, the face mask, the breast-plate, the sleeves, the shin guards, and the loin guard.

Samurai

Merchants and traders were not given much respect, in spite of their wealth.

Merchants

Lowest of the low were the peasants. They worked on the farms of the Daimyo and were treated like slaves.

Peasant

NEWCOMERS TO THE AMERICAS

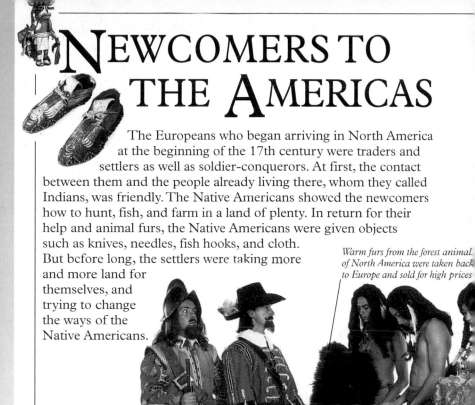

The Europeans who began arriving in North America at the beginning of the 17th century were traders and settlers as well as soldier-conquerors. At first, the contact between them and the people already living there, whom they called Indians, was friendly. The Native Americans showed the newcomers how to hunt, fish, and farm in a land of plenty. In return for their help and animal furs, the Native Americans were given objects such as knives, needles, fish hooks, and cloth. But before long, the settlers were taking more and more land for themselves, and trying to change the ways of the Native Americans.

Warm furs from the forest animals of North America were taken back to Europe and sold for high prices

European weapons, tools, and machines completely changed hunting and warfare for Native Americans.

European cloth was prized for its bright colors and silkiness.

Creek
(Southeast)

Iroquois
(Northeast)

Tlingit
(Pacific Northwest)

Hidatsa
(Plains)

Hopi
(Southwest)

Sauk
(Great Lakes)

Paiute
(Great Basin)

ive Americans used
ers and animal
n to decorate
selves.

Warriors and hunters

The work that men and women did varied from tribe to tribe, but usually the men were the hunters and warriors, while the women were the farmers and homemakers. Most Native Americans wore their hair long and they enjoyed decorating their bodies and clothes.

Tepees, longhouses, and pueblos

There was great variety in the lives of the Native American peoples. How they lived—their clothes, their food, their religious beliefs— depended on the land and the weather. Some of the differences between the tribes are shown by their homes.

r comfort
d protection
nst ants, snakes,
other dangers,
ive Americans
slipperlike leather
s called moccasins.

corn, squash, and
kins were among
otic American foods
that the European
settlers tasted for
_ the first time.

Tlingit cedar-plank house

Hidatsa animal-skin tepee

Sauk mat-covered dome lodge

Paiute brush and reed encampment

Iroquois wooden longhouse

Hopi stone and sun-baked mudbrick pueblo

Creek storehouse

THE ASHANTI KINGDOM

The Ashanti kingdom

The Ashanti kingdom flourished for 200 years after its emergence in the 17th century, in what is now Ghana in West Africa. The Ashanti were a highly organized people: the king had his own civil service, which carried out his commands throughout the country. The Ashanti were also fine warriors, and much of their wealth was based on selling slaves from the prisoners they captured in battle. They had vast quantities of gold which was used to make jewelry and as decoration for musical instruments and weapons. Ashanti goldsmiths were highly skilled in their craft. They used a special method to cast the metal, called the lost-wax technique.

The item to be cast in gold was modeled in melted beeswax.

The wax was made into thin sheets. These were cut into strips, which were used to make the model.

Clay was molded around the model and a hole made in the clay. As the mold was baked, the wax melted and poured out through the hole. Molten gold was then poured into the space.

When the metal had cooled and hardened, the mold was smashed open. The gold object was taken out and cleaned up.

Beautifully made
These royal sandals have flowers of gold sewn onto them.

Ashanti goldsmiths worked gold into all kinds of objects. The handle of this sword was covered in a fine sheet of gold.

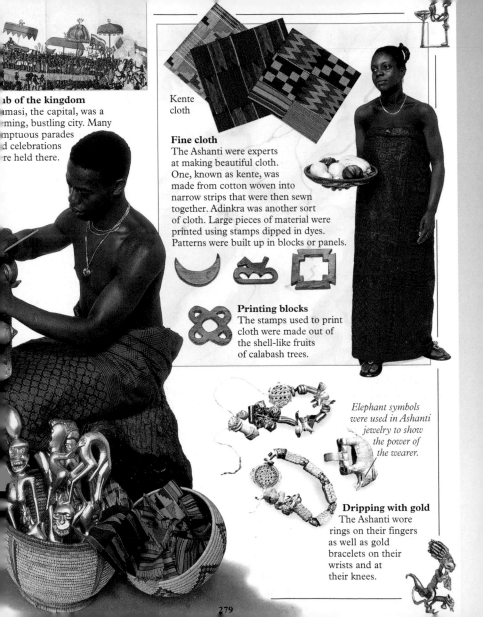

...b of the kingdom
...masi, the capital, was a
...ming, bustling city. Many
...mptuous parades
...d celebrations
...re held there.

Kente
cloth

Fine cloth

The Ashanti were experts
at making beautiful cloth.
One, known as kente, was
made from cotton woven into
narrow strips that were then sewn
together. Adinkra was another sort
of cloth. Large pieces of material were
printed using stamps dipped in dyes.
Patterns were built up in blocks or panels.

Printing blocks

The stamps used to print
cloth were made out of
the shell-like fruits
of calabash trees.

*Elephant symbols
were used in Ashanti
jewelry to show
the power of
the wearer.*

Dripping with gold

The Ashanti wore
rings on their fingers
as well as gold
bracelets on their
wrists and at
their knees.

CATHERINE THE GREAT

Catherine II, Empress of Russia during the 18th century, was called "Great" because she made Russia a great European power. She asked the advice of many of the major thinkers in Europe and, because she was interested in education, she started the Russian school system.

Catherine also loved clothes and spectacular entertainments, and so did her nobles. Under her rule they became even more powerful than they had been before. They were the owners of land and of people. These people were known as serfs and, like slaves, they had to do whatever their masters wanted. Serfs could be bought and sold by their masters.

Miserable existence
Nine out of ten Russians were serfs and life for them was grim. Often, they lived in poor log huts with only one room for an entire family.

Catherine's palaces and the homes the nobles were filled with furnitur ornaments, carpets, and other luxuries in the latest fashions.

The Hermitage

Catherine built the Winter Palace in St. Petersburg. She called it the Hermitage, because it allowed her to shut herself and her court away like hermits. Today it is a famous museum.

During court entertainments the wearing of masks became popular.

The court entertainments were dazzling to look at, with gorgeous costumes.

The playing of music was encouraged at court. Catherine invited foreign musicians to Russia to perform their work.

...bles dressed ...hes that came ...shionable France. ...were the finest ...money could buy.

Revolt of the serfs

In 1771, a Cossack soldier named Emilian Pugachev set himself up as a rival emperor to Catherine. The Cossacks were a warlike people who lived in southern Russia. Thousands of serfs who wanted to get rid of the nobles joined in their revolt.

The number of rebels under Pugachev grew and, in 1773, they swarmed across Russia, destroying the city of Kazan. Catherine ordered her army to attack the rebels and, in July 1774, the serfs were defeated. Pugachev was captured, brought to Moscow, and executed. The revolt was over.

THE JOURNEYS OF JAMES COOK

In the 18th century, a great explorer named James Cook made three voyages that mapped the Pacific Ocean, the world's largest and deepest sea. On his first voyage he sailed around New Zealand and down the east coast of Australia. On the second journey he explored the Antarctic and mapped many South Pacific islands. On his last trip he discovered Hawaii.

Cook's voyages were important because he tried to find out about the people, plants, and animals of the countries he visited. On his ship were scientists and artists, as well as officers, crew, and servants.

South Sea paradise
Throughout the 18th century, artists and writers presented life in the South Pacific as being easy and perfect.

Cook and his compa were members of the Royal Navy, so they wore naval uniforms

first voyage to the South
ment was made to watch the
movement of the planet Venus.
scientists looked through
a telescope like this.

*This very accurate
astronomical clock was used
for timing the observations
of the stars and planets.*

Art for all

Drawings and paintings made
by the artists on Cook's voyages were
published. People in Europe could see
illustrations of new plants and animals
discovered on the explorations.

Erythrina

Hibiscus

Wild cat

*This is a
quadrant. It
was another
means of
helping sailors
find their way.*

Butterfly fish

Blue-crowned lory

*Artists were taken on the voyages
to draw the plants and animals
they saw, just as a photographer
might take pictures today.*

REVOLUTION

The revolutionaries u
against organized rel
and many clergymen
the country.

Detail from a French revolution poster

In the 18th century, an important revolution started in France. It happened because the king, Louis XVI, and his nobles held all the power and wealth in the country. He could rule the people as he pleased. The way he chose to do so was unfair. For example, the nobles, who were already rich, paid no taxes while the poor peasants did. In 1789, the king had nearly run out of money. He wanted to increase taxes. At the same time, food was very scarce because of bad harvests. The ordinary people had had enough and decided that they didn't want to be ruled by the king. Louis was executed and a new government was set up.

Nobles were though
to be enemies of the
revolution. Some
were arrested and
went to the guilloti

The revolution was supported by people who thought they had been badly treated by their rulers. They included lawyers, traders, small farmers, workers, and ordinary soldiers.

The nobles made fu
of the simple clothe
the revolutionaries
They called them
"sans-culottes," pe
without the fine k
length breeches
the nobles wore. -

Women played a
important part i
revolutionary ei
They led many
the marches.

The guillotine

Anyone who was not loyal to the revolution faced arrest and possible death by guillotine. The guillotine cut off the heads of the victims. It was made of a heavy, sharp blade that fell between two posts. Death by guillotine was very quick. It caused less suffering than other methods of execution.

Victims of the guillotine rode to the place of execution in open carts, called tumbrels.

The revolutionaries wore a red hat that looked like a nightcap. It was decorated with a blue and white ribbon.

American revolution

In the 1770s, British colonists (settlers) in America grew sick of being ruled by the British king. They fought for their independence and won, setting up a Republic—a state without a king. The French revolutionaries were encouraged by the American success.

This painting shows colonists fighting the British in Massachusetts in 1775.

RICHES OF INDUSTRY

Modern photography was invented by the British scien[tist] William Fox Talbot during [the] 1830s. It soon became popu[lar] for people to have their photograph taken.

One of the biggest changes in the history of the world, the Industrial Revolution, started in Britain in the late 18th century. As the "Workshop of the World," Britain was the first home of new machines, new types of materials, and new ways of making power. This was the age of coal and iron, of gas and electricity, of railroads and factories.

Within 50 years this series of mighty inventions had dramatically changed the way in which people lived. Railroads and steamships made it possible to travel quickly from place to place. Instead of living in the country, many more people lived in towns and cities. There they worked in factories where machines made things in vast numbers, quickly and cheaply.

Grim conditions
The big industrial cities were very smoky, and many people were crammed together in badly built houses.

The railroads and cheaper paper provided many more readers with news of events from all over the world.

th the arrival of
ns, which had
un according to
tables, people
un to live their
s by the clock.

Iron foundry
Abraham Darby replaced charcoal (made from wood) with coke (made from coal) for making a new kind of tough iron.

Ironbridge

The invention of electroplating made it possible to coat iron objects with silver. They looked like solid silver but were far cheaper to make.

Made of metal
In 1779, Abraham Darby III built the first iron bridge across the river Severn. The place is now called Ironbridge. The Eiffel Tower was built in Paris in 1889 and is more than 980 feet (300 meters) high.

Eiffel Tower

Vast numbers of machine-made cups and plates were turned out for everyday use.

The invention of artificial dyes in the 1850s meant that cloth did not fade when it was washed.

The Great Exhibition
In 1851, the Great Exhibition was opened in London, inside a huge glass building called the Crystal Palace. The Exhibition displayed all the latest industrial developments.

Factory life
he first factories were built ontain the heavy machinery ed to produce cotton cloth. Vhole families—even young nildren—kept the machines going night and day.

PIONEERS

During the 19th century, European settlers traveled across America in search of land to farm. They were called pioneers. Some of them traveled in wagon trains so long that they stretched as far as the eye could see. The wagons were packed tight with provisions—food, tools, plows, household goods, and even chamber pots. There was often only enough room for small children, the sick, and some women to ride in the wagons. Everyone else walked alongside.

Tormented by the heat and dust, or by winds, rain, and snow, the pioneers trudged across prairies and climbed over mountains. They lived and slept outdoors, and often went without food and water. The pioneers also faced attacks from Native Americans who resented the Europeans taking their land from them.

The wagons were pulled by teams of horses, mules, or oxen

The lure of gold
Prospectors were people who hunted for gold. They would fill a shallow pan with gravel from a riverbed and wash the stones out of the pan with water. Then they looked for any gold that might have sunk to the bottom.

When gold was discovered in Australia, America, South Africa, and Canada in the 19th century, Europeans flocked to these countries to make their fortune.

The wheels in the fron were made smaller th those in the back, so t the wagon could be st more easily.

Self assembly

When the pioneers came to set up home, they had to build their own houses. Some made them out of logs, but others used chunks of dry earth cut from the ground.

The Great Trek

In 1835, Dutch settlers in South Africa moved in wagons to new land to escape being ruled by the British. This journey was called the "Great Trek." For safety against the Africans whose land they had entered, the settlers would carefully form their wagons into a circle at night.

top was made of
was held up by a frame
oops. It helped
out rain
dust.

The hoops were made of strong and flexible hickory wood.

The pioneers had to bring all their cooking equipment with them.

e wheels were made of wood
the rim was covered in iron.
eels often broke and held up
wagon train.

THE AMERICAN CIVIL WAR

In 1861, a civil war started in America between states in the South who owned slaves and states in the North who thought this was wrong. The South tried to break away from the Union to form a separate nation, but the North went to war to prevent this. After four years of bitter fighting, the North won and the South was forced to return to the Union. But the price paid by both sides was terrible. More than 600,000 soldiers died, more than half of them victims of disease, not of battle. When they got sick or were wounded, their treatment was as likely to kill them as cure them. The field hospitals were filthy and the surgeons often poorly trained.

If they lucky, so were drugs to them uncons during su But often had noth ease the

- Northern states
- Confederate states
- Border states that fought on the Northern side
- Areas with the most slaves
- Other territories

The Confederates
The soldiers of the South, or Confederacy, were given uniforms of gray coats and caps, and blue trousers. When uniforms were in short supply the men wore whatever they could find.

he Unionists

he soldiers of the orth, or Union, wore dark blue coats or jackets and light blue trousers. They had more and better weapons than the troops from the South because most of the factories making weapons were in the North.

e surgeons who treated liers often worked h dirty hands and hes spattered with blood.

The slave states

The wealth of the Southern states of America came from plantations producing cotton, sugar, and tobacco. The work on the plantations was carried out by slaves—the descendants of those who had been captured and shipped over from Africa. Their masters could do what they liked with them and they were often treated badly. Slavery was finally abolished in America in 1865.

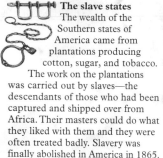

Slaves could be bought and sold at market like animals. Often families were split up.

Women volunteered to help the wounded. In the North, teams of trained nurses were set up.

Most medicines were not very effective, and a few were actually dangerous.

Special kit

With its pliers and saw, this box looks like a tool kit. In fact, it was a surgeon's case used during the American Civil War.

IN THE SCHOOLROOM

The blackboard double-sided. It on wheels so it c be moved easily.

Until 1870, children in England did not have to go to school. Children from rich families went to school, but poor families could not afford to pay for education. Poor children had to go to work to help their parents. After 1870, the government made school places available to young children for a very small fee. By 1902, education was free and every child between five and thirteen years old had to attend school.

The globe of the world was used to teach geography to the children.

At school, children were taught reading, writing, arithmetic, and religion. The children sat at their desks, chanting spellings and tables over and over again, and copying words onto slates. At other times they did some geography and history, drawing, singing, and physical exercise. Discipline was very strict and children were beaten if they made mistakes in their work.

A wooden hoop used for playing.

Playtime

When they were not in school, children amused themselves with outdoor games like the ones played today—marbles, skipping, hopscotch, and football. Hoops were popular, too—they were rolled along the ground, thrown in the air, or whirled around the body.

China inkwells in a tray were filled and given out to the older children by a monitor. The children wrote with pen and ink in a special copybook.

The ink to fill the inkwells was kept in a special containe that looked like a small watering can.

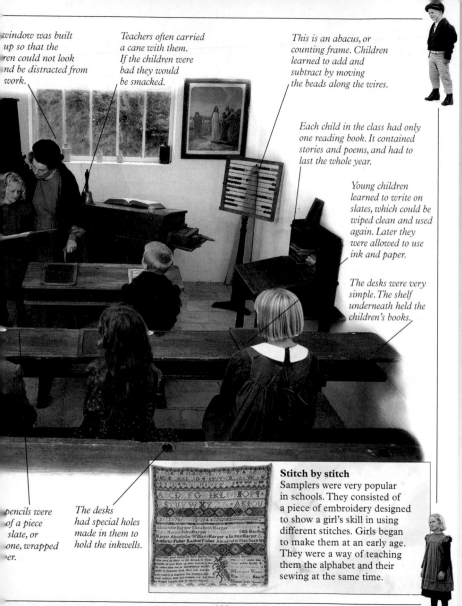

window was built up so that the [child]ren could not look [arou]nd be distracted from [their] work.

Teachers often carried a cane with them. If the children were bad they would be smacked.

This is an abacus, or counting frame. Children learned to add and subtract by moving the beads along the wires.

Each child in the class had only one reading book. It contained stories and poems, and had to last the whole year.

Young children learned to write on slates, which could be wiped clean and used again. Later they were allowed to use ink and paper.

The desks were very simple. The shelf underneath held the children's books.

[The] pencils were [made] of a piece [of] slate, or [st]one, wrapped [in pap]er.

The desks had special holes made in them to hold the inkwells.

Stitch by stitch
Samplers were very popular in schools. They consisted of a piece of embroidery designed to show a girl's skill in using different stitches. Girls began to make them at an early age. They were a way of teaching them the alphabet and their sewing at the same time.

ARTS AND ENTERTAINMENT

 Since earliest times, people have entertained themselves with dance, songs, and storytelling. When people lived in small groups, everybody would join together in a dance. Later, the rise of civilization saw the first professional performers, who danced, played music, or acted to please audiences.

Over time, more types of entertainment were invented. Today we can create and enjoy exciting plays, films, music, and ballets, and amazing photographs, paintings, and sculptures.

Recorder   Violin   Trumpet

Swan Queen in the
ballet *Swan Lake*

Camera

The Secret,
a sculpture by Auguste Rodin

Powder pigments

Artists' brushes

THEATERS

People have enjoyed going to the theater to watch plays for thousands of years—the first theaters were built by the Greeks about 2,500 years ago. Stone seats were carved into the hillside. The actors did not need microphones, because sound carried right up to the back row. Until the 17th century, most plays were staged out in the open. But by the 1650s, bare stages had been replaced by elaborate sets that had to be kept inside, so indoor theaters became common. Lights transformed theaters, too. Realistic acting began with the invention of the spotlight—for the first time, players' expressions could be seen.

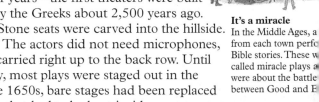

It's a miracle
In the Middle Ages, a from each town perfo Bible stories. These w called miracle plays a were about the battle between Good and E

Ancient art
Noh is an old, traditional type of Japanese theater. Religious stories and ancient myths are performed on a stage that has very little scenery. The plays, some of which are more than 500 years old, can go on for as long as six hours!

The upper gallery was about 25 feet (8 meters) above the ground.

Stage door

The Globe Theatre was first built in 1599.

More than 2,000 people could crowd in to watch a play. Only a few could afford to sit in these galleries.

e Globe Theatre

lliam Shakespeare, the most
nous of all playwrights, acted
the Globe's wooden stage.
e theater was rebuilt and
ned again in June 1997.

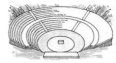

Stage

The Globe
was octagonal.

Entrance

*Musicians played
on this balcony.*

*When the flag was raised,
people knew that a play was
going to be performed.*

*There was no scenery
on the stage.*

*This model of the
Globe Theatre has
been cut in half to
let you see inside.*

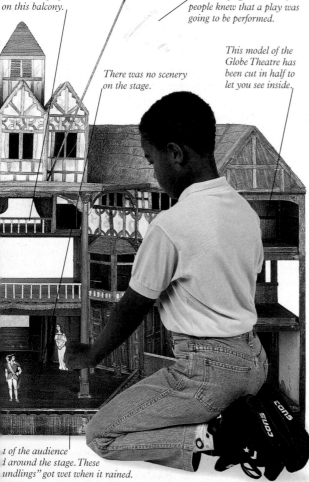

*t of the audience
l around the stage. These
undlings" got wet when it rained.*

Setting the scene

Theatres come in all sorts
of shapes and sizes. Early
ones were out in the open.
Most modern stages have
roofs so that plays can be
staged when it is raining.

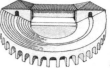

Greek theater
200 BCE

Roman theater
100 CE

Elizabethan theater
16th century

"Modern" theater
19th century

297

PLAYS AND PLAYERS

Not a word
Marcel Marceau was a famou French mime artist—he acts out stories without speaking.

Playwrights write stories, or plays, that are performed on stage by players, called actors and actresses. Molière and Shakespeare both lived more than 300 years ago but their plays, such as *L'Avare* and *Macbeth*, are still popular. Laurence Olivier, one of the last century's most famous actors, starred in *Henry V* by Shakespeare and also in more modern plays, such as *The Entertainer* by John Osborne. Like all good players, he could make an audience believe that what they are seeing is real, not just an act.

The actor playing Romeo shows that he likes Juliet by giving her a rose.

The players wear costumes like those worn by rich Italians in the past.

Happy ending
Plays that make people laugh are called comedies. Molière wrote many wonderful plays in the 17th century that are still funny today.

Sad ending
Tragedies are plays with sad endings. *Cat on a Hot Tin Roof* was written by Tennessee Williams and is a famous modern tragedy.

Setting the scene

Romeo and Juliet is one of Shakespeare's tragedies. The couple can never be together because their families hate each other.

Young

These are the first words Romeo ever says to Juliet.

Juliet replies—she is not upset at him holding her hand.

> ROMEO (to Juliet, touching her hand)
> If I profane with my unworthiest hand
> This holy shrine, the gentle sin is this:
> My lips, two blushing pilgrims,
>   ready stand
> To smooth that rough touch with a
>   tender kiss.   95
>
> JULIET
> Good pilgrim, you do wrong your hand
>   too much,
> Which mannerly devotion shows in this;
> For saints have hands that pilgrims'
>   hands do touch,

This line is not spoken— it tells the actors what to do.

There are 145 lines in this scene, or part of the play. This is line 95.

Makeup magic

To make an audience believe what they are seeing, players often change the way they look by using makeup.

Going grey

Talcum powder and special white mascara makes brown hair and eyebrows look gray.

The actress pretends to be shy, yet pleased to receive the rose.

Old

Pale powder takes away the rosy cheeks.

Lines are drawn on the face with a special dark pencil.

Staged in the East

Spectacular traditional Chinese plays are known as Peking opera in the West. Every action and color has a special meaning—the costume and makeup color show the sort of person the actor is playing.

299

MUSIC

Musical sounds can be made with your voice or by playing an instrument. The first instruments were played more than 42,000 years ago—people blew into shells and hollow mammoth bones! Today's instruments are more complicated. The sounds they make can be high or low: this is known as the pitch of the note. The way these sounds are arranged is called the tune. Rhythm is the pattern of long and short notes. A skillful musician can make the same tune sound slow and sleepy, or loud and jazzy.

Beat the clock?
A metronome can tick at different spe[e]
Musicians listen to
to make sure they a
playing at the right
speed. This is called
keeping the beat.

Music groups

Jazz band

Pop group

String quartet

Wired for sound
Electronic instruments are actually almost silent! When you twang the steel strings on an electric guitar, they vibrate. This movement is changed into tiny electrical signals by pickups beneath the strings. These signals are then increased by an amplifier and finally turned into sounds by an amplifier.

Electric drum

Elec[tric]
gui[tar]

Electric saxophone

A pickup

Note it
Music is written down in a special language. Instead of words, there are notes. These are the notes for "Here Comes the Bride."

Deeper notes are written on lower lines or in lower spaces.

This number tells you there are four beats in each bar.

The way a note looks indicates how long it lasts.

Notes are named letters. This one i[s] second space up

Bagpipes

A world of music

Different countries and regions have very different instruments and styles of music. This traditional music is played by local people, or folk, so it is often called folk music.

Banjo

Scotland is famous for bagpipes. They are played by blowing air into a bag and then squeezing the air up through the pipes.

People who live in the eastern mountains of the United States are famous for their banjo playing. Banjos were first brought to the United States by enslaved Africans.

Panpipes are made from pipes of different lengths and are popular in South America. You play them by blowing over the top of the pipes. Longer pipes make lower sounds.

Panpipe

Australian aboriginals are the only people to play the didgeridoo. It is made from a hollow bamboo branch. It is very difficult to play well.

Didgeridoo

ORCHESTRAS

Many musicians play music in groups called orchestras. Most orchestras have four sections: string, percussion, woodwind, and brass. The different sounds and notes, from as many as 120 instruments in a symphony orchestra, combine to form wonderful music. Orchestras usually play classical music, often written by great composers of the past, such as Mozart and Beethoven.

Percussion players play many different instruments, such as drums, triangles, and gongs.

Cymbal

Princi
violin

Clari

Violin

Set the beat

Most of the instruments in a gamelan orchestra from Indonesia are percussion instruments. They also have bamboo flutes and plucked string instruments.

The leader of an orchestra is always a violin player who sits near the conductor.

*Woodwind instrum
including recorders
are played by blow
down a tube that h
holes in it.*

Two beats to a bar

Three beats to a bar

Four beats to a bar

Keeping the beat
If all the instruments in an orchestra played at different speeds it would sound terrible. The musicians keep in time by watching a conductor who waves a baton to the beat of the music.

Conductor

Short stick, called a baton

conductor ...ds in front of ...usicians so ... they can see ...aton.

The French horn, like a trumpet or a trombone, is a long, curved tube that is made of brass.

Bow

This cello, like the violin, is part of the string section. It is played by drawing a bow across the strings.

*...ch Section?
...clarinet player is sitting
...yellow seat. By using
...ey shown below, you
...ee that a clarinet is
...odwind instrument.*

Strings

Child genius
Wolfgang Amadeus Mozart wrote, or composed, more than 600 pieces of music. He completed his first symphony when he was eight years old!

...tring   Percussion   Woodwind   Brass

DANCE

Dancing is a way of moving your body in time to music. Early peoples danced as a way of uniting and uplifting a group of people. It was not until the 12th century that dancing in pairs became popular. The arrival of the waltz in the 1800s was shocking—it was the first time that couples had held one another closely as they danced. In the 1960s dance changed again, when many people began to dance solo, often making up their own moves instead of following set steps.

This is a imaginar "bow."

The dan pulls bac an "arro

Proud to dance
The spectacular flamenco dance comes from the gypsy peoples of Spain. The dancers hold their heads up high as they stamp their feet and turn around. The women wear long, colorful dresses, but the men wear black.

There are about 55 specific finger positions— each one has a different meanin

Head over heels
Jive dancing is a fas and lively couple dance. The dancers twist, spin, jump, le around—whatever music makes them like doing!

Taking a bow

The dance begins

Taps are attached to the heel and toe of each shoe.

Tap, tap, tap
Fred Astaire was one of the most famous dancers of the 20th century. He tap-danced his way through many movies. Small pieces of metal, called taps, were attached to the soles of his shoes. When his feet touched the ground, you could hear the quick clatter of clicking metal.

Classical Indian dancers use their entire body. Their neck, wrists, and even their eyes move to the rhythm of the music.

As she pretends to put a clip in her hair, the dancer looks into the "mirror."

Her hand is held out flat to form a "mirror."

Moves matter
Classical Indian dance has been performed for more than one thousand years. Sometimes the dancers just create shapes and patterns with their body. In other dances they use hand movements and mime to tell stories of Hindu gods.

She stamps her bare foot in time to the drumbeat of an instrument called a tabla.

The pleats in the special dance dress let the dancer move freely.

One, two, three
The waltz is danced in triple time—each bar of music has three beats. As the dancers swirl around and around they bring their feet together once every three steps.

BALLET

Ballet is a graceful type of dance that uses particular positions and steps. It began in Italy but was developed by the French into the style you see today. Louis XIV of France started the first ballet school in 1661. But the dancers in his "ballets" at the French court sang and recited poems! The first true ballet, without words, was not performed until 1789. The basic steps and jumps taught by Louis' school are still used today—which is why many of them have French names. *Glisser* means to glide, and *pas de chat* means cat step!

Louis XIV

At the barre
Ballet dancers must warm up their muscles before they dance. They do this by stretching while holding onto a pole, called a barre.

This short, stiff skirt is called a tutu. It allows the dancer's legs to be seen.

Hopping frogs
The Tales of Beatrix Potter is an amazing ballet. The dancers wear wonderful costumes and animal masks.

Women did not dance in ballets until 1681. The they had to wea long, flowing d

"Turning feet out" takes years of practice.

First position
(en première)

Second position
(en seconde)

Third position
(en troisième)

Fourth position
(en quatrième)

Fifth position
(en cinquième)

The five positions
In the 17th century a ballet teacher name Beauchamps devele five feet positions th enabled dancers to their balance and s look elegant. Later, positions were adde too. Most ballet ste begin or end with c of these positions.

g hair is
ays tied
k in a bun.

*Male dancers need to be
strong. They have to
lift ballerinas high
up in the air.*

This is ballet, too!

During this century some very adventurous
ballets have been performed. These modern
ballets use many of the classic steps, but
often have no story. The imaginatively
dressed dancers simply express a mood.

*Ballerinas sew on
their own ribbons.*

*The ballerina
keeps her foot
pointed.*

*The leg is
held very
still and
straight.*

*male
et dancer
alled a
erina.*

Ballet shoes

To dance on tiptoe, or *en pointe*,
ballerinas wear special satin
slippers with stiffened toes. Girls
have to be at least twelve years
old before their feet are strong
enough to dance like this.

*ncing on
es makes
ballerina's
look
er and
graceful.*

*Ballerinas
put cotton
wool inside
their shoes
so their toes
don't hurt.*

*Ballet dancers
wear tights.*

*Male dancers'
shoes do not have
stiffened toes.*

OPERA

Inside Paris opera house

Operas mix music with theater in a most spectacular way. The performers on stage act out a story, but instead of speaking the words they sing them. A performance usually begins with an overture. This is a piece of catchy music that features snatches of the tunes that will be heard during the rest of the opera. As well as singing the story, the stars on the stage also perform solo songs, called arias. These are often the most beautiful songs.

Smashing note
When you rub your finger around the rim of a glass it makes a high sound. If a person with a strong voice sings this note loudly, and for a long time, the sound waves can shatter the glass!

Stylish surroundings
Operas are usually staged in special buildings that are designed to help the whole audience hear the sound clearly. The Sydney opera house in Australia is one of the most famous in the world. It was finished in 1973.

Paris opera h

The jagged roof looks like waves or the sails on a yacht.

The main concert hall holds more than 2,000 people.

Sydney opera house model

Crowded stage
Operas sometimes have spectacular stage sets and, as well as the soloists, a large group of singers, called the chorus.

A choice of voices

The soprano is the highest female voice. It is a brilliant and exciting sound.

The contralto, or alto, has a slightly lower voice than the soprano. It has a warmer tone.

The tenors sing many of the important male songs in an opera.

The bass sings the lowest notes. His voice is deep and strong.

Dressed to impress
Opera singers wear incredible costumes to play their parts. In *The Cunning Little Vixen* their makeup is amazing, too.

Tuneful tenor
Luciano Pavarotti was one of the world's greatest tenors. He had a powerful and beautiful voice.

Operas are mostly sung in Italian, French, or German.

Powerful lungs enable the singers to sing without a microphone!

...y tale
...as tell stories. *The Cunning Little ..., by Leoš Janáček, is about a crafty ...le fox who escapes from a forester ...has many exciting adventures.

PAINTING

This says "Jan van Eyck
was here, 1434." It may
to prove the artist was a
witness to the marriage.

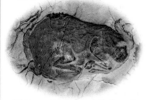

This cave painting is believed
to be 30,000 years old.

Painting began about 40,000
years ago when people painted
pictures of bulls, horses, and
antelopes on the walls of their
caves. We will never be sure why
they did this—perhaps it was
to make magic and bring people
luck in their hunting. Since then,
artists have painted pictures to record events, to honor
heroes and heroines, to make people wonder about the
world, to tell stories, or simply for pleasure. All artists
have their own painting style, and you may not like
them all—it's simply up to you.

*If you look closely in
the mirror you can se
the reflections of two
other people. Perhaps
one is the artist himse*

Hills and valleys
Paintings of the
countryside are called
landscapes. This
Chinese scene looks
very different than a
Western landscape.
It is painted on silk,
using a fine and
detailed style.

*Things that are
farther away lo
smaller, so the a
has made the s
in the front bigg
than those in the back. Thi
gives the picture depth.*

King Ramses II

by an unknown Egyptian artist

Lucrezia Panciatichi

by Il Bronzino

Self-portrait

by Vincent Van Gogh

Weeping Woman

by Pablo Picasso

Arnolfini Marriage, painted by Jan van Eyck in 1434

Looking for clues

This painting records a couple's marriage. But if you look closely you will see it is much more than just a wedding picture.

One candle is left to burn, even though it is daylight, to show that the couple will always love each other.

Like the merchant, his wife is wearing expensive clothes. It was the fashion to hold your skirts this way.

Action painting

In this painting, modern American artist Jackson Pollock was not trying to show objects or people, but feelings. He worked by dripping and splattering paint on the canvas.

Son of Man

by René Magritte

Marilyn Monroe

by Andy Warhol

The light shines on the couple's hands, and the artist has shown every tiny line.

Painting portraits

For thousands of years artists have enjoyed painting pictures of people. Not all of them painted the person true to life—there are many different styles of painting.

SCULPTURE

Sculptures are three-dimensional, not flat like paintings. Bricks, plastic, even rubber tires, have all been used by sculptors, but the traditional materials are wood, stone, bronze, and clay. Some sculptors build up their image by adding small pieces of material, such as clay. Others start with a big block of wood or stone and cut away material. When Michelangelo carved, it was as if he was setting free somebody who was trapped in the stone.

Mystery from the past
Strange statues were carved on Easter Island more than 500 years ago. Nobody knows for sure how the heavy heads were moved into place.

Many of Moore's sculptures are based on natural shapes, such as smooth pebbles.

In touch with nature
Some of the sculptures created by Henry Moore (1898–198?) look like people, but many are just interesting shapes.

This rounded sculpture is meant to be touched.

If you walk around a sculpture you see different exciting sh...

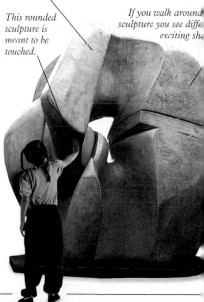

Mountain men
Mount Rushmore has the heads of four American Presidents cut into it. It took 14 years to blast and drill Presidents Washington, Jefferson, Roosevelt, and Lincoln out of the rock.

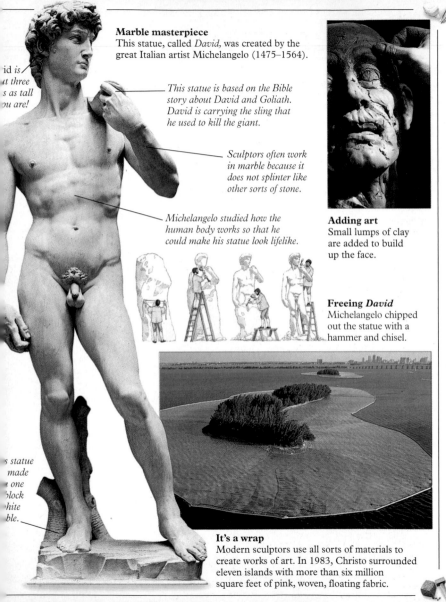

Marble masterpiece
This statue, called *David*, was created by the great Italian artist Michelangelo (1475–1564).

This statue is based on the Bible story about David and Goliath. David is carrying the sling that he used to kill the giant.

Sculptors often work in marble because it does not splinter like other sorts of stone.

Michelangelo studied how the human body works so that he could make his statue look lifelike.

...id is ...t three ...s as tall ...ou are!

...s statue ...made ...one ...block ...hite ...ble.

Adding art
Small lumps of clay are added to build up the face.

Freeing *David*
Michelangelo chipped out the statue with a hammer and chisel.

It's a wrap
Modern sculptors use all sorts of materials to create works of art. In 1983, Christo surrounded eleven islands with more than six million square feet of pink, woven, floating fabric.

PHOTOGRAPHY

Every day, all around the world, billions of photographs are taken. These are not just photos of birthdays and holidays, but pictures of goals being scored, models in studios, and important news events. All photographs are made in much the same way as when the process was invented more than 150 years ago. A camera is basically a box with a hole in it. Light that enters through this hole is captured as a digital image you can see on a screen, but cameras originally used film. Lots of photos are now taken on mobile phones.

Say cheese!
In early photographs took a long time for t picture to form. Peop had to stay still for u to 20 minutes to keep the picture from blur

Camera

Right time, right place
News photographers have to be ready for action all the time. They may not get a second chance to capture an amazing event or famous person.

Spare camera with flash

Click—A sinking bus is snapped

Camera Collection

35mm professional camera

High-quality studio camera

Instant camera

Underwater cam

...ind, rain, and bad light can ruin your shots
...hen you take pictures outside. This is why
...hotographers work in studios. Many of the
...ctures in this book were taken in a studio.

The photographer takes pictures when the model is in the right position.

The flash is much bigger than the flash on your camera!

White paper reflects light back onto the model.

...e person ...ving their ...oto taken is ...led the model.

...e makeup artist ...s the model ready ...e photographed.

...lecting umbrellas ...duce a diffused and soft ...t due to the larger size ...e reflecting surface.

This camera is connected to a laptop by a cable. This allows the photographer to look at the images in more detail.

Three-legged frames or tripods prevent the camera and equipment from moving around.

Different camera lenses

FILMS

From the first flickery film, people have loved the world of movie make-believe. The early films were made in black and white and did not have any sound. They were called silent movies. In the theater, a pianist played along with the film and the audience had to read words on the screen. It was not until 1927 that the first "talkie," called *The Jazz Singer,* came out. Color films, such as *The Wizard of Oz* were made in 1939, but only became common in the 1950s.

A star is born
The dry weather in California is id for filming. Hollywood, once a slee suburb of Los Angeles, was the cer of the American film industry by 1

Silent star
Charlie Chaplin (1889–1977) was one of the first movie stars. He starred in more than 80 films. His most famous character, "the Tramp" had a funny walk.

Cue clapboard
When a clapboard is clicked shut it is seen on the film and heard on the soundtrack. The pictures words can then be match

Moving pictures
Most films are now shot digitally, but like the first films, they are made of many still pictures called frames. The frames pass before your eyes so quickly that the pictures look as if they are moving.

Creative hub
Almost 2,000 films a year are made in India— more than double the number made in Hollywood. Streets in Mumbai and Delhi are lined with bright posters that advertise these dramatic films.

The lighting crew s up the lights so tha the actor looks as if he is outside and n inside a bright stu

This "mountain" was built inside a studio.

The camera rolls forward on a wheeled truck called a dolly.

is pole, which has a microphone the end of it, is called a boom. s held up high so that it does appear in the film.

The director is in charge of shooting the film.

Films for everyone

Romance

Western

Horror

Science fiction

Between shots, the makeup artists make sure that the actor looks right.

317

SPECIAL EFFECTS

Have you ever wondered how alien worlds are filmed, or how actors and actresses survive death-defying leaps? These amazing events are not real, they are created by special effects. With CGI (computer-generated imagery), clever camera work, and special equipment, such as wind machines, film directors can make us believe that what we are seeing is real. These tricks of the trade are used when shooting the action in the normal way would be too expensive, too dangerous, or just impossible!

Size isn't everything
This tiny, detailed model of a Y-wing spaceship appeared in *Return of the Jedi*. On screen it looked big enough to carry people

Green screen

Virtual reality
Green screens are an important part of making sp effects for television or film. The process is called chroma-key and it uses technology to superimpos actors and props onto a virtual background.

A wind machine can make a gentle breeze or a howling gale.

Cuew
Filmmakers can't wait for the right weather. In this scene from *The Mosquito Coast*, giant fans whipped up the waves that battered the boat.

Total transformation

Prosthetic makeup is used in television and film to turn actors into all kinds of characters. A sculpture of the character is created, which is then covered with plaster to make a mold. Liquid latex is poured into this to make the prosthetic; this is glued to the actor's face, then makeup is used to cover all the edges.

Finished movie

Fire!

Filmmakers don't just throw bombs to make flames and smoke. Explosions are carefully set up and controlled.

Smoke cylinders

This can makes orange smoke.

Explosives

Fuse

Falling for you

Jumping from a high building is dangerous and difficult! In films, it is either digitally simulated or done by experts, called stuntpeople. They take the place of the actor who is supposed to be falling to the ground in the story.

Actor

The highly trained stuntperson leaps from the building.

The audience must think that the actor is falling so the stuntperson wears the same clothes.

The stuntperson waves their legs and arms around, to look as though they are terrified.

The camera stops running when the stunt-person prepares to land.

The stuntperson twists in the air so that their shoulders will hit the bag first.

The stuntperson hits the soft airbag at more than 50 miles per hour (80 km per hour)!

FOOD AND FARMING

Lots of people buy food in stores or from markets, but it has probably been produced somewhere far away. This could be a large farm in the country, or a small plantation halfway around the world.

We eat some things—fruit, raw vegetables, and nuts, for example—just as they are picked. Other types of food have lots of things done to them before we put them on the table. Cocoa beans, for example, which grow in huge pods on cacao trees, are made into delicious chocolate. Grains of wheat are threshed to separate them from their husks, then milled into flour. Flour is used to make the bread, biscuits, and pastry that lots of people eat every day.

Chocolate cake

Baby pigs are called piglets.

Baby sheep are called lambs.

320

Fruit and vegetables

Many different kinds of cheese are made from milk.

ccoli
ning

Wheat and bread

Tractor

WHEAT

What have breakfast cereals, breads, cakes, pastries, pasta, and couscous all got in common? The answer is that they are made out of wheat, the most important crop in the world. Wheat is so important that it is known as a staple food. It is a main everyday source of food for more than 35 percent of the world's people. Like barley, oats, rye, corn, rice, sorghum, and millet, wheat is a cereal. Cereals are grasses and we eat their seeds.

Crop rotation

If the same crop is grown on the same land year after year, the soil may lose its fertility and pests and diseases build up. The farmer can prevent this by changing the crops grown each year. In the first year, rapeseed may be grown, then wheat, field beans, wheat, and barley.

rapeseed

barley

wheat

field beans

wheat

Machine power

This is a combine harvester. It cuts the crop and separates the grain from the straw.

This is the unloading spout. It is used to empty threshed grain from the harvester.

In the harvester, the grain is shaken off the stalks. The stalks fall to the ground in the back.

These are straw walkers. They carry the crop through the machine.

322

Edible ears

Other cereal crops include oats, barley, and rye. Like wheat, these plants have an "ear" of grain on each stem. Each grain is protected by a husk and inside the husk is the seed. The grain can be eaten whole or ground into flour.

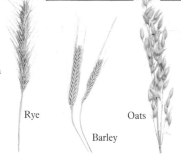

Rye

Oats

Barley

Wheat products

Wheat can be used for many different foods. You would never guess these items are all made from the same ingredient.

Wheat germ

Cracked wheat

Breakfast cereal

Pasta

Monsters on the move

These wheat fields in the prairies of Manitoba, Canada, are so vast that several combine harvesters can work the fields at the same time.

The cab is air-conditioned to keep the driver cool and also to filter out all the dust produced during harvesting.

The reel sweeps the crop into the cutter bar. The cutter bar cuts the crop.

An ear of wheat is made up of 40 to 60 grains. When wheat is ripe and ready for harvesting, it turns golden yellow.

Home sweet home

The wheatfield is a world of its own. It is home to mammals, insects, birds, and wild flowers.

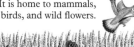

CORN

In many tropical and subtropical countries sweet corn is the main food that people eat. It is eaten as a vegetable or ground into flour or cornmeal. Corn is also made into oil for cooking and for salad dressings. Corn needs lots of sunshine to grow—it will grow in hot climates but also in cooler, mild ones, as long as there is plenty of sun. However, the varieties of corn grown in these different climates are not the same.

The flower at the top of the plant is called the tassel.

This is the stalk. Some kinds of corn have stalks as high as 20 feet (six meters).

Corn is, in fact, a huge grass.

These long, soft threads are called the silk.

The corn ear, or cob, is protected by a husk of tightly wrapped leaves.

The cob is covered in neat, straight rows of kernels. The kernels are the plant's seeds and the part you eat.

Pest problems
In warm and tropical areas, one of the pests most feared by farmers is the locust. They travel in huge swarms of more than 40 billion insects, stripping plants of their leaves and stems as they feed. Locusts can destroy crops and cause famine and starvation.

Short side roots spread over the surface of the soil. They anchor the tall plant like the ropes of a tent and stop it from falling over.

Deep roots go down into the soil and absorb the food and water the plant needs to grow.

Sun ripened

Corn is the staple food of the warmer parts of North, Central, and South America, and also of Africa. It can be grown in huge fields with the help of machinery, or tended by hand.

Sweetcorn

Mountain of corn

After the corn has been harvested, it is sorted. Some will be kept as seed for the next crop, some kept for food, and some used as animal feed.

Breakfast cereal

Amazing corn

Corn comes in all sorts of colors and it may even be striped, streaked, speckled, or spotted.

Tortilla chips

Tough grains

In dry parts of Africa and Asia, people mainly eat sorghum and millet. These cereals are tough and will grow with little water. This woman is pounding sorghum grain. It is mixed with water or milk until it becomes soft and sticky, like semolina. Sorghum is eaten with spicy stews, which give it flavor. It is also ground into flour. Millet is cooked like oatmeal, baked into a flat bread, or used in soups and stews.

Taco

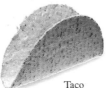

Corn oil

RICE

Like corn and wheat, rice is a staple food. It is the main food of almost half the world's population. As much as 90 percent of the world's rice is grown in Asia. However, the Asian countries eat most of what they grow. The US also produces huge amounts of rice, but sells a lot of what it grows to the rest of the world.

Rice is a swamp plant. It grows with its roots in water. It has hollow stems which take oxygen to the roots.

In Asia, the work of sowing, planting out the seedlings, and harvesting the rice is usually done by hand.

How the rice plant is used

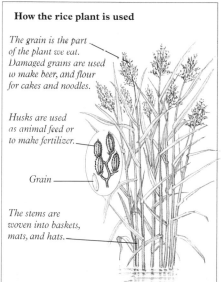

The grain is the part of the plant we eat. Damaged grains are used to make beer, and flour for cakes and noodles.

Husks are used as animal feed or to make fertilizer.

Grain

The stems are woven into baskets, mats, and hats.

Preparing the fields
The paddy fields are flooded, plowed, raked, and flattened. In Asia, buffaloes are sometimes still used to do the heavy work.

Planting out
The presprouted seedlings are moved to the paddy fields. They are planted far apart so they have plenty of space to gro

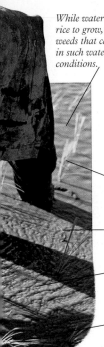

While water helps the rice to grow, it kills off weeds that can't grow in such watery conditions.

Rice is a type of grass.

Most rice is grown in flooded fields called paddies.

The fields are flooded for most of the growing season.

The rice is planted in straight lines.

Machine power

In the US, growing rice is highly mechanized. Tractors prepare the fields, the seed may be sown from airplanes, and combine harvesters gather the ripe plants.

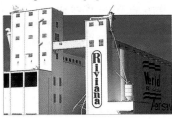

Safekeeping

Special buildings are used to store the rice until it is needed. They are called granaries. A granary keeps the grain dry and safe from hungry animals.

All rice

Rice noodles

Puffed rice cakes

Sticky rice cakes

Rice paper

Harvesting

The rice is ready for harvesting in three to six months. The fields are drained and the plants cut down, tied in bundles, and left to dry.

Winnowing

The rice is beaten to remove the grains. The grains are crushed and then sieved and tossed to remove any fine pieces of husk.

VEGETABLE OILS

Vegetable oils are made from the seeds and fruits of many plants growing all over the world, from tiny sesame seeds to big, juicy coconuts. The oils are used for cooking, as salad dressings, and to make cooking fats and margarine. Soybeans are the most important source of oil worldwide, especially in the US. In western Europe, the oil most widely produced is rapeseed oil.

Harvesting

Olives are picked in the fall when they are ripe. They are shaken from the trees and gathered up, usually by hand. Next, the olives are sorted out to remove the leaves and twigs, and taken to be pressed.

Olive trees are often quite small but can live for hundreds of years. They develop very wrinkled, knotty trunks.

How olive oil is made

The olives are ground to a thick paste which is spread onto special mats. The mats are then layered up on the pressing machine which will gently squeeze them to produce olive oil.

Olive trees are planted in rows. Fields of olive trees are called groves.

Edible olives

There are many varieties of olives—black and green, large and small. Most are used for making oil, but some are eaten whole, too. Raw olives are very bitter, but once they have been treated, fermented, and pickled, they taste delicious!

Surprising sources

Oil can be produced from lots of very different fruits and seeds.

Groundnuts (Peanuts)

Cottonseeds

Sesame seeds

Rapeseed

Soybeans

The trees are shaken to make the olives fall. Sometimes, machines are used to do this job.

Each long, flexible branch has lots of flowers and about 30 clusters of fruit.

Sunflower oil

Every sunflower is made up of hundreds of tiny flowers, surrounded by a fringe of petals. It is the seeds of the flowers that are rich in oil. Sunflowers are ready for harvesting when the flowers are dead and the heads have dried out. Sunflower oil is good for cooking oil, salad oil, and for making margarine.

...are laid ...so that the ...fruit can be ...red easily.

CATTLE AND DAIRY FARMING

A cow gives milk for ten months of the year, then she rests for two months. Most cows are milked twice a day.

Cattle are very popular domesticated animals because they provide us with a lot of food. They are kept for their meat, which is called beef, and also for their milk. Milk is full of calcium and protein, which makes it a very complete and nourishing food. Because of this, milk-giving animals are kept all over the world— but they are not always cows. Goats, sheep, camels, reindeer, and llamas give us milk, too!

To produce milk, a dairy cow must have a calf once a year.

Milky ways

To make just two pounds (one kilogram) of butter, you need around six gallons (22 liters) of milk! The liquid that is left over is buttermilk.

A calf born to a dairy cow stays with its mother for just 48 hours.

Hard cheese!

Foods made from milk, such as butter, cheese, yogurt, and cream, are known as dairy products. Making cheese is the best way to turn milk into a food that can be stored for some time. Thousands of different cheeses are made all over the world. Soft, creamy cheeses must be eaten promptly, but hard, crumbly cheeses will last for months and even years.

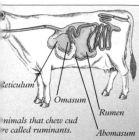

Reticulum

Omasum

Rumen

Abomasum

nimals that chew cud
re called ruminants.

Second helping
Cows eat grass without chewing it properly. It goes to the rumen and reticulum to be broken down into cud. The cow coughs this up and chews it again. When it is swallowed, the cud goes through the stomachs in turn, being finally digested in the abomasum.

This is the udder, where the milk is produced. It is in four parts. Each part has a teat.

In the milking parlor
When cows are milked, special suckers are attached to the teats. They squeeze the milk gently from the cow just like a calf does. A cow can give between 7 and 9 gallons of milk every day.

Bred for beef
g, heavy breeds of cattle
re kept for beef because
they have more meat on
hem. The world's largest
herds of beef cattle are
und in North and South
America. Here there are
ots of wide-open spaces
here the cattle can graze
until they are fat and
ready for eating.

Dairy cattle

Holstein Friesian

Jersey

Beef cattle

Hereford

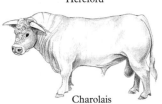

Charolais

Dairy and beef

Simmental

SHEEP

Sheep are raised for their meat, for the foods that can be made from their milk, and for their wool. There are more than 200 breeds of sheep and different sorts are able to live in very different places—in lands that are hot with little water, in areas that are cold and wet, in the lowlands, and on the hills. The kind of place where it lives affects the quality of the sheep's meat and wool.

All in a day's work
An experienced shearer can sh
a lot of sheep in one day.
At shearing time, shearers
travel from farm
to farm to clip
the animals.

Sheep produce
Sheep provide yogurt and cheese, and wool for clothing. The wool contains a fat called lanolin. It is used in ointments and hand creams.

Lanolin

Yogurt

Cheese

Milk

Hand-operated shears or electric clippers are used by the shearer.

Sheep are shorn in the spring and early summer when they no longer need their long coats to keep them warm.

It takes the wool from one average-sized fleece to make this sweater.

The fleece is made into wool for knitting and for making carpets and fabr Sometimes, it is even use to fill mattresses.

Bathtime

Once or twice a year, the farmer drives the sheep through a chemical dip. This keeps them free of pests and diseases.

Domestic sheep

Suffolk

Mummy!

Some lambs are orphaned or not wanted by their mother. These may be bottle-fed by the farmer or shepherd, or adopted by another ewe.

Wensleydale

Working dogs

Dogs are used to gather the sheep in flocks and move them from place to place. Sheepdogs naturally like to herd animals, but they need to be trained to follow instructions. The shepherd controls the dog using special calls and whistles. Sheep are timid, so the dog will run low in the grass to avoid frightening them.

Karakul

Scottish blackface

In a spin

To produce wool for knitting or weaving, many strands are twisted together to make one long thread. Spinning was first done by hand using a spindle. Later, the spindle was attached to a wheel, and wool could be spun more quickly. Now, most spinning is done by machine.

Wild sheep

Bighorn

hearer
the sheep
the fleece
off in
ece.

PIGS

Domestic pigs are mainly kept for their meat, especially in China, which has the most pigs in the world. Pigs raised for their meat are usually kept in pens and are fed on cereals, potatoes, fish meal, and skimmed milk. Pigs kept for breeding often live outdoors in fields. The farmer feeds them but they also search for their own food. They like worms, snails, roots, and plants.

Duroc

Mud, glorious mud
Despite their reputation, pigs are not dirty anim
They cannot sweat so in hot weather they roll
around in mud to help cool themselves.

A female pig is called a sow.

The piglets go to the same teat every time they want to feed. When they are six weeks old, they move on from milk to solid food.

Intensive Farming
When pigs leave their mothers, they are normally housed in piggeries. The pigs are fed a special diet, and because they have less space to run around, they put on weight quickly.

A sow makes a "nest" before she has her litter. In a pen, she paws straw into a heap. In a field, she lines a hole with leaves and straw.

Landrace

British saddleback

Piétrain

Vietnamese potbellied pig

Domestic pigs don't have a hairy coat to protect them—just a few short bristles. Because of this, pink pigs can get sunburned. Black pigs are protected by their dark skin.

Pig products

The meat from pigs, which is called pork, is used to make a variety of foods, including sausages, spiced meats, and all kinds of hams.

The last piglet born is often smaller and weaker than the rest. It is called the "runt" and it might not survive.

Detective work

Pigs have a good sense of smell and use their snouts to dig up food. In France, pigs are used to search for truffles, which are difficult to find because they can grow as much as 12 inches (30 cm) under the ground.

Truffles are like mushrooms and are a great delicacy.

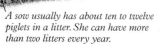

A sow usually has about ten to twelve piglets in a litter. She can have more than two litters every year.

CITRUS FRUITS

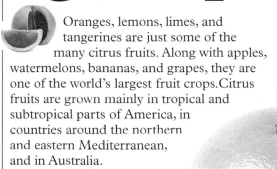

The ugli fruit is a [...] between a tangeri[...] orange, and a grap[...]

Oranges, lemons, limes, and tangerines are just some of the many citrus fruits. Along with apples, watermelons, bananas, and grapes, they are one of the world's largest fruit crops. Citrus fruits are grown mainly in tropical and subtropical parts of America, in countries around the northern and eastern Mediterranean, and in Australia.

A tree can produce a thousand oranges each year.

This is a white grapefruit. The flesh inside is a pale yellow.

Lemons, like other citrus fruits, are rich in minerals and vitamins, especially vitamin C.

Tangerines are like small, sweet oranges. They have several small seeds.

Limes have thi[...] skins and very tart juice.

Fighting frost

Citrus trees need just the right climate to produce good fruit — sun to make them sweet, and then cold to make them tart. But the trees' greatest enemy is frost, which will kill the fruit. So modern plantations often have wind machines and special orchard heaters in case it is frosty.

Orchard heaters protect the trees from frost.

...is a pink grapefruit.
...le it has a sweet,
...flesh.

The perfect package
Citrus fruits are perfectly packaged foods. In the middle is the juicy flesh, a wonderful source of food and drink that is rich in vitamin C. Next comes a spongy layer, called the pith, which cushions the flesh. On the outside is a protective skin.

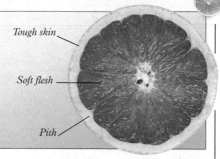

Tough skin

Soft flesh

Pith

Navel oranges are very juicy. Usually they have no seeds.

Clementines, like satsumas and tangerines, have a loose skin that is easy to peel.

Satsumas are like tangerines, except they don't have seeds.

You can eat kumquats whole, including the rind.

Mix and match
By mixing pollen from the blossom of different citrus trees, new varieties can be developed. The limequat, for example, is a cross between a lime and a kumquat.

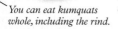

Juicy fruit
These oranges are being sorted and packed, and will be sold for eating. Many oranges are pulped to be made into juice. This pulp is frozen for transporting around the world.

Fresh orange juice contains lots of vitamins and nutrients.

GRAPES

Grapes need rain to swell them and sun to ripen them.

There are two different types of grapes—black and white. But black grapes are really dark red, and white grapes are light green. Grapes are delicious to eat fresh, and keep their sweetness when dried, too. But most of the grapes grown in the world are used for making wine. Grape plants are called vines, and they are planted in rows in vineyards. Vines need a lot of care, and it takes lots of hard work and skill to produce a bottle of fine wine.

Pruning
As vines grow, they are often cut back so they have a few strong branches rather than lots of weaker ones. This work is called pruning and must be done by hand.

Broad vine leaves shade the grapes from the direct glare of the sun and the battering rain.

Bitter wine
Red and white wine can also be made into vinegar. It is produced when special vinegar yeasts ferment the wine and turn it sour. Vinegars can be made from other liquids, like cider or malt, and are used as a flavoring. They can also be mixed with foods to pickle and preserve them.

From grapes to wine
First the grapes are crushed and pressed to mix the yeast with the sugar in the grapes. This is called fermentation. Then the juice is filtered and poured into vats. These are left in a cool place for the flavor of the wine to develop.

Grapes   Press

There is a natural yeast on the grape skin that is needed to turn the grape juice into wine.

Black grapes can be made into red or white wine. To make red wine, the skins of black grapes are left in the wine mixture.

Dried goods
Grapes for drying must be very sweet because it is their natural sugar that preserves them. They can be dried on racks, in the sun, or in ovens. Only seedless grapes are used for drying. Sultanas are dried white grapes. Raisins and currants are dried black grapes and are usually smaller.

Currants

Raisins

Sultanas

Grapes grow in tight bunches.

Grape harvesters
Most wine grapes today are picked by machine, except in small or sloping vineyards. Special grapes for making rare wines are carefully picked by hand.

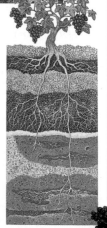

Digging deep
The type of soil in a vineyard is very important and affects the flavor of the wine. Yet some of the best wines are produced from poor soils. This is because the vine can find regular supplies of food and water by pushing its roots deep into the earth.

...ats

Wine

UNDERGROUND VEGETABLES

Some plants are not grown for their leafy tops, but for the parts of them that grow beneath the soil. Carrots, turnips, radishes, and parsnips are the fat roots of plants, and are known as root vegetables. Potatoes are the swollen part of the underground stem of the plant. They are called tubers. Onions, too, grow in the dark earth, but it is the bulb of these plants that we eat.

The flowers produce seeds that can be r to grow new plan but it is more usu to use seed potato

Farming with nature
Many farmers use chemical fertilizers and pesticides to help them grow crops efficiently, but some farmers use only natural products. They use fertilizers such as manure, and encourage pest controllers like ladybugs, which eat all sorts of flies and larvae. This helps to stop a buildup of chemicals in the environment and is called organic farming.

Potato plants grow well in cool climates, but are killed by frost.

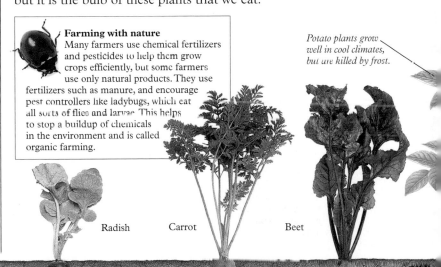

Radish

Carrot

Beet

These are the tubers. Each plant has between 15 and 20 tu

pes of tubers
bers come in all
pes and sizes.

Sweet potato

Cassava

Yam

Taro

Harvest time
In the fall, the potatoes are fully grown and special harvesters, pulled by tractors, are used to lift them carefully from the soil.

Tasty bulbs
Bulbs, like onions, are not roots. Instead, they are made up of clumps

Garlic

of tightly curled leaves. Leeks, garlic, shallots, and scallions are all members of the same plant family, and they are all valuable for the flavor that they can give to many other foods.

Shallot

When the leaves wither in the fall, the farmer knows the potatoes are ready to harvest.

Stem

Some potatoes may be harvested and set aside. These will then be used to grow new plants, and are called seed potatoes.

From these tiny scars, called eyes, new shoots will grow.

Onion

Roots

HOTHOUSE VEGETABLES

In countries with cool climates, usually there is not enough heat to grow the most delicate or exotic vegetables. But in special hothouses, with glass or clear plastic walls, a farmer can grow almost any crop. This is because the temperature inside a hothouse can be controlled. Hothouses are useful in warmer countries, too. They mean the farmer does not have to follow the seasons of the year, and summer vegetables that do not store can be grown fresh all year round.

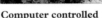

Computer controlled
Tomatoes are quite fragile plants, so this hothouse, where the temperature and feeding are controlled by a computer, is a good place to grow them. Tomatoes grown in hothouses are usually top quality and are picked by hand.

Nature's "hothouse"
Some of the world's hottest spots are dry deserts. But if a water supply can be set up, the desert heat can be put to good use. Fertile gardens can be created, like this fruit orchard in Jordan.

Short showers
Most of the work in large hothouses today is done by machines. These young sweet pepper (capsicum) plants are watered by overhead pipes. Hothouse c must also be sprayed to protect them from the pe and molds that like the damp, warm conditions.

carpet of seedlings

...ds germinate quickly in the warmth and protection of the ...ouse. These are ...tuce seedlings. ...thouses can be ...ge and some are ...half the size of a football field.

Water gardens

Some vegetables can be grown without soil. The plants are carefully supported and supplied with water which is automatically mixed with plant foods. This way of growing plants is called hydroponics.

This material does not feed the plants, but helps to support them.

Water full of plant food flows past the roots.

Mixed vegetables

Here are some other vegetables that would normally need lots of sun to grow, but can be farmed in hothouses in cool climates.

Cucumbers

French beans

Eggplant

...rs must fit ...ly to keep ...drafts.

These panels may be opened if the hothouse gets too hot.

...e hothouse has ...nsparent sides to ...in as much light ...possible.

This hothouse only uses natural heat, but some have special heaters.

Okra

Zucchini

Red and green chillies

COFFEE, TEA, AND COCOA

Coffee, tea, and cocoa are drunk in most countries of the world. Cocoa is also used to make chocolate. Coffee and cocoa grow in the tropics. They are grown on huge plantations, but a lot is produced on small farms as well. Tea is grown on plantations in the tropics and subtropics. Altogether, millions of people are employed to produce these crops. Coffee, tea, and cocoa are important to the countries that grow them because they are cash crops. This means they are grown to be traded with other countries rather than for home use.

Picky pickers

Tea comes from evergreen trees that are pruned into bushes. This makes it easy to pick the leaves. The best-quality teas are produced by plucking only the bud and the first two leaves on each shoot. A skilled plucker can pick enough leaves in one day to make 3,500 cups of tea.

Green tea   Black

Special treatment

The leaves are made into black or green te For green tea, the lea are dried, heated, and crushed. For black te. the leaves are dried, crushed, fermented, and dried again.

coffee tree produces
out 2,000 fruits each
ar. It takes twice this
ount to make two
unds (one kilogram)
roasted coffee.

The fruits are called cherries
because of their color and size.

There are two green
coffee beans inside
each cherry.
They only turn
brown after they
are roasted.

The coffee is harvested
twice a year.

The trees are pruned to stop them
from growing more than 10 feet
(three meters) high.

When the fruits first
appear, they are green.
Gradually, they turn bright
red. They are then ready
to be picked.

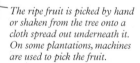

The ripe fruit is picked by hand
or shaken from the tree onto a
cloth spread out underneath it.
On some plantations, machines
are used to pick the fruit.

Heavy load
Cocoa pods are large and heavy.
They grow on the trunk of
the cacao tree or from its
thick branches.

The pod has a thick skin.

Each pod may contain
20 to 50 cocoa beans.

The pod grows up to 12
inches (30 cm) long, about
the size of a football.

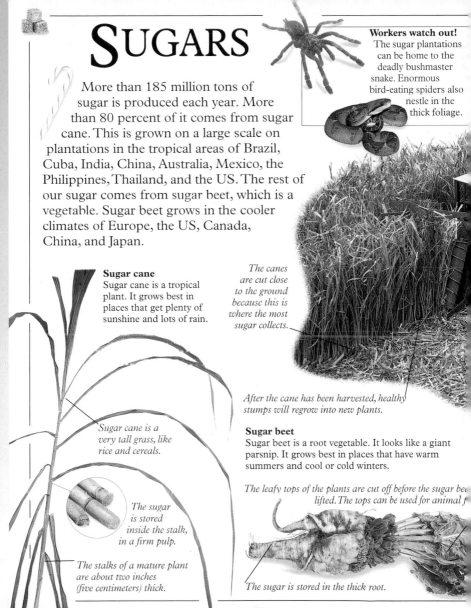

SUGARS

More than 185 million tons of sugar is produced each year. More than 80 percent of it comes from sugar cane. This is grown on a large scale on plantations in the tropical areas of Brazil, Cuba, India, China, Australia, Mexico, the Philippines, Thailand, and the US. The rest of our sugar comes from sugar beet, which is a vegetable. Sugar beet grows in the cooler climates of Europe, the US, Canada, China, and Japan.

Workers watch out!
The sugar plantations can be home to the deadly bushmaster snake. Enormous bird-eating spiders also nestle in the thick foliage.

Sugar cane
Sugar cane is a tropical plant. It grows best in places that get plenty of sunshine and lots of rain.

The canes are cut close to the ground because this is where the most sugar collects.

After the cane has been harvested, healthy stumps will regrow into new plants.

Sugar beet
Sugar beet is a root vegetable. It looks like a giant parsnip. It grows best in places that have warm summers and cool or cold winters.

The leafy tops of the plants are cut off before the sugar beet is lifted. The tops can be used for animal f...

Sugar cane is a very tall grass, like rice and cereals.

The sugar is stored inside the stalk, in a firm pulp.

The stalks of a mature plant are about two inches (five centimeters) thick.

The sugar is stored in the thick root.

canes are
hen they
4 to 16
5 to 7
s) high.

*The canes are ripe
when they look dry.*

Sugar production

In a sugar factory, sugar from the canes or beet is taken out, cleaned, and boiled. This leaves a syrup which is turned into brown sugar crystals. These can be refined to make white sugar.

Sorts of sugar

Sugars differ in color and in the size of their crystals, or grains.

Granulated

Demerara

Dark soft brown

Muscovado

*Sugar cane is often harvested by
machine, but in some places it is
still cut by hand.*

Maple syrup

Maple syrup is made from the sap of sugar maple or black maple trees. Holes are made in the trunks in winter when the trees are dormant. When a thaw follows a freeze, the sap is collected from the wounds in buckets. Maple syrup is only produced in North America.

PEOPLE
AND PLACES

In lots of ways, people are the same everywhere: they build homes, they wear clothes, they eat meals, and they have fun. However, people in different countries have developed their own languages and customs, which vary widely from place to place.

Did you know that in Spain there is a festival in which people throw tomatoes at each other? Did you know that the Chinese language has more than 50,000 written characters? Did you know that India produces more films each year than any other country?

Learning about other ways of life is not only interesting, it also helps you to understand and get along with people in other countries who may be very different from you.

Inuit boy from
northern Canada

African jewelry

The Eiffel
Tower in
Paris,
France

Indonesian boy on
a water buffalo

Talking drum
from Nigeria

Vegetable market in Guatemala

Antipasto
from Italy

Buckingham Palace in London, England

Woven bag
from Peru

Indian cricketer

THE ARCTIC & ANTARCTICA

The Inuit, Saami, Aleut, and other indigenous people live in the icy lands of the Arctic North. For many generations, they have found ways of coping with their cold surroundings. But no one has settled for very long on the southern extremes of the planet. Antarctica is the coldest and windiest place in the world. This huge continent is lashed by freezing blizzards and gales, with temperatures almost as low as -148°F (-100°C).

Icy city
Norilsk in the Arctic Circle is the farthest north city in the world. The sun does not rise in this Russian city between November and the middle of January.

Homes in the north
In the past, the Inuit were self-sufficient and lived a life on the move, hunting and fishing to survive. They built temporary homes, called igloos, from solid snow. Today, most Inuit live in wooden houses and earn a living by working for other people, often in fish-canning factories or for mining companies.

Speedy Ski-doos
Today, the Inuit people get around on snowmobiles called Ski-doos. This is much faster than using dogs to pull a sled, which is the traditional method of travel.

Warm clothes are vital in the Arctic.

Long-lost relatives
For many years, Inuit families on either side of the Bering Strait were not allowed to meet, for political reasons. Nowadays, the North American Inuit and their relatives in northern Asia can visit each other once again.

The Bering Strait is a narrow stretch of sea that separates northern Asia from North America.

The Arctic

Antarctica

Antarctic science

Scientists from all around the world
are the only people who live and work
in Antarctica. Some study the effect of
the enormous sheet of Antarctic ice
on the world's weather patterns. Others
observe the behavior of living things in
the freezing conditions.

*This scientist is
measuring the density
of Antarctic snow.*

*This emperor
penguin lives
in the Antarctic.
No penguins live
in the Arctic.*

Exploring the unknown

Antarctica was the last continent to be explored.
The first successful expedition in search of the
South Pole took place in 1911, led by a Norwegian
called Roald Amundsen. The British expedition led
by Captain Scott ended in disaster, when the team
froze to death on the trek home.

*A windshield protects the
riders from the biting wind.*

Climate change

The west coast of the Antarctic Peninsula
is one of the fastest-warming places in the world.
Rising sea temperatures mean plants and animals
must adapt, including penguin colonies that now
have less ice to live on.

*Runners on the front of the
Ski-doo spread the weight
of the vehicle evenly, to stop
it from sinking into the
soft snow.*

ski-doo

CANADA

Totem poles can be enormous or very small, such as those that guard the doorways to village homes.

Canada is an enormous country. A journey from the east to the west coast on one of the world's longest highways will take you through almost 5,000 miles (8,000 kilometers) of beautiful landscape. Canada's population of 37 million is small for the country's huge size. Most people live in cities in the warmer southern part of the country, close to the border with the United States.

Some carvings show off the family possessions.

Quebec City
Quebec City is the capital of the province of Quebec. It is Canada's oldest city and the only walled city in North America. Many of its distinctive buildings are in the original French style.

The animals are symbols of the family's ancestors.

Timber!
Half of Canada's 1.5 million square miles (4 million square kilometers) of forest are used for timber. Logging is a very important Canadian industry. On the west coast, large areas of forest are disappearing. Logging companies are being asked to slow down the destruction and to replant more trees.

Totem pole
The First Nations of British Co[l]... on the west coast of Canada, car... giant totem poles out of trees. S... totem poles celebrated special ev... or the lives of leaders.

Modern machinery fells giant conifer trees.

Canada

Inuit victory

Indigenous people have lived in Canada's Arctic north for thousands of years. In 1993, the Inuit people regained control of native land when a territory called Nunavut was formed and put under their control. Nunavut covers more than 20 percent of Canada's land mass and is home to almost 40,000 people.

Is there anybody out there?

The first long-distance phone call was made in Canada in 1876. A century later, Canada was the first country to set up a satellite network. Satellites provide a vital link to many remote communities.

Two languages

Canada has two official languages, English and French. The first Europeans to settle in Canada were the French, followed by the British. Today, the majority of Canadians speak English, but French is the official language in Quebec, Canada's largest province.

Winter sports

Winters are very harsh all over Canada. Ice hockey and skating are national sports—some families flood their back gardens in winter, so that the water freezes to make a temporary ice rink.

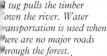

l tug pulls the timber own the river. Water ansportation is used when here are no major roads hrough the forest.

The timber is taken to a riverside sawmill, where it is cut into planks or pulped for papermaking.

THE UNITED STATE

The United States of America is an exciting mixture of different cultures and traditions. Over the last 500 years, tens of millions of people from all over the world have made America their home. The families of the new arrivals now help to make up the American population of about 326 million. The United States is a superpower, and is probably the most powerful nation in the world.

Leading light
The Statue of Liberty has been a welcoming sight to many immigrants arriving in America for more than one hundred years. The statue is a symbol of freedom, and was built to celebrate the 100th anniversary of American independence. It was given to the Americans by the French in 1884.

Lots of languages
Most Americans can trace their family trees back to other parts of the world. Four out of five Americans speak English, but other European and Asian languages are also widely spoken. The country's second language is Spanish.

Many Americans live in cities. This is San Francisco, in the West Coast state of California.

United States

Jeans are made of tough material called denim.

American icon
Jeans are an American invention. The first pair was made in 1874 by Levi Strauss. Jeans are now one of the most popular pieces of clothing ever invented, and Levi jeans are still sold all around the world today.

Drive time
America is a huge country, and many Americans are used to driving long distances to visit friends or family. Driving is a popular American pastime. Large cars are not as fashionable as they used to be. This is because smaller cars use up less gasoline and are better for the environment.

Many American children grow up in suburbs. It is easy to drive from the suburb to the nearest shopping mall or city.

More corn is grown in America than in any other country. A lot of the farming is done by machines, so less than two percent of the labor force work on farms today.

Native American Languages Act
In 1990, Congress made it US policy to "preserve, protect, and promote the rights and freedom of Native Americans to use, practice, and develop Native American languages."

MEXICO, CENTRAL AMERICA, & THE CARIBBEAN

Central America is made up of a narrow strip of eight countries that link the continents of North and South America. Just like the long chain of islands that makes up the Caribbean, Central America is surrounded by clear blue oceans. Today, the beautiful Caribbean Sea and the sunny, sandy beaches attract many tourists. In the past, the sea brought visitors who were less welcome, like the Conquistadors and colonizers from Europe 500 years ago.

Weaving for a living

About 40 percent of the people of Guatemala are Amerindian. Their ancestors go back a thousand years to the days of the ancient Maya. Guatemala now sells Mayan crafts to the rest of the world.

Horizontal weaving loom

The end of the loom is tied to a tree.

Carnival time

The Caribbean is famous for its carnivals. For two days and nights just before the Christian festival of Lent, people dance through the street wearing fantastic costumes.

It is often possible to tell which village a weaver lives in from the patterns in her cloth.

A strap around the weaver's back holds the loom steady.

Costa Rica Cuba Dominica Dominican Republic El Salvador Grenada Guatemala

Haiti

The Day of the Dead
Every year in Mexico, a festival is held to remember people who have died. It is called the Day of the Dead and takes place at the end of October. Families have picnics by the graves of their relatives. When night falls, they keep watch over the graveyard by candlelight.

Honduras

Jamaica

A sugary souvenir of the festival.

Mexico

Nicaragua

of chocolate
densely populated
co City is built on a lake
d Texcoco. Its indigenous
s were some of the first
e world to turn cacao
s into tasty chocolate
st 4,000 years ago!

Panama

A modern mix
Many Caribbean people are descendants of African slaves who were forced to work on sugar plantations. Slavery was stopped in the 19th century, and many Asians then came to work in the Caribbean. Their descendants still live there today.

St. Kitts-Nevis

St. Lucia

Terrific temples
More than 1,000 years ago, the ancient Mayans built impressive temples, especially in Mexico. Mayan society was very sophisticated long before the Spaniards invaded in the 16th century.

Natural disasters
Central America has many natural hazards, such as volcanoes, earthquakes, and hurricanes. Volcanoes have become popular with tourists, and some now have trails and cable cars up them.

St. Vincent and the Grenadines

Trinidad and Tobago

bbean people
e than fifty
ent ethnic
ps live on
lands of
Caribbean.
are just a few.

Asian Arawak Afro-Caribbean European

357

SOUTH AMERICA

Argentina   Bolivia   Brazil   Chile

Most South Americans are Catholics. A huge statue of Christ towers over the Brazilian port of Rio de Janeiro. This is a reminder of three centuries of European rule, when the first peoples of South America were almost wiped out. Most South Americans still speak Spanish or Portuguese. South America is home to diverse landscapes from the Amazonian rainforests to the Andes and the Galapagos Islands.

Galloping gauc[hos]

Large areas of northern and ce[ntral] Argentina are covered with a gr[eat] plain, called the pampas. Huge h[erds] of cattle are kept on the pampas, [and] are looked after by cowboys know[n as] gauchos. Most gauchos are descend[ants] of European settlers in South Ame[rica.]

These gauchos from northwest Argentin[a are] wearing tradit[ional] Spanish hats a[nd] neckerchiefs.

Stiff, flared leather flaps protect the gaucho's legs from high-growing thistles when he is riding his horse in the pampas.

Hea[vy] leath[er] ridin[g]

Rich and poor

São Paulo, in Brazil, is South America's biggest industrial city. The city center is very modern and wealthy. Many people from the surrounding areas travel to São Paulo in search of work. Their children often end up living in terrible poverty on the streets.

mbia
 Ecuador
 Guyana
Paraguay
Peru
Surinam
Uruguay
Venezuela
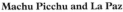

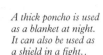

uchos are very proud
heir horses. They
rk on ranches
ed "estancias."

A thick poncho is used
as a blanket at night.
It can also be used as
a shield in a fight.

Machu Picchu and La Paz

South Americans have always been good at building cities in the mountains. Machu Picchu is hidden 7,700 feet (2,350 meters) up in the Andes, in Peru. The city was built more than 500 years ago, without the help of modern machinery.

La Paz is the capital city of Bolivia. It is the world's highest capital city, 12,000 feet (3,636 meters) above sea level. The city's steep streets are surrounded by snow-capped mountains. The thin mountain air often makes visitors breathless.

The Yanomami

In 1991, an area of the Brazilian rainforest about the size of Portugal was set aside for the Yanomami tribe. This did not stop miners from invading the land, bringing diseases that have wiped out large numbers of the Yanomami population.

South Americans

South America is a huge continent, with a wide mix of different people.

Highland Amerindian

Lowland Amerindian

South American of African descent

South American of European and Indian descent

NORTHERN AFRICA

The spectacular pyramids and priceless treasures of Ancient Egypt are world famous. Art and culture are still very important to people all over northern Africa. A great range of musical and artistic traditions have been passed down through families for generations.

The Berber people

Berbers are an indigenous people of North Africa. They have their own language and religion, but through conquests have also learned Arabic and become Muslim. Many live in cities, but others have a traditional nomadic way of life.

The big bass drums are called brekete drums.

Making music

African rhythms have influenced modern jazz and blues music, and are now an important ingredient of African pop music. These drummers are from Ghana in West Africa.

Famine

Up to 233 million Africans suffer from a lack of food. When the rains don't come, crops fail and disaster strikes, but this isn't the only cause. Sadly, humans are responsible, too. War and the need to move to avoid conflict, corruption, lack of planning, and misuse of aid can all result in starvation. These children in the Sahel region of northern Africa are in danger of starving.

Eritrea | Ethiopia | Gambia | Ghana | Guinea | Guinea-Bissau | Ivory Coast

City growth

...ore than 50 percent ...northern Africans ...e in cities. Some ...the largest cities ...the world, such as ...iro in Egypt, are in ...rthern Africa. Lagos ...Nigeria is Africa's ...test-growing ...odern city.

...drummers' clothes ...music come from ...bon, in northern ...na.

The smaller drums are called talking drums. The tighter the strings are squeezed, the higher the note.

Chocolate center

Well over half the world's cocoa is grown in western Africa. More cocoa is grown in the Ivory Coast than anywhere else. About a fifth of Ivory Coast farmland is used to grow cocoa crops.

African crafts

Wood carving, weaving, and jewelry making are traditional African crafts.

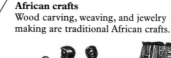

Nigerian wood carving

Narrow-strip woven pants from Ghana

Bronze bracelet from Mali

Algerian silver jewelry, with enamel decoration

Brass bracelet and earrings from Sudan

 Liberia

 Libya

 Mali

 Mauritania

 Morocco

 Niger

 Nigeria

 Senegal

 Sierra Leone

 Somalia

 South Sudan

 Sudan

 Togo

 Tunisia

SOUTHERN AFRICA

A rich variety of peoples make up the African countries in this region. Huge grassland savannahs support an amazing variety of wildlife. Game parks were first set up in Kenya to protect animals from hunters. Today, these parks are big tourist attractions. Across the whole region, traditional lifestyles, like those of the Kalahari Bushmen, have slowly been replaced with new ways. There have been many personal and political changes for the peoples of southern Africa.

A new start

The San people live in the Kalahari desert. For about 20,000 years, they hunted animals and gathered plants to survive. Very few of them still hunt, and most now find work on local farms or in nearby towns.

Today, most San people settle in one place. They have given up a life on the move.

On the move
Only a few groups of San still hunt in the Kalahari desert. Each group has a territory of up to 385 square miles (1,000 square kilometers). The men hunt while the women find tasty fruit, nuts, and roots.

Much of the San people's la now used for fa cattle ranches, a nature reser

na Burundi Comoros Congo Equatorial Guinea Gabon Kenya Lesotho Madagascar

 Malawi

 Mauritius

 Mozambique

Market day

African women often earn money by selling surplus vegetables from the family farm at the market. Village markets are lively and noisy occasions, where friends meet to exchange the latest news.

Namibia

 Rwanda

São Tomé & Príncipe

History of apartheid

In 1948, the white government of South Africa passed apartheid laws that were unfair to most people. The African National Congress fought the laws and their leader, Nelson Mandela, was jailed 27 years. He was let in 1990 and in 1994 he became the first black president of South Africa.

Going to school

Many African children have a long trek to school. A bus takes these Zimbabwean children part of the way, and they have to walk the last few miles.

 South Africa

 Swaziland

 Tanzania

 Uganda

Chatterboxes

The countries of southern Africa are home to many differents groups of people, each with their own language. European languages like English, French, and Portuguese are also spoken as a result of colonialism. The Constitutional Court in Johanessburg is shown here with its name written in all eleven official languages of South Africa.

 Dem. Rep. Congo

of the Zulus

hundred years ago, the Zulus were all clan of a few hundred people, but fought wars with similar clans to become big Zulu nation. Today, the Zulus are argest ethnic group in South Africa.

Zambia

 Zimbabwe

THE MIDDLE EAST

The Middle East has always been a very productive area. Its age-old civilizations have exported farming techniques, beautiful crafts, and three major religions all around the world. The discovery of oil has made parts of the Middle East very rich and powerful. Huge oil refineries are a common sight in the region. But the oil will not last forever, and other industries are being developed to keep the money coming in when the oil has run out.

Turkish bazaar
In the Middle East, many people shop in markets and bazaars. This shopkeeper is hoping to sell some of his brassware at the Great Covered Bazaar in Istanbul, Turkey.

Dressed for the heat
Parts of the Middle East reach temperatures in excess of 113°F (45°C) in the summer, so people wear loose-fitting clothing and cover their heads to protect themselves from the sun's rays.

White clothes reflect bright sunlight and help people keep cool.

Some Mus women we head scarz

Refugee Crisis
War has forced large numbers of people in the Middle East to flee their homes in order to seek safety. Millions of people are living in refugee camps around the Middle East as temporary shelter from the danger of war.

...ing on a kibbutz
...srael, big farms, called
...utzim, were set up so
...y Jewish families could
...and work on the same
... and share the produce.

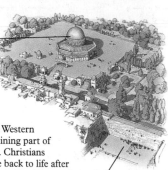

The Dome
of the Rock

City of faith
Jerusalem is a
special city for
Jews, Christians,
and Muslims. Jews
come to pray at the Western
Wall, the only remaining part of
the ancient Temple. Christians
believe Christ came back to life after
his death in Jerusalem. The Dome of
the Rock marks the spot where Muslims
believe Muhammad rose to heaven.

*The Western
Wall is the holiest
site in Judaism.*

*The traditional
male robe has
many names,
including thobe,
kandora, and
dishdasha.*

Trip of a lifetime
At least once in a lifetime, every
Muslim must try to make a special
journey, or Hajj, to Mecca in Saudi
Arabia. During the Hajj, visitors
crowd into the Great Mosque, and
walk seven times around the shrine,
called the Ka'ba.

Afghanistan

Bahrain

Iran

Iraq

Israel

Jordan

Kuwait

Lebanon

Oman

Qatar

Saudi Arabia

Syria

Yemen

United Arab
Emirates

Turkey

SCANDINAVIA

Scandinavia is the name given to the countries of northern Europe. The far north of this region lies inside the Arctic Circle, so the winters are very harsh.

The people of northern Scandinavia enjoy winter sports in the cold climate. Cross-country skiing was invented in Norway, and is still a quick way of getting around during the snowy winter months.

City slickers
About a quarter of th
Danish population li
in Copenhagen, the
capital of Denmark.
Most Scandinavians
choose to live in citie
in the warmer south
of the region.

Sweat it out
Saunas are wooden rooms, steaming with heat from a stove. Invented in Finland more than 1,000 years ago, they are found in many homes in Scandinavia. After a sauna, people often enjoy a cold shower or a roll in the snow.

Escape to the coun
Many Scandinavians
enjoy a high standard
living. Some can affo
to buy or rent a seco
home in the mounta
in the forest, or by th
sea. They escape to
these "holiday huts"
weekends and durin
the summer months

Land of the midnight sun
Imagine waking at midnight, to find the sun shining outside! At the height of summer, Earth's tilt causes northern countries to get more of the sun's light. In northern Scandinavia, it doesn't get dark at all in the middle of summer.

*It is still ligh
at midnight,
because the s
hasn't set.*

Lighting up the sky
The northern lights, or aurora borealis, can be seen in many parts of the Arctic Circle, especially the far north of Scandinavia. The colorful, dancing lights appear in the sky when a cloud of gas released from the sun collides with the magnetic field around Earth.

Denmark Finland Iceland Norway Sweden

Out in the cold
The Saami people are traditionally nomadic, traveling throughout northern Scandinavia and Russia herding their reindeer. It is getting harder to make a living this way, so many young Saami have become fishermen and farmers.

Building success
Denmark is the home of Lego®, one of the world's most popular children's building toys. The first Lego® theme park was built near Billund in 1968, but there are now many more all around the world.

Earthly energy
These Icelanders are swimming in waters warmed by energy deep under the Earth. This geothermal energy is also used to generate electricity and heat houses.

At midday, the hot sun is at its highest position in the sky.

...seven o'clock in ...morning, the ...is already far ...n the sky.

It is six o'clock, and the long, light evening is just beginning.

THE UK AND IRELAND

The Republic of Ireland, also called Éire, is an independent country, with its own government and traditions. England, Scotland, Wales, and Northern Ireland make up the United Kingdom. Many aspects of British life, such as its historical buildings and customs, have been preserved. But the United Kingdom is also good at adapting to change. A rich variety of ethnic groups now live in the United Kingdom's multicultural society.

By the sea
Britain is surrounded by the sea. British seaside vacati[ons] first became popular in the 1[9th] century. Today, many British people go on vacation abroad where it is less likely to rain!

Democratic center
The Houses of Parliament in London have been the home of British democracy since 1512. The political party with the most representatives, called MPs, forms the government. MPs are voted in at national general elections.

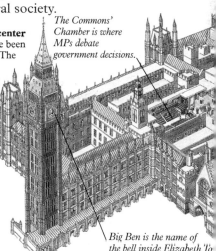

The Commons' Chamber is where MPs debate government decisions.

Big Ben is the name of the bell inside Elizabeth To[wer]

Howzat!
Sunday afternoons in summer would not be the same in many English villages without the familiar sight of a cricket match on the village green. Cricket is an English invention, and is usually followed by another well-known English tradition, afternoon tea!

Guy Fawkes nig[ht]
A plot to blow up the Houses of Parliament alm[ost] succeeded in 1605, but the ringleader, Guy Fawk[es,] was caught and executed. Guy Fawkes Night is s[till] celebrated all over Britain on November 5, wh[en] homemade straw dummies—called guys— burned on big bonfires at firework part[ies]

Arty Edinburgh

For three weeks every August, a big arts festival takes place in Edinburgh, the historic capital of Scotland. The fringe festival gives amateur and part-time entertainers the chance to perform, and also attracts some of the world's best musicians, theater companies, and artists.

Music masters

Traditional folk music is extremely popular in Ireland. The fiddle is a typical folk instrument, often played to accompany singers. Irish bands have been very successful on the world pop scene. Many songs were first written in Gaelic, the original language of Ireland.

Possible new laws are debated in the Lords' Chamber.

A divided community

Northern Ireland is part of the United Kingdom but remains politically divided, mostly along religious lines. Unionists (mostly Protestants) consider themselves British and want to stay part of the United Kingdom, whereas Republicans (mostly Catholics) see themselves as Irish, and want to be part of a united Ireland.

National pride

The Welsh are proud of their culture, and enjoy celebrating national festivals. St. David is the patron saint of Wales, so on St. David's Day, children go to school wearing traditional Welsh costumes.

The daffodil is the national flower of Wales.

FRANCE & THE LOW COUNTRIES

The Netherlands, Belgium, and Luxembourg are sometimes called the Low Countries, because much of the land is flat and low-lying. France and the Low Countries are powerful farming and trading nations, thanks to their good soil and large natural harbors. The people of the region are fond of good food. French chefs are world-famous for their fine cooking skills.

European dream
Many European countries are working together by being members of the European Union. The parliament is at Brussels, in Belgium, and also at Strasbourg, in France.

This stylish outfit is by Christian Lacroix, a top French fashion designer.

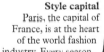

Style capital
Paris, the capital of France, is at the heart of the world fashion industry. Every season, famous designers display new creations at big shows.

Chocolate secrets
Many Belgian chocolate makers keep their recipes secret, so no one can copy them.

Brandy

Coffee

Mint

Nougat

Mixed nuts

City canals
Amsterdam is the capital of the Netherlands. It is built around a network of canals that were once used for trade and transportation. By tradition, many Dutch find their way around the city on bicycles.

At war with the sea
Nearly half of the Netherlands was once under seawater. Over the centuries, the Dutch have reclaimed this land from the sea, draining it by using a clever system of canals and sea walls, or dykes. Much of the reclaimed land is now used for intensive crop and dairy farming.

| Belgium | France | Luxembourg | Monaco | Netherlands |

...nd of wine

...ance produces some of the world's
...st wines. Each region has its own
...nes, with their own special flavors.
... the Rhône valley in southeast France,
...apes ripen in the summer sun. They are
...n harvested and fermented in vats.

...mall but rich

...xembourg is a tiny country nestled
...tween France, Belgium, and Germany.
... small population has a high standard
... living, because of the country's success
... a financial center.

Fabulous food

The French love their food, and take
care to buy it as fresh as possible. Most
French people are careful shoppers,
closely inspecting food and even
sampling it before they buy.

*Attractive vegetable
displays are
arranged to catch
the shopper's eye.*

*Many French
shops sell only
one kind of
produce, but
offer a wide
range of choices.*

*Crusty French
bread is bought
every morning,
as it does not keep
fresh for long.*

271

SPAIN & PORTUGAL

Both Spain and Portugal have warm, sunny climates and long coastlines. The blue skies and dazzling white beaches of Spain's

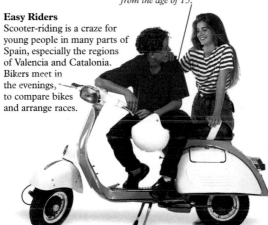

Mediterranean coast attract millions of tourists every summer. The sea is also an important source of food and employment. Fishing is a major industry in Portugal and on Spain's Atlantic coast.

Young Spaniards can ride scooters from the age of 15.

Easy Riders
Scooter-riding is a craze for young people in many parts of Spain, especially the regions of Valencia and Catalonia. Bikers meet in the evenings, to compare bikes and arrange races.

Fiesta!
Spain has more festivals than any other European country. Some are religious, others are just for fun. One of the messiest festivals takes place in Bunyols, in Valencia. The villagers pelt each other with tomatoes, to celebrate the time when a truck spilled its load of overripe tomatoes all over the village square.

Tide of tourists
Mediterranean countries are very popular with tourists. In 2018, about 82 million tourists flocked to the coast of southern Europe. Every the Spanish population do when tourists arrive to enjo the hot summer weather a sandy beaches.

| Andorra | Portugal | Spain |

City of seven hills
Lisbon, the capital of Portugal, is one of the smallest capitals in Europe. It is built on seven steep hills. Old electric trams carry the townspeople up and down the sloping streets.

Eating around Spain
Here are some tasty dishes from different regions of Spain.

Gazpacho—cold tomato soup from Andalusia

e your pick
ese Portuguese farmers grow
nges, lemons, and olives. Orchards
weet, juicy oranges are a common
t in the hot countryside of
thwest Portugal.

Cocido—meat stew from Castile and Estremadura

e dance
menco dancing was
eloped many hundreds
ears ago by the gypsies
Andalusia. It is still
ular all over Spain.
ny Spanish children
n the dance from
oung age, and enjoy
ring the colorful
nenco costumes.

Zarzuela de Pescado—
seafood stew
from Catalonia

First communion
Most Spanish people
are Roman Catholics.
From the age of seven
or eight, children are
taught the main beliefs
of the Catholic church,
and are ready to take
their first communion at
the age of 10. The
ceremony is a religious
and social occasion—an
important event for the
entire family.

Paella—chicken, seafood, and rice from Valencia

Doughnuts—a popular treat all over Spain

GREECE & ITALY

Greece and Italy lie in southern Europe, where the warm summers and beautiful Mediterranean coastline draw millions of tourists every year. Many magnificent buildings, dating back to the days of the Ancient Greeks and Romans, are also popular attractions. A lot of these sites are in urgent need of repair. Both Greece and Italy are struggling to keep their ancient monuments in good condition.

Priests on parade
Greek Orthodox priests are allowed to get married, unlike Roman Catholic priests. Priests play an important part in both Greek and Italian society and are given great respect.

Chemicals from car exhausts are eating away at the ancient stone.

Parts of the Parthenon are being restored or replaced.

Café talk
In some parts of Greece and Italy, far away from the busy towns and cities, life carries on at a very relaxed pace. Many families rest in the strong heat of the day. In the cooler evenings, men often gather in cafés for a drink and a chat.

So many tourists visit the Parthenon that its steps are being worn away.

Temple under threat
The Parthenon in Athens is an ancient Greek temple, built to honor Athena, the goddess of wisdom. It is under threat from air pollution and visitors' feet, but work is being done to protect it.

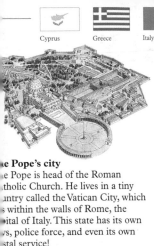

e Pope's city
e Pope is head of the Roman
tholic Church. He lives in a tiny
untry called the Vatican City, which
s within the walls of Rome, the
ital of Italy. This state has its own
vs, police force, and even its own
stal service!

Car Italia
Italy is world-famous for
its cars. They've produced
luxury sports cars including
the Ferrari and Lamborghini.
The Fiat car works in
northern Italy was once
among the largest car
factories in the world.

Pasta preparations
More types of pasta are
made in Italy than anywhere
else in the world. Flour, eggs,
vegetable oil, and salt are
mixed to make dough,
which is then rolled
out and cooked.
Pasta is often
eaten with a
tasty sauce.

*Spaghetti
Bolognese*

*Big arches reduce
the weight of this
typical Venetian
building.*

*Brick
foundations are
laid on wooden
posts, which are
driven deep
into the mud.*

Grand passions
Opera and soccer are two of Italy's
top obsessions. The soccer World Cup
took place in Italy in 1990. Luciano
Pavarotti, the world-famous Italian
opera singer, sang at a gala concert to
celebrate this important tournament.

Sinking city
Venice was built on the mudbanks of a lagoon on
Italy's northeast coast. The floating city is slowly
sinking. Many of its buildings have been damaged
by pollution and constant contact with water,
and need to be carefully restored.

GERMANY, AUSTRIA, & SWITZERLAND

Germany, Austria, and Switzerland lie at the heart of Europe. Central Europeans share a love of traditional food, drink, and festivals. They also share a language, as German is the most widely spoken language of the region. Germany is a powerful country. After years of separation for political reasons, East Germany rejoined West Germany in 1990 to become one big country. The wall dividing East from West Berlin was torn down amid great celebrations.

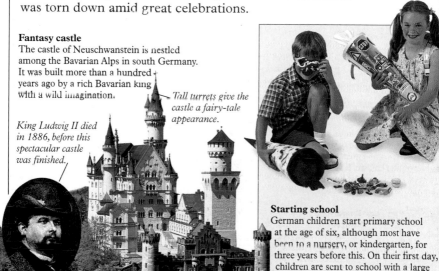

Fantasy castle
The castle of Neuschwanstein is nestled among the Bavarian Alps in south Germany. It was built more than a hundred years ago by a rich Bavarian king with a wild imagination.

King Ludwig II died in 1886, before this spectacular castle was finished.

Tall turrets give the castle a fairy-tale appearance.

Starting school
German children start primary school at the age of six, although most have been to a nursery, or kindergarten, for three years before this. On their first day, children are sent to school with a large cone stuffed with everything they will want, including candy, pens, and books.

The castle attracts tourists from all over the world.

| Austria | Germany | Liechtenstein | Switzerland |

...ming down the mountain
...e return of cows from the Alps
...elebrated in August. It is called
...Einabtrieb. The cows are usually
...orated in bright colors. But if
...ebody has died, the decorations
...black or dark blue.

...y Viennese
...e in five Austrians lives in Vienna,
...capital of Austria. The city was
...e at the center of the great
...tro-Hungarian empire. It is still
...mportant city, and is the home of
...ny United Nations organizations.

Four languages

Switzerland is surrounded
by Germany, Austria,
Liechtenstein,
France, and Italy.
The languages
spoken in Switzerland
are French, German,
Italian, and Romansch.
Most Swiss people speak
German, but many speak at least
two of these languages.

Snowy holiday
Every year, thousands
of skiers visit resorts in
Austria and Switzerland.
Some people worry that
mountain tourism spoils
the environment. But it
brings lots of money for
both countries and is a big
employer of local people.

*The highest point
of the wheel is nearly
213 feet (65 meters)
above the ground.*

The biggest wheel
The Riesenrad in Vienna is one of
the largest big wheels in the world.
The wheel is 200 feet (61 meters)
across, and it goes around at
30 inches (75 centimeters)
per second.

*Each carriage
takes up to
12 passengers.*

CENTRAL AND EASTERN EUROPE

Central and eastern Europe has been invaded many times, but is now a meeting place for different cultures and religions. The downfall of communism in the 1980s and 1990s has liberated the countries of the region, but has also allowed old tensions between many of the ethnic groups to flare up again. Several new countries have been created, including the Czech Republic, Croatia, Slovenia, and Bosnia and Herzegovina.

Lake Bled

The picturesque snow-covered mountains and clear lakes of northwestern Slovenia draw tourists to the area. Lake Bled, with its beautiful village overlooking the waterside, is one of the most spectacular vacation resorts in Slovenia.

Hungarian dr

This traditional dress is cove in detailed embroidery. Colo sewing is a typical Hunga handicraft. Today this costi is only worn on special occasi

Prague's town hall

Prague is the capital of the Czech Republic and one the most beautiful cities in Europe. The Old Town H looks huge, but is really a row of small adjoining bui

Fishermen of the Adriatic

These fishermen are from the island of Korcula, off the coast of Croatia. Local people have made a living from fishing since prehistoric times. Many families have their own boat and a private jetty.

Above the inscription "Prague, Head of the Kingdom" is the city's coat of arms.

Bosnia and Herzegovina

 Bulgaria

 Croatia

 Czech Republic

Hungary

Kosovo

Macedonia

Montenegro

tislava castle
tislava is the capital of Slovakia and is situated on the Danube River. The oldest parts of the city date back to the middle ages.

Poland

Romania

Serbia

Slovakia

Slovenia

City of learning
Many of Poland's buildings were lost in World War II, but Krakow's buildings escaped and the impressive streets are a reminder that Krakow was once the capital of Poland. The oldest university in Poland is situated in Krakow—the university of the Jagellonians.

Favorite foods
Here are some typical central and eastern European dishes.

To get to the steeple you have to enter the main doors, which are Gothic in style and carved from wood.

The face of this famous clock not only tells the time, but shows the movement of the sun and the moon through the twelve signs of the zodiac.

Pictures on the calendar show how the world changes with the four seasons.

Historic square
Warsaw, the capital of Poland, is more than 700 years old. Today its old town is a popular tourist attraction and people can explore the area in traditional horse-drawn carriages.

Red borscht

Pork with cabbage and dumplings

Goulash

Dalmatian bake

NORTHERN EURASIA

Eurasia is the name given to the combined landmass of Europe and Asia. Northern Eurasia stretches across a vast area, from Ukraine in the west to the frozen lands of Siberia. For centuries, northern Eurasia was controlled by powerful rulers and governments. But in 1991, the communist Soviet Union split into 15 independent states.

Daring dance
This energetic dance celebrates the courage of cossack soldiers from the Ukraine.

Musical entertainment
Named after the famous composer, the Moscow Tchaikovsky Conservatory is one of several conservatories in Russia. It is where the very best music students learn to master their chosen instruments.

Going to church
Orthodox Christianity has been the traditional Russian religion for more than 1,000 years. The cathedral of St. Basil is one of the most spectacular Russian Orthodox churches.

The cathedral lies in Red Square, right in the heart of Moscow.

St. Basil's was built for Tsar Ivan the Terrible in the 1550s, to mark his military successes.

Russian art
The Hermitage Museum in St. Petersburg is one of the largest museums in the world. It holds more than three million cultural artifacts and works of art in galleries totalling over 2.5 million sq feet (230,000 sq meters).

...ania Moldova Mongolia Russian Federation Tajikistan Turkmenistan Ukraine Uzbekistan

Moscow State Circus

Some of the most famous circuses in the world are based in Russia. The Bolshoi Circus on Vernadskogo opened in 1971 and can seat an audience of up to 3,400 people. It entertains audiences with exciting aerial feats, trapeze artists, and amazing costumes.

Northern Eurasians

The largest ethnic group of northern Eurasia is made up of Slavs. Next biggest is the Turkic-speaking population. Smaller groups include Mongols and Inuit.

A world of difference

The people of Central Asia look very different from the Russians who live farther north. They speak languages similar to Turkish and many are Muslims, like their neighbors in the Middle East. These women are selling bread at a market stall in Uzbekistan.

Ukrainian Slav

Yesterday's hero

Ancestors of these Mongol horsemen fought in the army of the fierce Mongol emperor, Ghengis Khan, 1,000 years ago. Today, Ghengis Khan is once again a Mongolian national hero.

Turkic-speaking Uzbek

Colorful, onion-shaped domes top the nine chapels of St. Basil's.

Mongol

Caucasus Mountains

There is a huge diversity of ethnicity and language in the Caucasus Mountains. People generally live long lives, which may be due to their active lifestyle and the high altitude.

Russian Inuit

CHINA AND TAIWAN

There are more than a billion people in China—more than any other country. In fact, almost a fifth of the world's entire population lives in China. Fifty-seven different ethnic groups live there, but by far the largest group is the Han, traditionally a peasant farming people.

Communism in China
The Communist governmen in China plays an active role in people's everyday lives. This official government po encouraged couples who live cities to have only one child.

Food and farming
Two-thirds of the Chinese people are farmers, growing crops on every spare patch of suitable land. Up to three crops of rice may be grown on the same paddy field each rice-growing season.

Rice is the basic food for China's huge population.

Bringing up baby
For many years there was a "one child per family" rule in China. It was introduced in 1979 try to control the f population growt Since 2016, couples can have two children.

Words and pictures
The Chinese written language is based on pictures, which describe objects, actions, and ideas. There are about 50,000 pictures, or characters. A simplified list of about 2,000 is commonly used today.

男
人 *Man*

女
人 *Woman*

Lettering brush

China   Taiwan

Folk art in Taiwan
Taiwan has some colorful folk
traditions. A sticky mixture of rice
and flour is dyed and molded to
make these decorative figures. In
the past, the flour and rice recipe
was used to make children's snacks.
Today, the figures are kept, not eaten.

Hong Kong
More than seven million people live in
the 403 square miles (1,045 square kilometers)
of Hong Kong, making it the world's
most crowded place as well as a busy
trading center.

Get well soon
This street trader is
selling herbal medicines.
Ancient, natural ways of
treating illnesses are
very common
in China.

Angelica root

*Most Chinese mothers
work full-time. Their
children are looked after
in day care at the
workplace, until
they are old enough
to go to to school.*

Buddhist Tibet
Most people living in Tibet are Buddhists.
They believe their past leaders are alive
now in the body of their present leader,
the Dalai Lama. In 1959, the Dalai Lama
fled his home, the Potala Palace, to escape
the invading Chinese army. He now lives
in exile in India.

JAPAN & KOREA

Japan is famous for its electronic gadgets and machines. In the last 50 years, Japan has become one of the world's richest countries, and many Japanese people enjoy a high standard of living. Its neighbor, Korea, is split into two separate countries. North Korea has cut off its links with the South and is one of the world's most secretive societies. South Korea is a successful industrial country, like Japan, and trades with the rest of the world.

Fish food
The traditional Japanese diet of fish is very healthy. Many Japanese people live to be very old—in 2010, more than a quarter of the population was over 65 years old.

Children on parade
The Seven-Five-Three Festival in Japan is named after the ages of the children who take part. Every year on November 15, girls and boys are dressed up in traditional costumes and taken to a Shinto shrine. It is a very sociable occasion.

Dinnertime
The evening meal is an important time for busy Japanese families to get together and relax. Parents often get home late from work, and children have lots of homework to do in the evenings.

Rice is cooked until it is sticky, so it is easy to eat with pointed chopsticks.

An electric rice cooker sits close to the table.

Japanese tea is drunk without milk, and is called green tea.

Watch your head
These pupils are not hiding from their teacher! They are practicing what to do if there is an earthquake. Earthquakes do not happen often in Japan, but they could happen any time. In the past, they have caused terrible damage.

書店

Japan

North Korea

South Korea

Colorful Koreans
This woman is wearing the national costume of South Korea. It is made of brightly colored material. South Korea sells huge amounts of material to the rest of the world. Millions of square yards of cotton are produced in South Korea every year.

Selling ships
Most of the ships in Asia are made at the Hyundai shipyard in South Korea, the biggest shipyard in the world. It has 9,000 employees, and in 2015 it became the first shipbuilder to deliver its 2,000th ship.

The food is placed on the table before the family sits down to eat.

The family sits on cushions around a low table to eat their meal.

Watch this space
The big cities of Japan can get extremely crowded. Space is often very hard to come by, but the smallest places are always put to good use. This electronics shop had hundreds of gadgets for sale in a tiny kiosk in Tokyo.

Chopstick rest

esentation is very portant in Japanese oking. Portions are ays small.

Climb every mountain
Japanese people work hard, but they also enjoy their hobbies. Japan has some stunning mountain ranges, and many Japanese people keep fit with mountain climbing. These hikers are on Mount Furano-Dake, on the island of Hokkaido in northern Japan.

書店

THE INDIAN SUBCONTINENT

Bound by the Himalayas in the north and the Indian Ocean in the south, the Indian subcontinent is a region that includes the nations of India, Pakistan, Bangladesh, Bhutan, Nepal, and the Maldives. Most of these countries are young, having formed after the end of European colonial rule in the 20th century. Hinduism, Islam, and Buddhism are the most common religions practiced in the subcontinent.

Railroad network
Stretching over an amazing 41,861 miles (67,368 km), the railroad network in India is one of the largest in the world. Most people in India prefer to use trains to travel between towns and cities. Trains are run by the government-owned organization called Indian Railways, which employs more than 1.4 million people and is one of the largest employers in the world.

Urban life
A booming economy underlines India's rapid growth into one of the world's fastest developing nations. Almost a third of India's population now lives in urban areas, mainly in big metropolitan cities such as New Delhi and Mumbai. Skyscrapers frame parts of the skyline of Mumbai, which has a population of more than 22 million.

Bangladesh Bhutan India Maldives Nepal Pakistan Sri Lanka

Floods in Bangladesh

Bangladesh is a very low, flat country, crisscrossed with rivers. After heavy rain, flooding can cause terrible damage. This farmer is helping to push a tricycle taxi, called a rickshaw, through a flooded village in northeastern Bangladesh.

A world of films

India has one of the most successful film industries in the world, and produces the highest number of films in a year—1,986 films were produced in 2017 alone. The Hindi branch of this industry – Bollywood—is centered in Mumbai. Bollywood films are famous around the world for their vivacious song-and-dance routines, glamorous sets, and colorful dresses.

Playing cricket

Introduced by the British in the 19th century, the sport of cricket has millions of followers across the subcontinent. Many children start playing cricket from a very young age, and can often be seen on the streets and in the parks. Becoming a cricketer is now a well-paid job!

The land of tea

Sri Lanka is one of the largest exporters of tea in the world, and the country is famous for the Ceylon tea it produces. Tea is consumed in most households, and it has become a major source of revenue for the people.

SOUTHEAST ASIA

Brunei   Myanmar

It is hard to get away from water in most parts of Southeast Asia!
The twelve countries that make up the region are linked by waterways
and surrounded by oceans. The hot, wet environment is ideal for
farming rice, the staple crop of the region. It also
supports large areas of tropical rainforests.
Sadly, heavy logging has forced many forest
people to move into towns, where the way
of life is very different.

People power
The Penan people live
in the rainforests of
Sarawak. They have
tried to stop the
destruction of their
forest home by blocking
roads into the rainforest.
Sarawak has the world's
highest rate of logging.

The secret of success
The small island state of Singapore
is a powerful trading nation.
Singapore became successful
because of its position. It was built
up as a key trading post between
the Far East and the West, and is
now one of Asia's richest countries.

Living with water
Many houses in Malaysia and
Indonesia are built on stilts. This
helps protect them from floods
during torrential rainstorms.

*The houses are called "long"
houses. Behind each door
is a large room, or "bilik,"
where the family lives.*

*The houses are made
from natural and modern
materials. Some roofs are
made from palms, others
from corrugated iron.*

Bali dancers

The Indonesian island of Bali is famous for its exciting dances. Historical tales of local princes and heroes are acted out in a masked dance called the Wayang Topeng. The dance is very entertaining, with lots of clowning around as well as serious storytelling.

A Topeng dancer acts out the character of the mask.

Every movement is carefully controlled.

Floating market

Much of Bangkok in Thailand is below sea level, and the city has a busy network of canals. Floating markets are colorful occasions—local traders bring their goods to market by boat, and shoppers paddle up to take a look at what is on display.

Religious teaching

The vast majority of Thais are Buddhists. Every male Buddhist is expected to become a monk for a while, to study religious teachings and prepare for adult life.

Extreme weather

In 2004, an earthquake caused a tsunami in Southeast Asia. With waves 100 feet (30 meters) high, entire towns, villages, and cropland were destroyed across 14 countries. Communities have pulled together to rebuild the many schools, hospitals, and homes that were lost.

ts are the main form of sportation. Rivers provide s between small communities.

Notched tree trunks or ladders are used to get down to the water level.

AUSTRALASIA & OCEANIA

Most Australians live in big cities like Sydney, the capital of New South Wales. Both Australia and New Zealand are big economic powers, trading mainly with Asia and the United States. By contrast, many Pacific islanders of Oceania live in isolated communities that have little contact with the outside world.

Emergency!
The Royal Flying Doctor Service is a lifesaver for people living in remote pa of Australia. Few patients are more than a two-hour flight away from a hospita

Aboriginal art
Aboriginal peoples were the first to settle in Australia, more than 50,000 years ago. They have strong artistic traditions, and Aboriginal art is now sold around the world, making much-needed money for their communities.

Australian megamix
British settlers first came to Australia about 250 years ago, but in the last 70 years there have been many new arrivals from other parts of Europe and Asia.

Many Italians moved to Australia after World War II.

The majority of Australians share a love of the outdoors, and live by the sea.

A large numb Australians h British ancest

New Europ arrivals inc many Greek

New Zealand | Papua New Guinea | Samoa | Solomon Islands | Tonga | Tuvalu | Vanuatu

Teaching in Tonga

Tonga is one of the independent nations among the Pacific islands of Oceania. English and Tongan are the two official languages for the small population of around 106,000. In Tonga, children have to go to school between the ages of five and eighteen.

First people

These people were some of the first settlers in Australasia and Oceania.

Pacific islander

Stone money

Some Pacific island tribal traditions have not changed for thousands of years. The people of Yap island still use stones like this one as money when they make important property deals.

...s boy has ...namese parents. ...lish is his second ...guage, just as it is ...ne in five other ...Australians.

This girl's parents are Chinese. Many Australians are of Asian descent.

Papua New Guinea tribesman

Rugby dance

The Maoris settled in New Zealand about 1,000 years ago. The New Zealand rugby team, the All Blacks, has borrowed some Maori traditions. They use an old Maori war chant, called a haka, to get them in the mood for matches.

Surfing is popular along the coast of Australia.

Maori woman

Aboriginal tribesman

CHAPTER 4

SCIENCE AND TECHNOLOGY

Through the centuries, people's lives have changed enormously. Today, the way you live is completely dominated by technology, from the electric toaster that produces your breakfast to the bus that takes you to school. Computers, devices, and apps have become central to how you learn new things, play games, entertain yourself, meet new people, and keep in touch with family and friends.

Science and technology have helped us in lots of ways. Because of them, we can grow and distribute food cheaply, manufacture clothing and household goods in huge quantities, treat illnesses of all kinds, travel from place to place quickly, and communicate with people all over the world in an instant.

But we have to be very careful to use the technology we have in a responsible way. The same knowledge that saves lives and makes our world better can also lead to the development of dangerous weapons, chemicals that make us sick, and pollution that harms our planet.

**Science and Machines
Energy and Industry
Transportation**

SCIENCE AND MACHINES

You don't need to walk into a laboratory to see science in action. Science is all around you, every day of your life. There are three main kinds of science. The science of the natural world—plants and animals— is called biology. The study of what things are made of, and what happens when they are mixed together, is chemistry. The third science, physics, is about how everything in the universe works.

The world of physics includes the study of machines. Machines help us to perform tasks using less effort. For example, one of the first machines, the wheel, makes it easier to move things from place to place. From scissors to smoke detectors, machines are all around us, making our lives easier and safer.

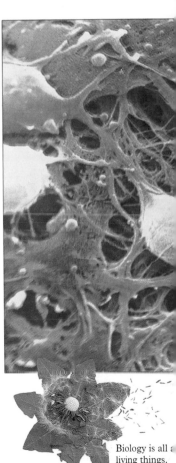

Biology is all a[bout]
living things.

The laws of flight are studied in physics.

Cooking an egg is everyday chemistry. When you heat it, a chemical reaction turns the runny part hard and white.

Tunneling machine

Light bulb

The development of the wheel

Colored image of nerve cells from the brain.

Quartz clock

Portable video game

LIVING THINGS

You are a living thing. All living things are made up of cells, and your body is made up of many billions of cells. Your cells join together to make tissues, for example muscles. Tissues combine to make organs, such as your heart. Biologists are scientists who study living things. They have divided the world of living things into groups called "kingdoms." The study of plants is called botany, and the study of animals is called zoology.

Cherries

Seaweed

Moss

Fly agaric fungus

Bacteria and fungi kingdoms
Bacteria are so tiny they can't be seen without a microscope. They have a simple, one-cell structure. Bacteria and fungi feed on other living things and recycle the remains.

A kitten grows up into a cat. All living things grow.

Splitting up
Living things are made up of at least one cell. For a living thing to reproduce and grow, its cells must keep on splitting into identical pairs. This single-cell bacterium divides every 20 minutes. Look how many bacteria there are after one hour.

Now

20 minutes later

40 minutes later

One hour later

All living things make copies of themselves. This process is called reproduction.

Living things all find some way of breathing. A cat breathes through its nose.

Livir thing food stay

Plant kingdom

There are many different kinds of plants. Some are soft and small enough to hold in your hand. Others are enormous and woody. Some plants have flowers, but others don't. Green plants use sunlight, water, and carbon dioxide to make their own food.

Sweet chestnut

Poppy heads and seeds

living things get rid of waste products.

Gerbera flower

Raft spinner

Hoverflies

Badger

Animal kingdom

Animals have billions of very complex cells. Most of the world's animals, like insects, do not have backbones. Animals with backbones include mammals, birds, reptiles, amphibians, and fish.

Hen with chicks

Grass snake

Lovely lashes

Some people have tiny mites living in their eyelashes. The mites feed on liquid from the eye, cleaning the lashes at the same time. The mites need people, and people need them. Many living things depend on each other.

Spotted salamander

All living things move, but you can't always see the movement.

A cat hears with its ears. Every living thing is sensitive in some way to the world around it.

Cuban hock

Shore crab

Rudd

SOLIDS

Hydrogen atom

Uranium atom

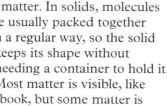

Everything is made up of matter. Molecules are the building blocks of matter. In solids, molecules are usually packed together in a regular way, so the solid keeps its shape without needing a container to hold it. Most matter is visible, like the pages of this book, but some matter is invisible, like air. Matter may be solid, liquid, or gas, and change from one state to another.

Amazing atoms
The smallest amount of a pure substance is called an at[...]
The simplest atom is hydrogen, bu[...]
other atoms are more complex. Atoms are incredibly tiny—about 100,000 million atoms fit on this period.

Molecules in a solid
Each of these children is acting the part of a molecule in a solid.

The children are all wearing red T-shirts, to show that the molecules are all the same.

The molecules in most solids make up a very regular pattern.

Ice

Water

Steam

In a state
Ice, water, and steam are made up of the same molecules. They are not alike because their molecules are spaced differently. Solid ice melts into liquid water. When water is boiled, it turns into a gas called steam.

Solids on show
You can tell these solids apart because they do not look, feel, weigh or smell the same. They all have different properties.

A flower is soft and delicate.

A cake is crumbly and tasty.

Larger than life

These long, thin wax molecules are shown about 3 million times larger than they are in real life. The tiny blue dots are atoms that have joined together to make up the wax molecules.

Sugar

Crystal clear

Grains of sugar are solid crystals. Their atoms are close together and arranged in a regular pattern called a lattice. Many solids that look smooth actually have a crystal structure, like these vitamin C tablets.

king molecules

ms link up to make molecules.
o atoms of hydrogen join
ether to make one molecule
ydrogen gas.

The molecules in a cool solid do not move around very fast. If a solid is heated, the molecules move around faster and faster.

Vitamin C crystals, seen through a microscope.

Vitamin C tablets

There are strong links between the molecules in a solid. This means that solids have a fixed shape.

Graphite and diamond

Graphite is soft and is used in pencils, and diamond is the hardest solid in the world. But diamond and graphite have a lot in common! They are two different forms of carbon. This means they have the same molecules, but they are arranged in different ways.

shell is hard
nd brittle.

A spider's web is light and strong.

LIQUIDS

If you spread some butter on hot toast, the butter melts. When a solid gets hot enough to melt, it turns into a liquid. Liquids behave differently than solids. The heat that melts a solid breaks down some of the strong links between molecules, so that the molecules can move around more freely. A liquid flows because its molecules can't hold together strongly enough to form a solid shape.

Syrup flows slowly.

Car oil flows fairly well.

Ink flow very easi

Sticky spoonful
Some liquids flow much more easily than others. Liquids that are "viscous" do not flow well.

Molecules in a liquid
These children are behavir like molecules in a liquid.

Fair shares?
Who has more milk to drink? It may not look like it, but these glasses hold the same amount. Containers of different shapes can hold the same volume, or amount, of liquid.

Liquid levels
Liquids flow to fill containers of any shape or size. The surface of liquid always stays level howeve much you may tilt the container

Too hot to handle?

Ice creams melt very easily, but not all solids have such low melting points. Some only melt if they are heated to very high temperatures. The steel in this factory melts at 2,732°F (1,500°C).

On the boil

When a liquid is heated to a certain temperature, it turns into a gas. This temperature is called the boiling point. Different liquids have different boiling points. The water in this pan boils at 212°F (100°C).

In a liquid, the molecules are separate from each other.

Moving molecules can get into all the corners of a container. This is why liquids take up the shape of the container that holds them.

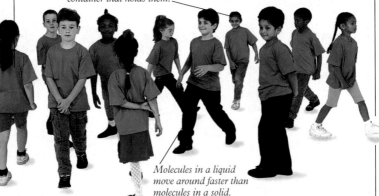

Molecules in a liquid move around faster than molecules in a solid.

Molecules in a liquid are not arranged in a regular pattern, so they can move around freely.

the surface

olecules near the surface of a liquid
l toward each other. A drop keeps
shape because of this surface
sion. If some dishwashing
uid is added to a water drop,
surface tension is made
aker, so the drop spreads out.

Good mixers

Cranberry juice mixes well with water. It dissolves completely.

Bad mixers

Some liquids do not mix at all. Oil does not dissolve in water.

GASES

Gases are all around us and can't usually be seen or felt, but some can be smelled. All smells are molecules of gas mixed in the air. If you smell some tasty soup, you are actually sniffing in molecules of the soup. When you heat a liquid, it turns into a gas. The heat makes the molecules in the liquid move around faster and faster. The gas molecules fly off in all directions, spreading through the air.

Lighter than air
When a gas gets hot, it takes up more room and gets lighter. A hot-balloon rises up in the air because air inside it is hot, and much lighter than the air outside.

Molecules in a gas
Each child is acting like a molecule in a gas. Look how they are bumping into each other.

There are no links between any of the molecules in a gas.

Dancing on air
When a shaft of light shines through a gap in the trees, specks of dust look like they are dancing in the sunlight. What is really happening is that the molecules in the air currents move around, flicking the dust in all directions.

As a gas spreads, the molecules get farther and farther apart. Gases will always spread to fit the space they are in.

Carbon dioxide
Other gases
Oxygen
Nitrogen

In the air
There are a number of different gases in the air we breathe. 78 percent of air is nitrogen gas. Oxygen makes up 21 percent. Carbon dioxide and a variety of other gases make up just one percent of the gases in the air.

Pumping air

It is easy to squash together, or compress, gas molecules. When you pump up a tire, you compress air molecules into a small space. The more air molecules you pump in, the more they push against the inside of the tire. The tire gets harder because pressure increases inside it.

High pressure

Air presses on everything on Earth. You can see air pressure at work. If you suck juice out of a carton, the carton buckles. This is because the air pressure pushing on the carton is greater than the air pressure inside the carton.

Molecules in a gas move very quickly, darting around in all directions.

Out of breath

Gases can dissolve in liquids, and oxygen from the air dissolves in water. Fish need oxygen to breathe, so they use the oxygen in water to survive under water. Humans also breathe oxygen, but unlike fish, we can't breathe under water without a supply of compressed air.

Night and day

Plants help keep the balance of gases in the air. Night and day, they take in oxygen and "breathe out" carbon dioxide, as we do. But by day, they also take in large amounts of carbon dioxide—which they need to make their food and give off oxygen.

ENERGY

Energy is needed for life, and for every single movement in the whole universe. When you have run a race, you may feel that you have used up all your energy. But your energy has not been lost, it has changed into different kinds of energy: movement and heat. When work is done, energy is never lost, but it changes into other kinds of energy. Movement and heat energy are just two of the many different kinds of energy.

Jumping jack
When the lid is closed, the puppet's spring is coiled up, ready to push the puppet out of the box. We say the spring has potential energy. When you open the lid, the spring's potential energy turns into movement energy.

Energy change
We can't make energy, or destroy it. Instead, energy can change from one kind to another. This toy robot shows how energy may not stay in one form for very long!

Eating energy
We get our energy from food, and we need to eat plants, or animals that have eaten plants, to stay alive. Plants get energy to grow from sunlight, so our energy really comes from the sun.

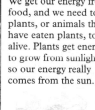

Sun power
Living things that grew millions of years ago were buried under rock, where they slowly turned into coal, oil, and gas. Energy from these fuels comes from the sun, shining long ago.

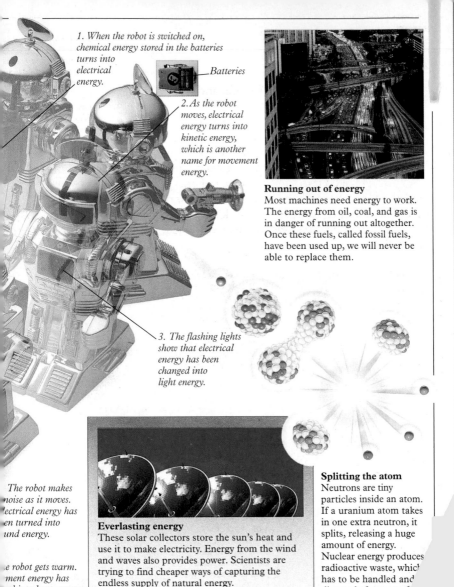

1. When the robot is switched on, chemical energy stored in the batteries turns into electrical energy.

Batteries

2. As the robot moves, electrical energy turns into kinetic energy, which is another name for movement energy.

3. The flashing lights show that electrical energy has been changed into light energy.

The robot makes noise as it moves. Electrical energy has been turned into sound energy.

The robot gets warm. Movement energy has turned into heat energy.

Running out of energy
Most machines need energy to work. The energy from oil, coal, and gas is in danger of running out altogether. Once these fuels, called fossil fuels, have been used up, we will never be able to replace them.

Everlasting energy
These solar collectors store the sun's heat and use it to make electricity. Energy from the wind and waves also provides power. Scientists are trying to find cheaper ways of capturing the endless supply of natural energy.

Splitting the atom
Neutrons are tiny particles inside an atom. If a uranium atom takes in one extra neutron, it splits, releasing a huge amount of energy. Nuclear energy produces radioactive waste, which has to be handled and disposed of very caref

105

HEAT

The sun's rays can make you very hot. The way heat rays move through air is called radiation. You feel warm because the radiation makes the molecules in your skin move around faster than usual. Heat comes from molecules moving around. It moves through solids by conduction—the molecules in a solid vibrate, bumping the heat along. Heat travels through air and liquids in a circular movement called convection.

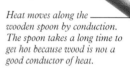

Heat moves along the wooden spoon by conduction. The spoon takes a long time to get hot because wood is not a good conductor of heat.

Snug as a bug?

Heat doesn't travel easily through air, so materials that trap air keep you warm. This polar explorer is wearing clothes made of materials that insulate his body. This means they keep his body heat close to his body, where he needs it.

Tricky fingers

If you dip one finger in hot water and another in cold, the hot water will feel hot and the cold water will feel cold. If you then dip both fingers in lukewarm water, your "hot" finger is tricked into finding the water cold, and your "cold" finger finds the water hot.

Good conductors
If you heat a solid, its molecules jostle around, passing the heat from molecule to molecule. Just as a whisper moves along a line of children, so the moving molecules pass, or conduct, the heat from one end of the solid to the other.

Building bridges
When most solids are heated, they get bigger, or expand. This is because the heat speeds up the molecules, and they get farther and farther apart as they move. Bridges are built with small gaps between the sections of the roadway, so there is room for them to expand on a hot day.

As the water reaches its boiling point, it evaporates into steam.

When the water near the heat source gets hot, it rises up toward the surface.

The cooler water near the surface will sink to the bottom of the pan, where it is then warmed up by the heat source.

flames a direct rce of heat.

Metal is a good conductor of heat.

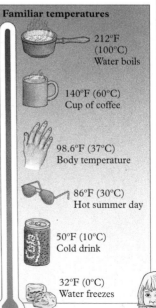

Familiar temperatures

212°F (100°C)
Water boils

140°F (60°C)
Cup of coffee

98.6°F (37°C)
Body temperature

86°F (30°C)
Hot summer day

50°F (10°C)
Cold drink

32°F (0°C)
Water freezes

LIGHT

You may need to wear sunglasses on a sunny day, because the bright light hurts your eyes. It is dangerous to look straight at the sun. The sun's light is not just blinding, it also travels to us very fast. In just one second, light travels 186,000 miles (300,000 kilometers). If a straight beam of light has to pass through obstacles such as convex and concave lenses, it changes direction. This is called refraction.

Hot stuff
Most light comes from hot objects. A very hot object makes a very bright light. The sun is white hot, and sunlight is the brightest natural light we have.

Concave lenses curve inward in the middle.

This beam of light comes from a flashlight. A flashlight is a man-made light source.

Light bends outward when it passes through a concave lens.

Retina

Pupil

Optic nerve

Lens

Con lenses b in the mi

How we see light
Light enters your eye through your pupil. It passes through a lens, which focuses the object you are looking at onto the retina. Millions of tiny cells inside the retina turn this upside-down image into electrical messages. The optic nerve carries these messages to your brain, which "sees" the image the right way up.

Light for life
Plants always grow toward the light, even if, like this plant, they have to grow around corners to reach it! Light is very important for life. Plants need light to grow, and we need to eat plants, or animals that eat plants, to stay alive.

The big bang!
Light travels faster than sound. When fireworks explode high in the sky, you see the lights before you hear the loud bang. Light reaches your eyes more quickly than sound reaches your ears.

Over the rainbow
Drops of rain act like tiny prisms. When light passes through raindrops, the colors of light are split up to form a rainbow.

When a beam of light passes through a prism, the colors split apart because each wavelength is bent a different amount.

Light travels in tiny waves. Light has a mixture of different wavelengths.

A prism is a solid, triangle-shaped piece of glass or plastic.

When light is reflected, the beams of light bounce off the mirror at the same angle as they hit it.

light passes gh a convex lens, ent, or refracted, d.

When light hits an object that it can't travel through, such as this mirror, a shadow forms behind the object where the light can't reach.

Busy line
When you talk on the telephone, your voice is turned into laser light signals and sent down very thin fiber glass tubes called optical fibers. Up to 150,000 different conversations can be sent down just one of these optical fibers.

COLOR

Imagine waking up in a world without color. There would be no beautiful paintings or rainbows to look at, and no bright shoes or clothes to wear. At night when you switch off the light, all the bright colors around you suddenly disappear. This is because you cannot see the color of an object without light. White light can be split into all the colors of the rainbow—shades of red, orange, yellow, green, blue, indigo, and violet. When all these colors are mixed back together, they make white light again.

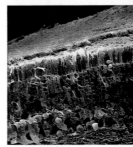

Color cones
The inside of the back of your eye looks like this through a microscope. You have cells in the back of your eyes called cones which send messages to your brain about the colors you see.

Seeing in color
If you don't have all the different types of cones in your eyes, you may find it hard to tell some colors apart. A color-blind person may not be able to see the number on this color blindness test.

White only color that can't be by mixing to the primary colors of

Seeing red
We see things because light bounces off them. Light is actually a mixture of all the colors of the rainbow. When light hits these shoes, all the colors sink in, except the red color that is reflected back to your eyes.

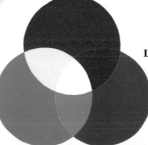

Light mixing
The colors of light behave differently than paint color When red, green, and blue light are mixed together, they make white light. Wh the same colors of paint ar mixed, it makes a dark color

nt mixing
can make new colors
mixing the primary
rs of paint together.

Blue, yellow, and red are the primary colors of paint.

Red and yellow mix to make orange.

Blue and red mix to make purple.

Different shades can be made by adding more of one color than another.

Blue and yellow mix to make green.

Tasty morsels
Which of these dinners do you prefer? Both meals would taste the same, but the food coloring in one puts you off before you start. Color can change our feelings about things, especially food.

Warning colors
Colors are often used as a warning. This moth is poisonous, and its bright wings warn hungry birds to leave it alone. We also use colors to warn us of danger. A red traffic light tells us to stop, but a green traffic light means that it is safe to go.

SOUND

Astronauts talk to each other by radio because their voices can't travel through empty space. Sound travels in waves. When these waves move through air, the air molecules move quickly, or vibrate. If there are no air molecules, no sound is made, because there is nothing to vibrate. When you shout, the vocal cords in your throat vibrate. These vibrations pass through your mouth into the air, making the air itself vibrate. Your ear picks up the vibrations and you can hear them as sound.

Deafening decibels
The loudness of soun is measured in decibel When airplanes land, reach a very high num of decibels. This grou controller is wearing ear protectors to prev being deafened by the noise.

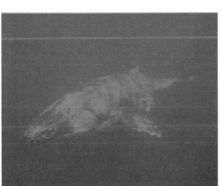

Wailing whales
Whales communicate under water over huge distances. The sound of a great whale may travel hundreds of miles under water. Sound travels faster and farther through liquids and solids than through air. This is because molecules in liquids and solids are more tightly packed.

The bottle tops clink together when the jingling stick is shaken.

Lentils inside the shaker make a soft, rattling sound.

Strings vibrate as the instrument is plucked. The tighter the string, the higher the note.

Seeing sounds
You can show that sound vibrations exist by hitting a tray next to a drum sprinkled with rice. The rice bounces up and down with the vibrations that the sound makes.

Bouncing sound
This pregnant woman can see her baby before it is born because of sound. High-frequency sound waves are reflected as they reach the baby, making an image on the computer screen.

ing a tin pan
kes it vibrate.
hear a loud
crashing noise.

What is frequency?
The number of complete sound waves that pass by in a second gives us the "frequency" of a sound. Frequency is measured in hertz. High notes have a high frequency. They make lots of vibrations, and have a high number of hertz. Low notes have a low frequency.

Hearing sounds
We cannot hear sounds of very high or low frequencies, but some animals can. It is impossible for us to hear these sounds because they are outside our hearing range.

When a wind instrument is played, the air inside the tube vibrates to make a sound.

Blowing into the pipe makes the air inside it vibrate all the way along to the funnel at the end.

Bat
up to 120,000 hertz

Mouse
up to 91,000 hertz

Cat
up to 64,000 hertz

Dog
up to 45,000 hertz

Young person
up to 20,000 hertz

FORCE AND MOVEMENT

A rocket can only take off because a blast of energy forces it to move. Things move if they are pushed or pulled, or if they are high up to start with. The movement they make has a speed in a particular direction. How quickly they speed up depends on how big the force is, and how heavy the moving thing is. Some forces make things move, but others stop things from moving. Friction is the name for the force that stops movement.

Push it

Playing with force
Forces can act in lots of different directions to change the shape of something. Try this for yourself with a lump of modeling clay.

Pull it!

Squeeze it!

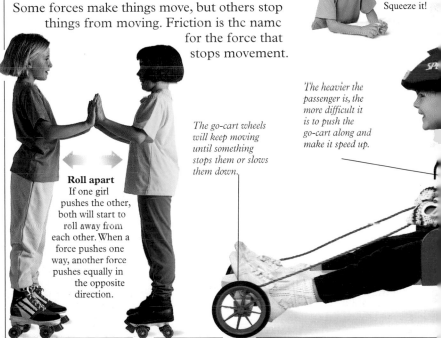

Roll apart
If one girl pushes the other, both will start to roll away from each other. When a force pushes one way, another force pushes equally in the opposite direction.

The go-cart wheels will keep moving until something stops them or slows them down.

The heavier the passenger is, the more difficult it is to push the go-cart along and make it speed up.

Speed and velocity

The time something takes to move a distance is called speed. Velocity is speed in a particular direction. A rocket's velocity is much greater than a snail's!

A snail moves at about 0,003 miles (0.005 km) per hour.

A fast sprinter runs at about 27 miles (43 km) per hour.

A race car reaches speeds of over 257 miles (413 km) per hour.

A rocket needs to travel 25,000 miles (40,000 km) per hour.

Down to earth

When you jump, a strong force called gravity pulls you back down to Earth. Earth's gravity gets weaker as you travel away from it. On the Moon, gravity is much less strong, so astronauts can jump high with heavy packs on their backs before gravity pulls them back down again.

Pushing is a kind of force. The harder the boy pushes, the bigger the force on the go-cart.

Quick stop

Without friction between its wheels and the ground, this truck would slip all over the road. The tires have thick patterns, called tread, to help them grip the ground.

More pushing power is needed to start the go-cart than to keep it moving.

Good performance

At high speeds, air rushes over the top of a racing car, pushing it down onto the track. This makes the wide tires grip the track better, so the car can take bends faster than an ordinary car.

MAGNETS

Magnets are pieces of special material which have an invisible force that can push things away, or pull things towards them. The biggest magnet of all is the world itself. Scientists think that as Earth spins around, electricity is made in the hot metal deep down in its center. This electricity gives Earth magnetic power. Earth has two magnetic poles, called the magnetic North and South Poles. Compass needles always point toward the magnetic North Pole.

Magnetic fields

A magnetic field is where a magnet has its power. If iron filings are sprinkled around a magnet, they gather together where the magnetic field is strongest. Two identical poles push each other away, so iron filings curve outward.
Two different poles attract. The iron filings run straight between them.

Left out
Magnets only attract some kinds of material. Not all metals are attracted by magnets.

Magnets are fun to play with! These magnets are called horseshoe magnets because of their curved shape.

The area where the magnet has its power is called the magnetic field.

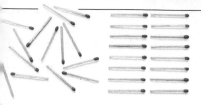

What are magnets?

Scientists think that atoms behave like tiny magnets. In a nonmagnetic material, the atoms face in different directions. In a magnet, all the atoms face the same way. Magnets lose their strength if they are hit, dropped, or heated, as this makes the atoms face in different directions.

The ends of a magnet are called its poles.

N
S

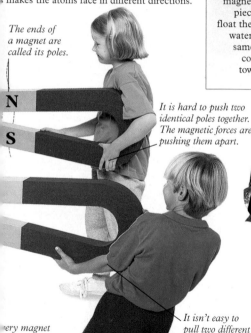

It is hard to push two identical poles together. The magnetic forces are pushing them apart.

Every magnet has two poles, a south pole (S), and a north pole (N).

It isn't easy to pull two different poles apart. The magnetic forces between them hold them close together.

Make a magnet
If you stroke a needle about 50 times with a magnet, it will become magnetic. Stroking the needle in the same direction turns its atoms to face the same way.

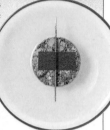

Simple compass
Compasses are made with magnets—see for yourself! Tape your magnetic needle to a piece of cork, and float the cork in some water. It points the same way as a real compass needle— toward the magnetic North Pole.

Electricity and magnets
Electricity is used to make magnets which can be switched on and off. The amount of electric current determines the strength of the magnetic field produced. Reversing the flow of electricity will also reverse the magnet's poles. This electromagnet is used to sort scrap metal.

MACHINES

When you solve a difficult math problem, you are working hard, but this is not what scientists call work! In science, work is only done when something is moved— for example, lifted or turned around. Machines make it easier to move things, so less effort is needed to do a job. Bicycles help us move quickly. Like most machines, bicycles are made up of a number of small, simple machines. Wheels, axles, pulleys, gears, levers, slopes, and screws are all common simple machines.

Forced apart
Wedges are simple machines that split things open. When a force hammers a wedge into a block of wood, the wood is pushed apart. A wedge is a kind of slope.

Fulcrum

Easy does it
Levers make it easier to move things. A seesaw is a kind of lever. It balances on a point called a fulcrum. The girl's weight moves the box up. Moving the fulcrum closer to the box will make it easier to lift.

Saddle sore?
It is possible to ride a long way on a bike—between 1922 and 1973, a Scot named Tommy Chambers cycled 799,405 miles (1,286,517 kilometers)!

Cables link the brake levers to the brake blocks. Pulling the brake levers makes the brake blocks stop the moving wheels.

Brake blocks press against the wheel. They use friction to stop the wheel from moving.

Wheel genius
The wheel is one of our most important machines. Two wheels can be joined together by a pole called an axle. A small movement of an axle makes a big turn of a wheel.

The wheel spins, or rotates, around an axle.

Difficult   Easy

Get into gear

A toothed wheel that turns another toothed wheel is called a gear. Gears change the speed or direction of the moving part of a machine. The small wheel spins around twice as fast as the big wheel, turning in the opposite direction.

Uphill climb

Slopes are simple machines. They make it easier to move things onto a higher or lower level. A screw is a kind of slope. If you could unwind the spiral grooves on a screw, they would flatten out as a slope.

A chain links the gears and the pedals to the back wheel. A small movement of the pedals is turned into a bigger turn of the wheel.

The chain is part of a pulley system.

Light as a feather?

Lifting up a weight with your bare hands is hard work. It is much easier to lift a weight by pulling down on the ropes of a pulley. If you double the number of pulley wheels, the same amount of effort will lift twice as many weights.

...power force that ...ou started.

ENGINES AND MOTORS

Engines and motors provide power to make things move. Motors usually run on electricity, and often drive small things, such as fans or hairdryers. Engines are usually more powerful, and run on heat. In steam engines—the first real engines—heat boils water to make steam, and the steam pushes the engine around, just as steam in a pan of boiling water pushes up the lid. Cars have "internal combustion" engines. In these, the engine pushed around by the gas produced from burning gasoline inside the engine.

A. DEAKIN & SONS, MODERN AMUSEMENT

Boiler to make steam

Letting off steam
Brightly colored steam traction engines like this one were often seen at fairgrounds up until around the middle of the 20th century. The steam traction engine drove the rides and made electricity for the lights.

Electric power
Electric motors work by magnetism. An electric current passing through a coil of wire turns the coil into a very powerful magnet. If the coil is set between another magnet, it is driven around at great speed to power machines, such as your hairdryer.

Magnet

Coil of wire spins around

Jet power
Most modern airplanes have jet engines. These push a blast of hot air out of the back, which drives the plane forward at enormous speed.

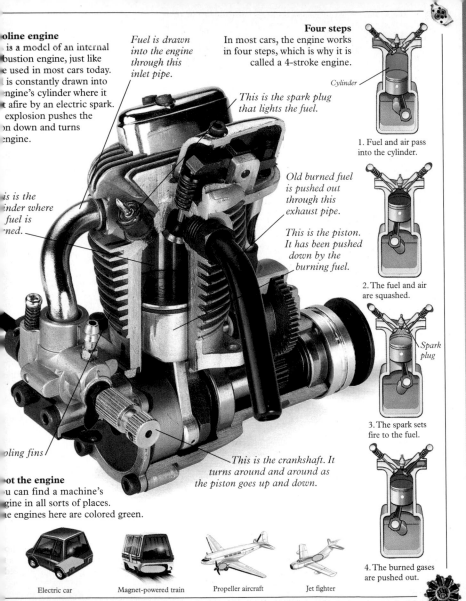

...oline engine

...is a model of an internal ...bustion engine, just like ...e used in most cars today. ...is constantly drawn into ...engine's cylinder where it ...t afire by an electric spark. ...explosion pushes the ...n down and turns ...engine.

Fuel is drawn into the engine through this inlet pipe.

This is the spark plug that lights the fuel.

...is is the ...nder where ...fuel is ...ned.

Old burned fuel is pushed out through this exhaust pipe.

This is the piston. It has been pushed down by the burning fuel.

...ling fins

...ot the engine

...u can find a machine's ...gine in all sorts of places. ...e engines here are colored green.

This is the crankshaft. It turns around and around as the piston goes up and down.

Electric car

Magnet-powered train

Propeller aircraft

Jet fighter

Four steps

In most cars, the engine works in four steps, which is why it is called a 4-stroke engine.

Cylinder

1. Fuel and air pass into the cylinder.

2. The fuel and air are squashed.

Spark plug

3. The spark sets fire to the fuel.

4. The burned gases are pushed out.

WAR MACHINES

An aircraft carrier

Hand grenade

Modern armies have all sorts of weapons, from rifles and grenades for fighting a single enemy, to bombs and missiles for attacking large targets. Soldiers can go into battle riding in a tank—a huge gun on wheels protected by heavy armor plating. But nothing can protect against nuclear bombs, the most powerful weapons of all.

Going bang!

Gunpowder was first used in China more than 1,000 years ago for making fireworks.

In 1605, Guy Fawkes tried to blow up the English Parliament with gunpowder.

In 1867, Alfred Nobel invented a very powerful explosive called dynamite.

The main gun can fire powerful shells that will travel nearly 10,000 feet (3,000 meters).

This is the turret. It turns around so the gun can be aimed in any direction.

The tank can carry a huge amount of fuel—around 420 gallons () 1,900 liters. But it is only enough to drive about 275 miles (440 kilometers) at 25 miles (40 kilometers) an hour.

The commander sits at the top.

The driver sits inside at the front, and uses mirrors to see what is happening outside.

The gunner aims the main gun using a thermal imaging sight. This picks up the heat given out by enemy targets.

The loader loads the main gun with explosive shells. He also operates the radio

...way at sea

...craft carriers are huge ships ...h flat decks which war ...nes use for taking off and ...ding. The carriers sail close ...nemy coasts so the planes ...launch attacks.

...ne of the crew uses a ...achine gun to defend ...e tank against ...emy aircraft.

Getting up speed

Muskets were used by soldiers in the 17th century. They needed reloading after each shot.

Heavy steel armor up to five inches (13 centimeters) thick protects the crew from enemy fire.

Handguns like this Colt 45 were carried about 150 years ago by cowboys in the American west. They could fire six bullets without being reloaded.

Machine guns were invented in 1884 by Sir Hiram Maxim. They could fire dozens of bullets one after the other.

The wheels run inside tough metal bands called caterpillar tracks. To steer, the driver makes one track run faster than the other.

Destruction caused by a nuclear bomb in Hiroshima, Japan, 1945.

Nuclear weapons

A single nuclear bomb can destroy a whole city, and the radiation it leaves behind can kill people and animals years later. There are now enough nuclear weapons to destroy the world.

... nuclear explosion

...As the bomb ...lodes, it ...akes a ...giant ...reball.

2. The explosion shakes the city below.

3. The blast and fire destroy buildings.

4. A cloud of rubble and dust mushrooms up high into the sky.

COMPUTER MAGIC

Computers are the world's smartest machines. Inside a computer are thousands of very tiny electronic switches, a bit like light switches. By switching them on and off in different combinations, computers can perform all kinds of tasks. They are used everywhere, from factories and hospitals to stores and offices. Some guide aircraft, ships, submarines, and spacecraft. Others are used just for having fun, such as playing games and watching movies.

Keeping your head up
A jet fighter pilot must not take their eyes off the view ahead, even for a second. All the information they need to control the plane and fire at targets is fed to a computer, and projected onto the pilot's face mask. This is called a "head-up" display.

Seeing inside
Doctors can use a CT (computed tomography) scanner to see inside a patient's body. A CT scanner uses X-rays to create images of "slices" through the body. These are put together on a computer to create a 3-D image, which doctors use to see what needs treating.

Bytes and megabytes
Computers can help
with homework,
or steer a rocket
into space.

Pocket brain
The first electronic computers
filled a large room. Now there
are smarter and faster
computers that
can be held in
your hand, such as
this smartphone.

Laptop computer

Shrinking switches
The switches in
computers have gotten
steadily smaller, and
more complicated.

Tablet computer

*The first computers
had glass valve
switches as big as
your thumb.*

Global positioning
system (GPS)

Gaming device

*Computers now have
microprocessors. They are
only the size of a small
fingernail, yet packed
with billions of switches.*

Data center

ROBOTS

Robots are machines that "think" with a computer brain that tells them what to do. Once they have been programmed, they can work entirely by themselves. Some people believe that one day we will be able to make robots that can do everything a human can—and they may even look like humans. Right now, though, most robots in use today are nothing more than mechanical arms or cranes.

The camera in Asimo's head allows him to see objects, plan routes, and even recognize faces.

Asimo automatically bends or twists his body to keep balanced while walking or running.

Mechanical men
Automatons are smart machines that move kind of like humans or animals. This one was made for a fair in Victorian times.

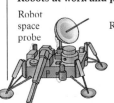

Factory hand
A factory robot is often just a moving arm. But a robotic arm can hold things, screw them into place, weld them, and check that they work. It can replace lots of human workers.

Robots at work and play

Robot space probe

Robot dog

Bomb-disposal robot

Robotic arm

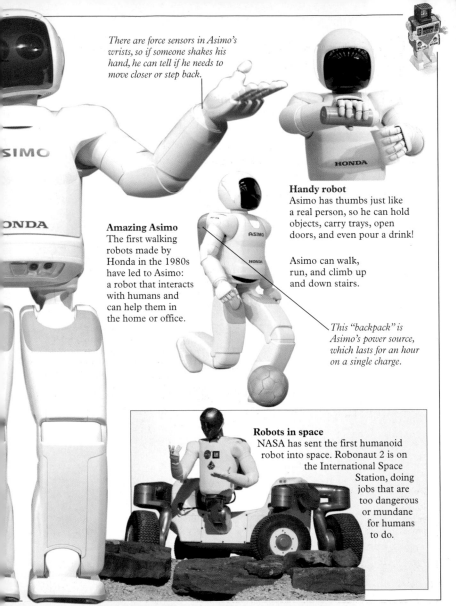

There are force sensors in Asimo's wrists, so if someone shakes his hand, he can tell if he needs to move closer or step back.

Handy robot
Asimo has thumbs just like a real person, so he can hold objects, carry trays, open doors, and even pour a drink!

Asimo can walk, run, and climb up and down stairs.

Amazing Asimo
The first walking robots made by Honda in the 1980s have led to Asimo: a robot that interacts with humans and can help them in the home or office.

This "backpack" is Asimo's power source, which lasts for an hour on a single charge.

Robots in space
NASA has sent the first humanoid robot into space. Robonaut 2 is on the International Space Station, doing jobs that are too dangerous or mundane for humans to do.

ENERGY AND INDUSTRY

Oil

In today's world there are thousands of different industries, and they are divided into three groups. Primary industries, such as farming and mining, take raw materials from the earth. Manufacturing industries make, or manufacture, things from the raw materials. Service industries are made up of people who sell these goods or supply skills, such as nursing or teaching. All industry needs energy, so as the world becomes more industrial, it needs more and more energy.

Energy for industry comes mostly from fossil fuels—coal, oil, and gas. Since these are quickly being used up, we are now switching to solar, wind, and ocean energy that will last forever.

Wind is a type of endless energy.

Oil

Coal

Natural gas

Nuclear energy

iron ore

Steel is made from iron ore.

Cars are made from steel.

Microchips manufactured on a silicon slice.

Nylon rope

Stores are part of the service industry.

Factories put things together, one step at a time, in production lines.

COAL

Like layers of icing in a cake, there are bands, or seams, of coal in the rocks beneath the ground. Some seams are near enough to the surface to be scraped out with diggers. This is called opencast mining. But most seams are found deeper down, and have to be dug up by miners using massive machines. About 40 percent of the nine billion tons of coal mined each year is burned in power stations to generate electricity.

Cooking coke
Coal is put into giant ovens and baked at more than 1,650°F (900°C). When the oven door is opened, coke topples out. Coke is needed to make steel.

Coke is coal minus tar, oils, and gases.

The tar that collects at the bottom of a coke oven is used to make soap!

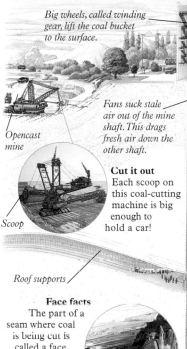

Big wheels, called winding gear, lift the coal bucket to the surface.

Opencast mine

Fans suck stale air out of the mine shaft. This drags fresh air down the other shaft.

Cut it out
Each scoop on this coal-cutting machine is big enough to hold a car!

Scoop

Roof supports

Face facts
The part of a seam where coal is being cut is called a face. The coal is ripped out by a spinning cutter with steel teeth.

Coal face

A big bucket carries coal to the surface.

Water is sprayed onto the coal to cut down the coal dust.

Conveyor belt

Pumps take water from the bottom of the mine.

Air in

Computer
control room

The coal is washed
and separated into
different-sized
lumps before it
leaves the mine.

Burning to go
Nonstop trains
take coal straight
to the power station.

Cages carry miners
down a deep shaft.

The main
shaft was
blown out of
the rock with
explosives.

All aboard!
Miners travel on trains
to coal faces that are
many miles away
from the shaft.

Long tunnels are
dug to reach new
coal seams.

Most of the coal
in this seam has
already been
dug out.

A breeze can always
be felt in the tunnel
as the air moves
through the mine.

Boring!
Big machines
chew through
the rock to open
up new tunnels.

Mine shafts can be
4,000 feet (1,200
meters) deep.

Down to earth

Not all coal is the same.
Hard coals, which are found
deeper underground, release
more energy when they burn.

Half-squashed coal, or
peat, is made into fuel bricks.

Soft, crumbly brown coal
is burned to make coke.

Black bituminous coal is
burned to generate electricity.

Anthracite coal is used in
houses and factories.

Davy's
safety lamp

Seeing the light
Miners once worked by candlelight,
but the flames often set fire to the
explosive gases that build
up in tunnels. In 1815,
a safety lamp was
invented. Its flame
was kept behind a
wire mesh. Modern
lamps are even
safer, as they are
battery powered.

OIL

In the rocks under hot deserts, snowy plains, and stormy seas, there is buried treasure: a "liquid gold" called oil. Most of this sticky, black fossil fuel is used for energy, but 12 percent of each barrel is turned into chemicals and plastics. All oil is brought to the surface by drilling deep holes called wells. On land this is fairly easy, but at sea, platforms as tall as skyscrapers have to be built.

Sandstone

Sandstone with oil

Solid "sponge"
Oil is found in the tiny spaces in rocks such as sandstone. This oily layer is often sandwiched between water and a layer of natural gas.

Each marble stands for a grain of rock.

Natural gas

Trapped oil

Water

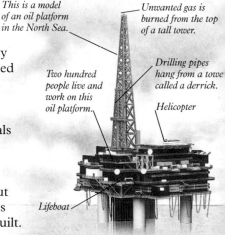

This is a model of an oil platform in the North Sea.

Unwanted gas is burned from the top of a tall tower.

Drilling pipes hang from a tower called a derrick.

Two hundred people live and work on this oil platform.

Helicopter

Lifeboat

Every day, one quarter of a million barrels of hot, freshly drilled oil are pumped into the hollow concrete legs to cool down.

Some o piped a giga underw sto t

Cooled oil is piped ashore.

A boring bit
A sharp-toothed metal cutter, called a bit, bores through rock to reach oil. Drill bits are replaced twice a day, as they wear out quickly.

During drilling, chemicals are pumped around the bit to carry rubble up to the surface.

Explosives are used to make cracks in the rock so that oil can flow into the wells.

Oil

Water

Gas

An arched layer oilproof rock, suc as granite, traps underneath it.

Wells fan out to reach the oil.

Only way out
A 769 mile long (1,287-kilometer-long) pipe snakes across the snowy wastes of Alaska. Oil takes a whole week to flow down the pipe to reach an ice-free port in the South.

Oil at sea
Huge structures, called rigs, drill down to find oil. At sea, some rigs float on the surface, while others stand on the sea bed.

Huge tankers "plug into" this oil store to take on oil.

Tankers can take oil all over the world.

Look how big this rig is compared to the Statue of Liberty!

Jack-up rig

Anchors keep the oil store on the sea bed.

Pump it up
Not all oil gushes to the surface naturally. Some is pumped up by machines called nodding donkeys! This "donkey" has been painted to look like a grasshopper.

Drill ship

This zigzag break in the picture is to show that oil is usually found under thousands of yards of rock.

Semisubmersible rig

Gas gushes out when the pressure is released.

Wildcat wanted?
Before a well is dug, geologists must be sure that the rocks below the ground are the right shape to trap oil. A test drill, or "wildcat," is only started if the surveys and satellite pictures look good.

Bubble trouble
Just like the fizz in soda pop, bubbles of natural gas are trapped in oil. If there is enough gas, it is piped ashore. If not, the gas is just burned.

NATURAL GAS

What a whiff!
Natural gas has no smell. Chemicals are added to it so that leaks can be smelled.

In 1918, a gas was discovered in an oilfield in Texas. It was named natural gas because it replaced a gas that was manufactured from coal. This new fuel is now used in factories and homes all over the world. Natural gas travels a long way before it reaches your stove, to burn as a bright blue flame. It has to be released from deep below the ground, cleaned, and piped countless miles.

The journey begins at a gas rig.

Gas terminal

Mostly methane
Natural gas contains three different gases. Butane and propane are taken out at a gas terminal. Methane, the part that burns best, is sent through pipes to houses and factories.

Giant fans waft natural gas along the pipes.

Pipe

Butane gas camping stove

"Pig"

Cool it
Ships take methane to places that are not connected to pipelines. The gas is cooled into a liquid so that it takes up 600 times less room.

If it is cooled into a liquid, a balloonful of methane gas can fit into a space the size of a pea.

Methane is cooled to -260°F (-162°C) to make it turn into a liquid.

Methane tank

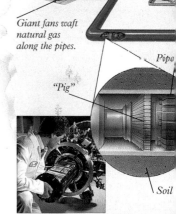

Soil

Very important pig
"Pigs," not people, check natural gas pipes!
A "pig" is a computer on wheels that whizzes down pipes to pinpoint cracks and other problems

On the way up
This big building, called a rig, gathers up gas that flows from deep under the sea bed. The drill to reach the pocket of gas may be nearly four miles (six kilometers) long.

Some gas is stored near homes to supply sudden daily demands—such as at dinner time!

The roof floats on top of the gas. So the lower the roof is, the less gas is left.

Iron pipe

The plastic gas pipe is dragged through the tunnel by the "mole."

Road

Gas is sent through pipes to homes and factories.

The "mole" smashes through the earth like a pneumatic drill.

Pumping stations keep the gas moving.

"Mole" hole

Growing gas
Farms off the coast of California grow a giant seaweed called kelp. It is harvested three times a year by special ships and then put in tanks and left to rot. The decaying kelp gives off methane gas.

Moles beat diggers
Small pipes can be laid without digging up streets by using a rocketlike machine called a "mole." Its route is guided by a computer.

What size pipe?

You could stand up in the pipe that travels between the rig and the terminal.

A dog could fit into the pipe that links factory pipes to gas-terminal pipes.

The pipes that take gas to factories is roomy enough for a cat to sit in.

A mouse could fit into the small plastic pipe that goes into your home.

NUCLEAR ENERGY

Super fuel
One handful of pure uranium can release as much energy as 72,000 barrels of oil!

Atoms are the tiny particles that make up the whole universe. Enormous amounts of energy are locked inside atoms. When billions of uranium atoms are torn apart in a nuclear power station, the energy that is set free can boil water. Steam from this hot water is used to generate electricity. People worry about nuclear power because when the energy is released from an atom, deadly rays, called radiation, also escape.

Not so fast
This drawing shows very sim how neutrons whizz around nuclear reactor and crash int uranium atoms in fuel rods.

2. The split uranium ato inside the fuel "shoot out" neutrons wh travel at 9, miles (16,000 per seco

1. Energy released w neutrons hit ato in the fuel r

Water warms up.

Fuel rod

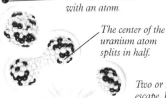

A neutron collides with an atom

The center of the uranium atom splits in half.

Two or three new neutrons escape. Each one can collide with another atom and set free more energy.

Energy and radiation

Old fuel rods are radioactive "garbage."

Cold water

Fission division
The heart of an atom, called a nucleus, is made up of neutrons and protons. These are held together by energy. When an atom is split, some of this energy is set free. Splitting an atom to release energy is called fission.

Cool it
Fuel rods are replaced every few years. Before the reusable uranium ca be removed from them, the rods are cooled in a special pond.

Moderator

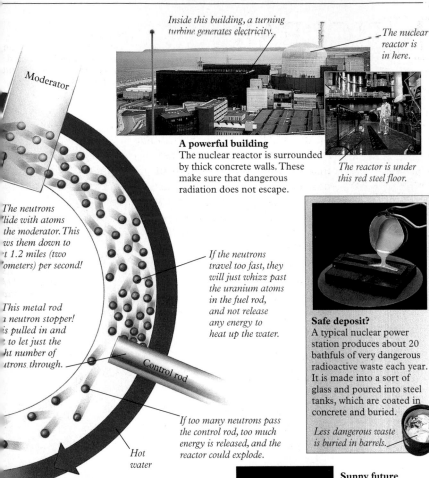

Inside this building, a turning turbine generates electricity.

The nuclear reactor is in here.

A powerful building
The nuclear reactor is surrounded by thick concrete walls. These make sure that dangerous radiation does not escape.

The reactor is under this red steel floor.

The neutrons lide with atoms the moderator. This ws them down to t 1.2 miles (two ometers) per second!

If the neutrons travel too fast, they will just whizz past the uranium atoms in the fuel rod, and not release any energy to heat up the water.

This metal rod n neutron stopper! s pulled in and to let just the ht number of utrons through.

Control rod

If too many neutrons pass the control rod, too much energy is released, and the reactor could explode.

Hot water

5. *Heat passes from the hot water inside the reactor to this flow of cold water. The cold water boils into steam.*

6. *The powerful jet of steam turns a turbine to generate electricity.*

Safe deposit?
A typical nuclear power station produces about 20 bathfuls of very dangerous radioactive waste each year. It is made into a sort of glass and poured into steel tanks, which are coated in concrete and buried.

Less dangerous waste is buried in barrels.

Laser beam

Sunny future
When superhot atoms collide, they fuse together and set energy free. It is this fusion that makes the sun shine. Scientists are trying to build "suns" on Earth by firing lasers at atoms.

RENEWABLE ENERG

When oil, gas, and coal run out, people will need other sources of energy to fuel their cars and light their houses. Wind and water are already being put to work, but the best hope for a renewable supply of energy is the sun. Light and heat from the sun pour down onto Earth all the time. Today, sunshine runs everything from watches to power stations. One day scientists hope to collect sunlight in space, and beam it back to Earth!

What a gas!
In some countries manure is collected, dumped into containers, and left to rot. The gas it gives off is piped into homes and used for cooking and heating.

Trick of the light
This is the world's first solar power station. It was built in 1969 at Odeillo in France. Electricity is generated by using reflected sunlight to boil water into steam.

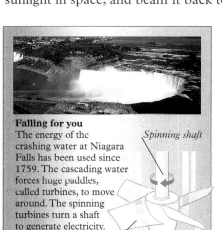

Falling for you
The energy of the crashing water at Niagara Falls has been used since 1759. The cascading water forces huge paddles, called turbines, to move around. The spinning turbines turn a shaft to generate electricity.

Spinning shaft

Whooshing water pushes the paddles around.

This enormous mirror is curved so that all the sunshine that hits it is reflected onto one small spot at the top of the tower.

Computers keep the 63 minimirrors facing the sun.

Not alone
The solar power station is faced by 63 small, flat mirrors. They reflect extra light onto the main mirror.

Whizzing in the wind

Strong, steady winds can be put to work turning windmill blades. As the blades spin, they turn a shaft that generates electricity. These modern windmills come in several shapes. Groups of them are called wind farms.

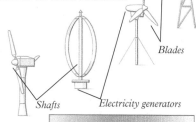

Blades

Shafts *Electricity generators*

Reflection of the ground

A solar power station does not need a chimney—there are no fumes or ash!

This mirror is 140 feet (42 meters) wide. It is built onto the side of a building.

Water inside this tower turns to steam.

It can get as hot as 6,900°F (3,800°C) inside this tower.

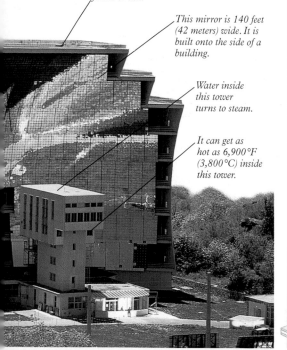

No need for a plug

Solar cells, made from slices of wafer-thin silicon, turn sunlight into electricity. This remote jungle telephone is powered by several solar cells.

Sunlight knocks electrons from the top layer to the bottom layer of silicon. This generates an electric current that is collected by the metal layers.

Sunlight *Metal*

Silicon

Metal

ELECTRICITY

Electricity is used as a way of moving energy from place to place. It can take energy from burning a fuel, such as coal or gas, in a power station into your home to work your television. Most electricity is generated in machines. Small machines, called dynamos, light the lights on bikes. Huge generators in power stations light whole cities. Pedal power works a dynamo, but steam produces the electricity in a power station. This steam is made by using the heat from burning fossil fuels or splitting atoms. Sunshine, falling water, and whirling windmills can also generate electricity.

Dynamo

Mighty machine
The big blue generator inside this power station is about ten times as tall as you!

This magnet spins around because it is fixed to a rod that touches the turning wheel.

Electricity is generated in this coil of wire by the spinning magnet.

Chimney

3. Steam surges from the boiler into the generator. It pushes around huge paddles, called turbines.

2. The burning coal makes water turn into steam.

4. Turbines turn a massive magnet 50 times per second.

5. The moving magnet creates an electric current in the coils of wire.

First transformer

A pile of coal as heavy as 40 elephants is burned each hour.

1. Coal is crushed and then blown into the boiler to burn.

A condenser turns the hot steam into hot water.

Choice of fuels
A power station uses just one sort of fuel to generate its electricity. This one burns coal, but other power stations use oil, natural gas, or nuclear fuel.

Oil

Natural gas

Uranium

The cooling tower cools the hot water so that it can be used again.

In charge

Power stations can't be built near all the places that need electricity. So the electricity generated flows into a network of cables, called a grid. At the touch of a button, electricity is made to flow to wherever it is needed.

...ectricity is dangerous, ...tall pylons hold the ...g cables high above ...ground.

Second transformer

Electricity cables are laid under the ground in towns and cities.

A substation makes electricity safe for you to use in your home.

Aluminum cable

Energy travels down the cables at about 155,000 miles (250,000 kilometers) per second— almost as fast as the speed of light!

Going up or going down?

Machines called transformers change the strength of an electric current. The current that flows between pylons has to be decreased to stop the cables from melting.

...ese children
...pretending
...e tiny parts
...toms, called
...trons.

Each ball is a "parcel" of electrical energy.

Pass the parcel

People once thought that electricity flowed like water, which is why it was called a current. In fact, energy moves along a cable more like balls being passed down a line!

Watt is power?

The speed at which different machines use energy is measured in units called watts.

Electric clock
(10 watts)

Vacuum cleaner
(900 watts)

Welding machine
(10,000 watts)

111

METALS

Metals are found in the ground, hidden in certain rocks called ores. Tin, copper, and iron all have to be taken out of their ores before a factory can melt and shape them into a can, pan, or car. Pure metals, however, are usually too weak to be used in industry, and have to be mixed together to make better metals called alloys. Lead is soft, and tin breaks easily. Together they can make a strong, tough alloy known as pewter.

Iron ore

Copper pan

Not natural
Brass cannot be dug out of the ground. It is an alloy made by mixing together two weaker metals, copper and zinc.

Brass is stronger than zinc or copper.

Zinc-coated bucket and wire

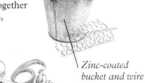

Precious metals
Gold and silver are used to make much more than just jewelry. Gold is sprayed onto an astronaut's visor to reflect sunlight. Silver is used in electronic equipment because it carries electricity very well.

Limestone

Crushed iron ore

Coke

Bla furr

Steel from iron
Iron has a lot of carbon in it, which makes it crack easily. If some carbon is removed, iron turns into superstrong steel. This change starts in a blast furnace.

Coke, limestone, and iron ore heat up and turn into iron and a waste material called slag.

H a

Iron

Slag

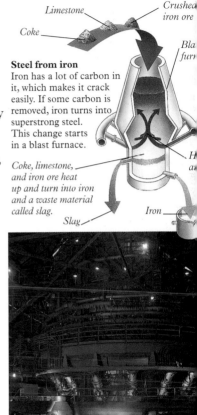

1. Blasted iron ore
A stream of iron is flowing from this huge oven, called a blast furr It has been burned out of iron or by blasts of hot air.

Plane wrapper
Aluminum is a marvelous metal. Thin sheets are wrapped around chocolate to preserve its taste. Thick sheets are made into jumbo jets. Aluminium is used to make planes because it does not rust, and it is very light. The aluminium is made as stiff as steel by adding a little copper.

g dipper
eel girders are dipped in a bath
melted zinc to stop them from
sting. This process is known
galvanizing.

Iron waiting to be converted

Oxygen rushes down this tube.

Upright converter

Scrap iron can be put into the converter, too.

In 40 minutes the converter can make 385 tons of steel.

Rust buster
You would not want to eat with rusty cutlery! So chromium is added to steel to make an alloy called stainless steel.

Tipped-up converter

When the strips of steel are cold they can be squashed by rollers into flat slabs.

Hot steel

2. Iron in, steel out
The liquid iron is poured into a converter. After a powerful jet of oxygen has burned out the impurities and most of the carbon, the converter is tipped up to pour out steel.

3. Taking shape
Hot, freshly made steel is poured into a big tray. When it has almost set, nozzles are opened and steel oozes out, like toothpaste out of a tube.

MAKING A CAR

Model T

Every few seconds, somewhere in the world, a brand-new car rolls off a production line and out of a car factory. Each car is made from raw materials, such as iron ore, sulphur, and sand, which have been shaped into more than 30,000 parts! Most of this "jigsaw puzzle" is put together on a kind of giant conveyor belt. Each area of the factory puts on a few particular pieces; for example, the body shop adds the roof, but never the seats. The first car made like this was the Model T Ford.

Stamp it out
Sheets of cold steel are stamped into shape by machines called presses. A press room can be the size of three football stadiums!

Each car body is made from more than 20 pieces, or panels, of steel.

Press

Steel

The start of the "conveyor belt."

About 65 percent of a car is made of iron and steel.

Start with steel
Steel is the most important ingredient for making cars. Rolling mills press hot steel into thin sheets. These are then rolled up and sent to car factories.

A roller test is used to check that the car is working.

Apart from their color, all the cars made on this production line are the same.

Cars are washed and polished before they leave the factory to be sold.

Ready to go
Cars were invented toward the end of the 19th century. There are now more than one billion of them.

Built to bounce
To make your journey smooth, tires are made of rubber and filled with air.

Strands of steel or nylon strengthen the tires.

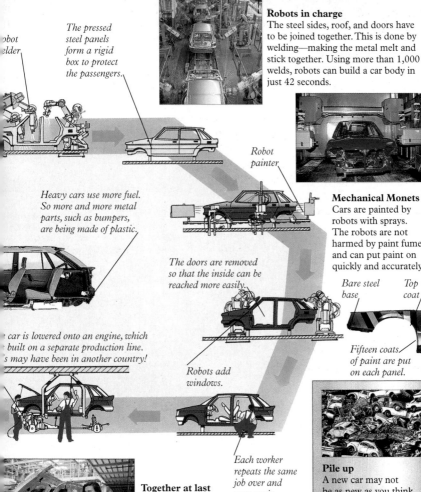

bot elder

The pressed steel panels form a rigid box to protect the passengers.

Robots in charge
The steel sides, roof, and doors have to be joined together. This is done by welding—making the metal melt and stick together. Using more than 1,000 welds, robots can build a car body in just 42 seconds.

Robot painter

Heavy cars use more fuel. So more and more metal parts, such as bumpers, are being made of plastic.

Mechanical Monets
Cars are painted by robots with sprays. The robots are not harmed by paint fumes, and can put paint on quickly and accurately.

The doors are removed so that the inside can be reached more easily.

Bare steel base   *Top coat*

car is lowered onto an engine, which built on a separate production line. s may have been in another country!

Fifteen coats of paint are put on each panel.

Robots add windows.

Each worker repeats the same job over and over again.

Together at last
The engine is the heart of the car, but it is not added to the body until near the end of the production line.

Pile up
A new car may not be as new as you think. Up to 25 percent of the steel may have come from old cars! Recycling scrap steel saves raw materials and energy.

CHEMICAL INDUSTRIES

Soap, fertilizer, and glue are just a few of the useful products of the chemical industries. They are made by combining different substances. Crude oil (unprocessed oil taken straight from the ground) is the main raw material for these industries. The carbon and hydrogen in oil can be made to combine in different ways to make more than half a million things, such as gas, paint, or pills! This manufacturing starts in large factories called refineries.

Oil refinery

Distillation tower

230°F (110 °C)

Split it up!
Crude oil is split into useful oils inside a distillation tower at a refinery. The oils are separated by being boiled into a gas, and then cooled back into a liquid.

Cooling oil drips from the edge of this "saucer" into the tray below.

Kerosene is the fuel used by airplanes.

360°F (180 °C)

Liquid again
If you put a saucer over a cup of steaming hot liquid, droplets collect on the saucer. The liquid has turned into steam and then cooled back into a liquid when it hit the cold saucer.

The cloud of crude oil gets cooler and cooler as it wafts up the tower.

Lubricating oil makes machines run smoothly.

At 725°F (385 °C), crude oil turns into a gas.

Crude oil is pumped into a furnace to be boiled into a gas.

Very hot liquid turns into a gas.   Gas cools into a liquid.

All change

Chlorine keeps the water in swimming pools clean and safe to swim in. It is made in a factory by passing electricity through salty water. The electric current makes the atoms in the salt and water rearrange, and produces chlorine.

Catalytic cracker

Oil is made up of long chains of carbon and hydrogen atoms. Useful chemicals, called petrochemicals, are made by breaking up these chains. This is done by heating the oil in tanks called catalytic crackers. The small chains can be used to make useful things such as shampoo.

Carbon atom — *Hydrogen atom*

Hydrogen atoms are forced between the carbon atoms to break up the chain.

Antiseptic liquid

Nail polish

Shampoo — *Plastics*

The gases that come out of the top of the tower are made into plastics.

One-fifth of each barrel of crude oil separates into gasoline.

Gasoline is the most common fuel used to power cars.

When the cloud of crude oil reaches this height, it is cool enough for diesel to turn into a liquid.

Diesel is the fuel used by many trains.

A different oil flows out of each pipe because all the oils in crude oil cool into liquids at different temperatures.

Dark industrial oil is burned in factories and power stations.

Bitumen is the first oil to flow out of the tower.

Thick, sticky bitumen is spread on the surface of roads.

Super sulphur

About 165 million tons of sulphuric acid are used every year to help make things such as fertilizer, paper, and explosives. This acid is made by heating a yellow rock called sulphur.

PLASTICS

Plastics are amazing materials. They don't rot like wood or rust like some metals, and they are light and easy to shape. Plastic pens, shoes, and even surfboards are all made from oil or coal. Chemicals are taken from these fossil fuels and turned into small, white pellets. These are then melted and blown to form bags or rolled flat to make floor tiles. Buckets, bowls, and boxes are usually shaped by being injected into molding machines.

Get set or go?
Some plastics are like bread! Once they have been "baked" they cannot be reheated and made into new shapes. A mug made of melamine will not change shape when hot drinks are poured into it. Polystyrene and polythene are more like chocolate—they can be melted again and again. Each time the mixture cools, it sets into the shape of the mold it has been poured into.

The two halves of the steel mold lock tightly together.

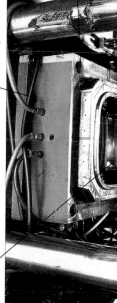

Bowled out
Plastic bowls are made by injecting melted plastic pellets into the space between two halves of a steel mold. The plastic cools inside the mold, and sets into a bowl shape.

Cold water cools down the plastic after it has been molded.

Coloring and plastic pellets are poured in.

Heaters help to melt the pellets.

New bowl

Mold

A screw pushes the squashed, hot pellets into the mold.

Melted plastic

Each bowl needs this amount of coloring.

Two handfuls of polypropylene plastic pellets make each bowl.

Temperatures of 540°F (280°C) are needed to melt the pellets and make them flow into this mold.

Don't throw it away

Plastic litter can create harmful pollution. It is best to reuse or recycle plastic because throwing it away is a waste of energy. Most plastic "garbage" can be turned into new things, such as filling for sleeping bags or coats.

Plastic products

Nose cone

Some planes' nose cones are made from composite plastic.

Many electronic gadgets, such as game consoles, are made of a tough plastic called ABS.

Each half of this bowl mold weighs as much as 20 eight-year-old children!

This half of the mold moves back to let the warm, newly shaped bowl drop onto a conveyor belt.

Four bowls can be made in a minute.

Under the rim, you may see a line. This is where the two halves of the mold met.

Jets of air blow the bowl off the mold when it is finished.

Every bowl that comes out of this machine is exactly the same shape.

Food slides off the slippery plastic, known as Teflon, used to coat the surface of nonstick pans.

Plastic packaging keeps food fresh for longer. For example, polythene bags stop bread from drying out.

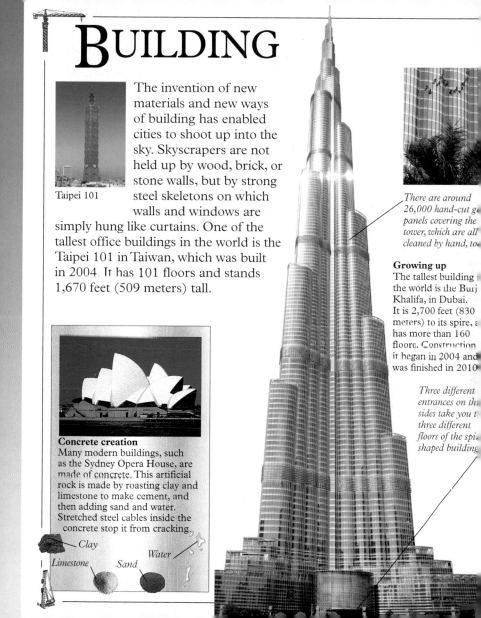

BUILDING

The invention of new materials and new ways of building has enabled cities to shoot up into the sky. Skyscrapers are not held up by wood, brick, or stone walls, but by strong steel skeletons on which walls and windows are simply hung like curtains. One of the tallest office buildings in the world is the Taipei 101 in Taiwan, which was built in 2004. It has 101 floors and stands 1,670 feet (509 meters) tall.

Taipei 101

There are around 26,000 hand-cut g... panels covering the tower, which are all cleaned by hand, to...

Growing up
The tallest building ... the world is the Burj Khalifa, in Dubai. It is 2,700 feet (830 meters) to its spire, a... has more than 160 floors. Construction it began in 2004 and was finished in 2010...

Three different entrances on th... sides take you t... three different floors of the spi... shaped building...

Concrete creation
Many modern buildings, such as the Sydney Opera House, are made of concrete. This artificial rock is made by roasting clay and limestone to make cement, and then adding sand and water. Stretched steel cables inside the concrete stop it from cracking.

Clay

Water

Limestone

Sand

It took about 22 million man-hours to complete the tower.

re are tages where ower gets ower as it taller.

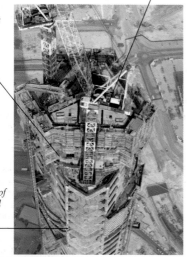

re are 00 tons of orced steel in the r—enough ach more a quarter of vay around vorld.

A team of more than 380 people worked to put on the glass and metal cladding— as many as 175 panels a day.

Building bridges

Simple beam bridges can span narrow streams, but bridge designs get more complicated.

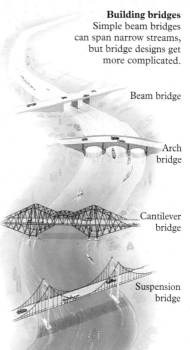

Beam bridge

Arch bridge

Cantilever bridge

Suspension bridge

Rock steady

Buildings need a strong base, or foundation, to stop them from sinking, slipping sideways, or being blown over by the wind. Tall buildings are held down by long steel or cement piles.

Steel frame

Concrete base

Piles are pushed into solid rock.

Soft rock

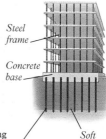

TRANSPORTATION

Transportation is so much a part of our daily lives that most of us take it for granted. Without it, we would all grind to a halt. Millions of people would not get to work, many children would not get to school, and no goods would be delivered to stores. Even the letters we send would never reach their destinations.

Early people relied on animal transportation, and this remained the only way of getting around until about 200 years ago, when the bicycle was invented. Cars didn't come into common use until the first part of the 20th century Today, though, a jet plane can fly you across the world in hours, and huge spacecraft take astronauts on exploratory journeys into space. Soon, you may be able to book a ticket to outer space!

Motor scooter

Electric car

Some pilots like to perform displays of flying called aerobatics, in which they twist and turn their planes.

Boeing 787 taking off

19th-century sailing ship

The TGV train is the fastest wheeled train in the world.

Container ship

BIKES

Bicycles were invented in the late 1700s. But they have changed their shape so much over the years that some early bikes such as the "ordinary" bicycle, also called the penny-farthing, look very strange to us today. Power for a bicycle comes from the rider, but sometimes the rider simply runs out of energy! In 1885 a German, Gottlieb Daimler, added an engine to the bicycle, and the motorcycle was invented. The very first motorcycles had tiny steam engines, but today they have gasoline engines, and can more than match cars for speed.

Fix it yourself
Bicycles are simple machines and one of the cheapest forms of transportation. Most repairs on bicycles are quite simple, too, and can be done cheaply and easily by their owners.

Pollution-free traffic
In the Netherlands, there are more bicycles than people. Nearly 40 percent of all trips taken in the capital, Amsterdam, are on bikes. Imagine the terrible fumes, and the effect on the environment if all these riders drove cars instead of pollution-free bicycles.

Protective helmet

Reflective strips help motorists to see cyclists at night.

The pedals are linked to the back wheel by a chain.

The brakes are operated by levers on the handlebars.

iding a motorcycle n be dangerous, and rider should wear uther clothes and special helmet for otection.

Working bikes

Scooters, which are motorcycles with small engines, are used for many jobs around the world. The Spanish Post Office uses yellow scooters for delivering most of its mail. Bicycles can also be adapted for carrying all sorts of things—even pigs!

There are storage compartments under the seat.

This part can be removed to make a seat for a passenger.

Hot wheels

Motorcycles come in all shapes and sizes for different jobs and sports.

World War II
US Army motorcycle

1966 police motorcycle

1983 Racing motorcycle

Motocross motorcycle

ie panels of this motorcycle are aped so the bike will cut smoothly rough the air. Its top speed is 8 miles (238 kilometers) an hour.

The motorcycle engine runs on gasoline.

The exhaust carries waste fumes from the engine.

CARS TODAY

It is hard to imagine a world without cars. They are all around us and are always being improved to make them more comfortable, more reliable, faster, and safer. And cars must continue to change. There are now so many cars in the world that they are one of the greatest threats to our environment. Experts are constantly thinking of new ways to make affordable cars that use less energy and produce less pollution.

Safety first
Engineers test all new car designs for safety by crashin the car and filming what happens to the dummies ins Most cars have airbags in th steering wheel that inflate i fraction of a second in a cra

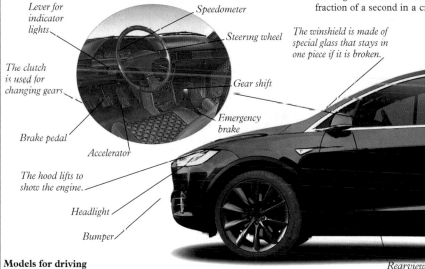

Lever for indicator lights

Speedometer

Steering wheel

The winshield is made of special glass that stays in one piece if it is broken.

The clutch is used for changing gears

Gear shift

Emergency brake

Brake pedal

Accelerator

The hood lifts to show the engine.

Headlight

Bumper

Rearview mirror

Models for driving
Cars are designed to suit the needs of many different people.

Mini car

Sedan car

Sports car

Family car

Record-breaker
Cars like this are the fastest around. In 1997, ThrustSSC set a new Supersonic World Land Speed Record, traveling at 763 miles (1228.5 kilometers) per hour.

Sticking to the road
Race cars have low bodies, an airfoil or "wing" at the back that pushes the car down, and wide, gripping tires. These are all designed to keep the car firmly on the road at speeds of up to 230 miles (370 kilometers) an hour.

*body is
ngthened to
like a
ective "cage."*

This door opens wide so that luggage can be stored in the back.

Cars of the future
Most gasoline engines are quite noisy and give off harmful fumes. Electric cars are quieter and cleaner, although their batteries need charging. Some futuristic cars, such as the Fun-Vii concept car (above), can even display pictures on their outsides.

Filling up with gas

These lights are used to tell the driver behind if the car is going to turn, brake, or reverse. They also show where the car is in the dark.

*ires grip the road
all weathers.*

Pickup truck

Stretch limousine

Camper van

זהירות! מטען חורג

TRUCKS

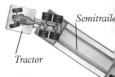

Trucks come in all shapes and sizes, and do very different jobs. Some trucks are very specialized and are used for essential services, such as collecting garbage and fighting fires. Most trucks, however, are used for transporting goods. Trucks are ideal for this job because they can deliver things right to your door. Even goods carried by trains, planes, and boats usually need trucks to take them on the last stage of their journey.

Semitrailer

Tractor

Tight corners
Long trucks are often made up of two parts that are hinged so they can tu tight corners. The front p is called the tractor, and pulls a semitrailer.

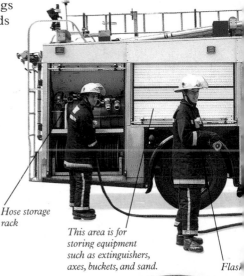

Floodlight for night emergencies

Warning light

Hose storage rack

This area is for storing equipment such as extinguishers, axes, buckets, and sand.

Flas

This gauge shows how much water is left in the fire engine.

Pump for the fire engine's internal water supply

Trains without tracks
Some of the world's biggest trucks are used to transport goods across the desert in Australia. They are called roadtrains because one truck pulls many trailers.

Amphibious truck

Cement truck

Earthmover

Car transporter

The equipment for cutting people out of crashed cars is stored in here.

The ladder can be raised automatically to a height of 44 feet (13.5 meters).

Blue flashing lights

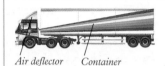

Air deflector   *Container*

A working arrangement
The same tractor can hook on semitrailers of many different types, so no journey is wasted. Air deflectors make some loads more streamlined to save fuel.

Tanker

Five crew members can sit in the front and rear of the cab.

This reflective strip makes the fire engine easy to see.

ver the top
ucks are not just used for work. ople often race them and perform azy stunts with them, too. This Foot truck is demonstrating how flatten a row of parked cars!

Cab comforts
At night, long-distance truck drivers usually sleep in their cabs, in an area behind the seats. Some have only bunks, but others have televisions, fridges, and even ovens.

ELECTRIC AND DIESEL TRAINS

In 1964 the Japanese opened the first high-speed electric railroad. These "bullet" passenger trains reached speeds of 130 miles (210 kilometers) an hour, a world record at that time. But railroad companies earn most of their money by moving goods, called freight. Freight trains are often pulled by diesel locomotives, and they keep a lot of traffic off the roads. The world's longest freight train had 682 cars and was more than four miles (seven kilometers) long!

Around the bend
Trains have to slow d[...]
to go around bends
safely. Some trains ca[...]
tilt inward on curves,
like a motorcycle lear[...]
into a bend. This mea[...]
they don't have to slo[...]
down so much.

*The Inter-City Express,
or ICE, is an electric
train from Germany.*

*On electric trains, the section that pulls
the coach cars is called a power car.*

*Pantographs pick up
electricity from overhead
wires to power the train.*

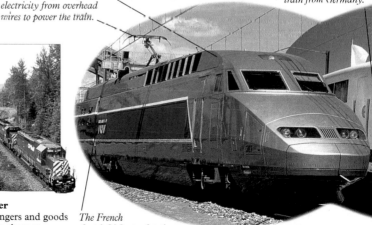

Diesel power
Many passengers and goods still travel by cheaper, diesel-powered trains, such as this long Canadian railroad convoy.

*The French
electric high-speed train
is called the TGV. On its
regular route it has a top
speed of 190 mph (300 kmh).*

*High-speed train routes are expensive [...]
set up because they need a special track
that has gentle curves.*

At the controls

The control center for Eurostar is in contact with the driver of every train. Controllers can warn the driver about any problems ahead, such as delays, signal failures, and electrification faults. In this way, the control center keeps the rail network running as smoothly as possible.

Grand Central Station

The largest railroad station in the world is Grand Central Station in New York. It has two levels with 41 tracks on the upper level and 26 tracks on the lower one.

On the tracks

A variety of engines and freight cars use the railroad tracks of the world today.

Breakdown train

Snowplow

typical ICE has eight ch cars with 16 power motors and can carry up to 500 passengers.

Coast to coast

One of the great railroad journeys of the world crosses Australia, from Sydney to Perth. The route covers 2,466 miles (3,968 kilometers) in three days and includes a world record 297 miles (478 kilometers) of completely straight track!

Passenger train

The streamlined shape of electric trains helps them speed along. In tests the E has reached 215 mph (345 kmh).

Freight train

UNDERGROUND AND OVERGROUND

As a city grows busier, the traffic on the roads becomes heavier and slower. This problem often can be solved by building a railway across the city, either over it, on tracks raised above the roads, or under it! There are underground trains all over the world, from London, where the world's first underground railway was built, to Moscow, where stations are like palaces. But they all do the same job—keep people moving.

No smoking

The first underground railroad opened in London in 1863. It used steam trains, but the smoke often made it impossible to see in the tunnels. The answer was electric trains, which were introduced in 1890.

A tight squeeze

So many people travel on the underground trains in Tokyo, Japan, during the rush hour, that special "pushers" are employed to squeeze passengers into the cars.

The London Underground is also called the "tube" because the deep tunnels are built using steel tubing. Tunnels near the surface are dug like ditches and then covered over.

Underground trains are powered by electricity picked up from extra rails.

Emergency stairs

SUBWAY

Riding a single rail

It is not always possible to build an underground railway system, so some railways run overground. Some trains run on top of a single rail, called a monorail.

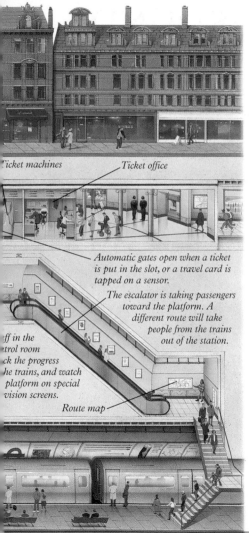

Ticket machines

Ticket office

Automatic gates open when a ticket is put in the slot, or a travel card is tapped on a sensor.

The escalator is taking passengers toward the platform. A different route will take people from the trains out of the station.

...ff in the ...trol room ...ck the progress ...he trains, and watch ...platform on special ...vision screens.

Route map

Hanging on

Not all trains run on top of the rail. The first monorail was built in Wuppertal, Germany, and the electric trains hang from the line.

Going up!

Special types of transportation are needed for getting people up steep slopes.

Rack railway

Cable car

Funicular railway

SAILING SHIPS

Nearly three-quarters of Earth's surface is covered by water, most of it in the seas and oceans. For thousands of years people have been finding ways to cross this water. At first they built rafts, and boats with oars, but around 3200 BCE the Egyptians began to use sails. From then on, sailing ships ruled the seas until a century ago. Today, big ships have engines, but small sailing ships are used for sports, fishing, and local trade.

China tea bundles

A quick t
A ship's speed is measure in knots—one knot is abo 1.85 kmh (1.15 mph). Th fastest sailing ships we clippers, such as the Cut Sark, which had a top spee of 17 knots. It transporte tea from China to England about 100 day

Sailors once used an instrument called a sextant to find their way in the middle of the ocean. A sextant helped navigate using the position of the sun or stars.

Sea charts
The sea often hides dangers, such as shallow waters or shipwrecks, so sailors must find their way using sea maps, called charts.

Tall ships
Many of the great ships of the past have been restored and are used today for special "Tall Ships" races.

Across the ocean
For hundreds of years, sailing ships have traveled the oceans of the world for exploration, trade, and war.

15th-century Portuguese caravel

16th-century Spanish galleon

17th-century merchant ship

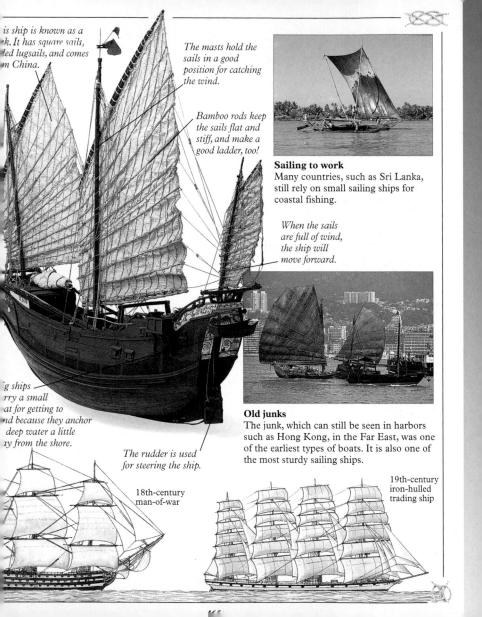

is ship is known as a
k. It has square sails,
ed lugsails, and comes
m China.

The masts hold the
sails in a good
position for catching
the wind.

Bamboo rods keep
the sails flat and
stiff, and make a
good ladder, too!

Sailing to work
Many countries, such as Sri Lanka,
still rely on small sailing ships for
coastal fishing.

When the sails
are full of wind,
the ship will
move forward.

Old junks
The junk, which can still be seen in harbors
such as Hong Kong, in the Far East, was one
of the earliest types of boats. It is also one of
the most sturdy sailing ships.

g ships
rry a small
at for getting to
nd because they anchor
deep water a little
y from the shore.

The rudder is used
for steering the ship.

18th-century
man-of-war

19th-century
iron-hulled
trading ship

SHIPS WITH ENGINES

Wind is not a very reliable form of power—sometimes it blows from the wrong direction, and sometimes it does not blow at all! But from around 1800, steam engines were used to turn paddle wheels or propellers. Steam power moved ships faster and was a more reliable way of transporting people and goods. Today, ships use mainly diesel engines, and their most important job is carrying cargo.

This part of the ship is called the bridge.

The cruising speed of a ship like this is around 15 knots or 17 mph (28 kmh).

Propeller power
The ship's engine turns a propeller at the back of the ship. This pushes the ship forward. On a big ship, these propellers can be enormous.

The ship is steered from the wheelhouse.

Living quarters

In the dock
In modern ports, like Singapore, most cargo arrives on trucks and trains, and is already packed in containers. These are stored on the docks and can then be neatly loaded onto the ships by cranes.

Pull and tug
Big ships are difficult to control, and from full speed can take several miles just to stop. So in ports and harbors, small powerful boats called tugs help push and pull big ships safely into position.

vacation at sea

uise ships offer passengers
uxury vacation as they travel.
e biggest cruiser today holds
arly 9,000 people. It is the length
4 football fields, and has 23
imming pools and 24 elevators.

A loading line
On the side of a ship is a row
of lines called a Plimsoll
mark. A certain one of these
lines must always be above
water or the ship may sink.
There are several lines, as
ships float at different levels
in salt or fresh water, in
summer or winter, and in the
tropics or the North Atlantic.

Plimsoll mark

*The front of the ship is
marked with a sighting mast.
Otherwise it would be hidden
from the crew in the bridge by
the cargo on the deck.*

*Containers are stacked
in racks on the deck.*

GRACECHURCH CROWN

Save our souls
In an emergency at
sea, passengers and
crew put on life
jackets and send an
SOS signal. Rescue
is carried out by a
lifeboat crew.

hip shapes
he seaways of the world are busy
th ships of all shapes and sizes.

Naval frigate

Roll-on/roll-off ferry

Oil tanker

Skimming Over the Water

Most boats travel very slowly because the water itself creates a drag on a boat's hull, or body, that slows it down. But hovercraft and hydrofoils just skim across the water, so they can travel at great speed. A hovercraft is not really a boat because it hovers above the surface of the water. It is also amphibious, which means that it can travel on both land and water.

Hovercrafts, lik this Landing C Air Cushion, a still widely usec the military.

Fan boating
People get around the reed beds and watery forests of the Everglades in Florida using flat-bottomed fanboats. These have raised fan motors that do not get caught in the weeds.

Control cabin

What a drag!
Water-skiers can speed over the water, but will slow right down if they fall in. This is because water is more than 800 times denser than air

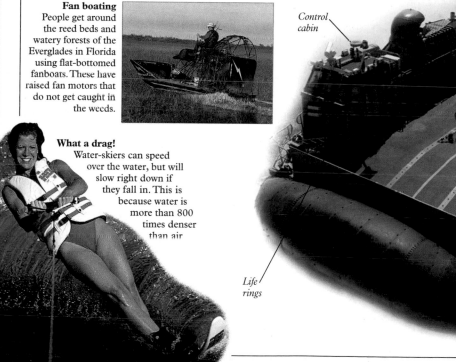

Life rings

Up and away
Hovercraft are also known as air-cushion vehicles because they float on a cushion of air.

When the hovercraft is sitting still on the tarmac, the skirt is flat and empty.

The engines start, and the skirt fills with air to become a thick cushion.

Hovering just above the surface of the water, the vehicle speeds on its way.

Military vehicles or cars drive in through the doors in the back.

Propellers push the vehicle forward.

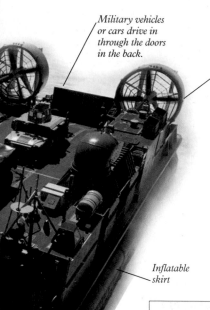

Inflatable skirt

Thin fins
Fins under a hydrofoil lift it out of the water so that it can skim over the surface at great speed.

Riding high
Catamarans have two thin hulls so there is very little of the boat in the water to slow it down.

Super speedy
Superboats have very powerful engines. They race at speeds of around 155 miles (250 kilometers) an hour—so fast that their hulls rise right out of the water.

PLANES WITH PROPELLERS

For hundreds of years people tried in all sorts of crazy ways to fly like birds and insects. But it was not until 1903, when the Wright brothers attached a propeller to a small gasoline engine, that people first managed to control a plane's takeoff and landing. Today, huge jet planes can fly hundreds of people around the world, but smaller, cheaper planes with propellers are still the best form of transportation for many jobs.

These propellers have three blades. As they spin around, they move the plane forward.

Skis have been attached to the wheels so the plane can land and take off from the snow.

BRITISH ANT...

Fresh air!
In 1927 Charles Lindbergh made the first nonstop solo flight across the Atlantic in the *Spirit of St Louis*. Like all pilots at that time, Lindbergh had to wear warm leather flying gear such as a helmet, gloves, a coat, and boots to protect himself from the cold.

Open cockpit

To the rescue
Light aircraft are relatively cheap to run and are ideal for transportation in large remote areas. In parts of Africa, for example, the only way doctors can get to their patients quickly is by plane.

470

Short take-off

Small planes only need short runways. This means they can go to places where larger planes could not land, such as this grassy airstrip on a mountainside in Nepal.

War and peace

Over the years, there have been many types of propeller-driven aircraft.

World War I triplane

This plane can seat up to 19 passengers.

The rudder moves the plane to the left or the right.

World War II Spitfire

This tailplane keeps the plane stable. Hinged flaps on the back of it move up and down to make the plane climb or dive.

Cessna light plane

This twin-engined "Otter" can take off and land in a small space.

Floatplane

Fighting flames

This Canadair plane is specifically designed for fighting forest fires.

Flying slowly and quite low, the pilot opens a hatch to release the water.

The pilot prepares to lower two pipes to scoop up water into the body of the plane.

As the plane skims the surface, up to 1,400 gallons (6,400 liters) of water are forced into the tanks in 10 seconds.

PASSENGER PLANES

The biggest airliner today is the Airbus A380, which can carry 853 passengers and enough fuel to fly 9,200 miles (14,800 km)—as far as England to Australia. Big planes have made flying much cheaper, and millions of people pass through the world's airports each year. The passengers simply step onto a waiting plane, but many jobs must be done to ensure every flight takes off and lands safely.

Join the line
The busiest airport in the world is Hartsfield–Jackson Atlanta International Airport in Georgia. More than 92 million passengers pass through it every year, as well as 950,000 planes.

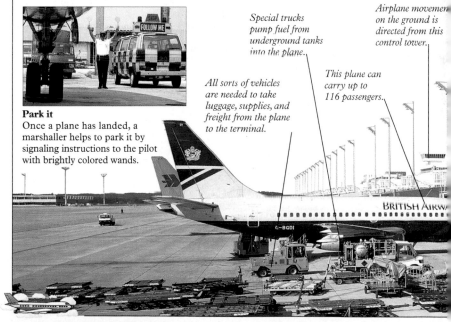

Park it
Once a plane has landed, a marshaller helps to park it by signaling instructions to the pilot with brightly colored wands.

Special trucks pump fuel from underground tanks into the plane.

All sorts of vehicles are needed to take luggage, supplies, and freight from the plane to the terminal.

Airplane movement on the ground is directed from this control tower.

This plane can carry up to 116 passengers.

BRITISH AIRWAYS

G-BQDI

Top speed
The fastest passenger plane in the skies today is the Boeing 747, also known as the jumbo jet. The average 747-400 plane takes off at 180 mph (290 kmh) and cruises at 565 mph (910 kmh).

Room with a view
At peak hours in major international airports, there is a plane taking off or landing every 45 seconds. Workers called air traffic controllers carefully organize planes for takeoff and landing.

Curious cargo
Goods may be loaded onto a plane with a scissor-action crane or a conveyor belt. Some cargo simply walks in and out of the hold!

A good checkup
Before each journey the ground crew give the plane a good cleaning, inside and sometimes outside! Engineers check that the plane is in perfect working order.

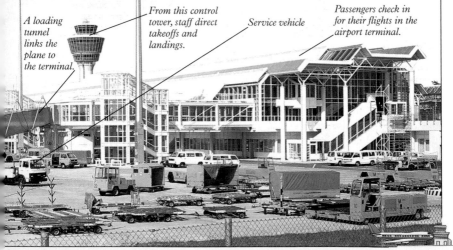

A loading tunnel links the plane to the terminal.

From this control tower, staff direct takeoffs and landings.

Service vehicle

Passengers check in for their flights in the airport terminal.

INDEX

PICTURE CREDITS

The publisher would like to thank the following for their kind permission to reproduce their photographs:

123RF.com: Aberration 396br, bloodua 369cr, deusexlupus 457br, Dinodia 349br, Grafner 295tr, Robert Klein 449cra, Iryna Linnik 369fbr, nerthuz 452br, Niphon Subsri 395br, 425crb, rawpixel 456bc, 456br, saiko3p 386br, Szilard Szanto 314br, Vladimir Kramin 456bl **A.F.P. Photo, Paris:** Mufti Munir 387cra; **Air France:** 473tl; **Alamy Images:** Chad Ehlers 366clb; **Alamy Stock Photo:** Andrew Bell 460tr, BonkersAboutTravel 363c, ClassicStock 266-267c, Design Pics Inc 386cl, Dinodia Photos 316bc, Friedrich Stark 387crb, Futuras Fotos 278tl, Juergen Freund 70bl, Mohamad Haghani 147b, Planetpix 37r, Rodolfo Arpia 314cl, Taigi 50clb, Tom Uhlman 407; **Allsport:** John Gichigi: 179cr, c; **Allsport/** Russell Cheyne 391cr, Yann Guichaoua/Agence Vandystadt 404tl, D.Klutho 459bl, S.Powell 261br, Pascal Rondeau 415br; **Ancient Art**

& Architecture Collection: 256tl, 260, 261c, 268bl; **Aquila Photographics:** C.Greaves 167cl; **Archiv Fur Kunst und Geschichte, Berlin:** Musee du Louvre, Paris 310bcr; **Ardea:** G.K.Brown 177l, D.Parer & E.Parer-Cook 13t, K.W.Fink 209cra, F.Gohier 102b, 103t, 105tc, 213cb, C.Haagner 13b, J.M.Labat 188c, Mike Osmond/ Auscape Int 102-3, J.Swedberg 170c, R.&V.Taylor 98b, A.Warren 203cr, 199b, A.Wearing 239tr; **Art Directors:** 352c; **ASAP:** Y.Mazur 365tl; **Australia House:** 461bc; **Australian Picture Library:** 371r; **Aviation Picture Library:** Austin J.Brown 472tr, 473tc. **Hans Banziger:** 119cl; **Michael Benton:** 137clb; **BFI Stills, Posters & Designs:** courtesy Productions La Fete Inc., Montreal, Canada 378tr; **Bibliotheque Nationale, Paris:** 267c; **Biofotos:** Heather Angel 29cr, 62br, 68br, 71tl, 78c, 78clb, 81tc, 106tr, 344ccb, Bryn Campbell 25, Brian Rogers 29cra; **Birmingham Museum:** 349crb; **Black Hills Institute of Geological Research:** Ed Gerken 138bl, 139tc; **BNFL:** 437crb; **Bridgeman Art Library:** Bibliothèque National, Paris 310cl, Christies, London ©1993. Pollock-Krasner Foundation 311cr, Forbes Magazine Collection 287tc, Galleria del'Academia, Florence 313l, Galleria degli Uffizi, Florence 310bcl, Giraudon 306tl, 310bc, Giraudon/ Louvre 303br, National Palace, Mexico City 272br, Guildhall Library 462c, Musee Rodin, Paris 295br, National Gallery, London 311tl, Phillips 311bc, Private Collection ©ADAGP, Paris & DACS, London 1993 311hl, Private Collection ©DACS 1993 310br, Tretyakov Gallery 280bl; **British Aerospace:** 424bl; **British Coal:** 430tl, cr, 431tc, cl, bl; **British Gas:** 434br, 435c; **Courtesy Trustees of the British Museum:** 250bl, 251bl, br, 258tl, 258-9c&b, 259r, 260t, 260-1t, 278-9t, 357cra; **British Steel:** 430cl, 442br, 443bl; **John Brown:** 447bra. **© Canon:** 314tl, 314bl; **J.Allan Cash:** 433c; **Christie's Colour Library:** 293bc; **Bruce Coleman Ltd.:** 170-1, D.Austen 212c, Jan & Des Bartlett 176cl, 182b, Erwin & Peggy Bauer 141tc, 175cr, M.N.Boulton 81tr, Mr.J.Brackenbury 122t, J.Burton 67bl, 78cla, 113bl, 194-5t, 204cr, J.Cancalosi 325cl, G.Cappelli 339cr, D.Chouston 180tr, A.Compost 198-9t, E.Crichton 114b, 145bl, 402cl, G.Cubitt 66tr, 69cr, P.Davey 216cl, A.Davies 200c, F.Erize 107tl, 178tr, 206tr, D.I.Everson 102t, MPL Fogden 75tl, 118tr, Jeff Foott 61cl, 104-5b, 176r, 209ca, C.B. & D.W. Frith 64tl, F.Furlong 170tl, J.Grayson 109tr, D.Green 158tr, F.Greenaway 171tc, U.Hirsch 72br, M.P.Kahl 65tr, S.C.Kaufman 67br, 201br, 347bc, S.J.Krasemann 115cb, 202-3b, 331bc, H.Lahhardt 126cb, H.Lange 61tr, G.Langsbury 171cl, F.Lanting 116br, L.Lee Rue 66br, 329tr, 363bl, M.Timothy O'Keefe 336bc, W.S.Paton 193tr, M.R.Phicton 137cra, 210cr, D.& M.Plage 10b, 217cr, Dr.E.Pott 74cr, 329br, Dr. Sandro Prato 66-7c, 115cr, M.P.Price 58-9c, J.Purcell 74bl, 109tc, M.Read 130t, H.Reinhard 60bl, 71tr, 106bl, 210tr, 215tc, F.Sauer 123b, J.Shaw

162-3, 151tl, K.Taylor 117bl, 123br, 127d, 258bl, N.Tomalin 192cr, M.Viard 335crb, J.Visser 205cr, R.William 119tl, 141c, K.Wothe 69bc, 201dl; **Bruce Coleman Inc.:** 113c; **Colorsport:** 375crb, Sipa Sport 469cr; **Comstock Inc.:** George Lepp 159cl; **Corbis:** Astier/BSIP 424cb, Dave Bartruff 367ftl, Blue Jean Images 424-5, Tami Chappell/Reuters 472tr, Leo Mason 472tl, Tom Sibley 425br; **Derngate Theatre, Northampton:** 380tr; **DLP:** D.Heald 342-3c, D.Phillips 301tc; **Dorling Kindersley:** Neil Fletcher 128, Kate Howey and Elgan Loane of Kentree Ltd, Ireland 426br, David Leffman/ Rough Guides 367crb, Gary Ombler/ Oxford Museum of Natural History 145cl, John Rigg/The Robot Hut 426bl; **Dreamstime.com:** Dreamstime.com/Christian Delbert/ Babar760 373tc, Orcea David 425tr, Dimbar76 380bl, Fred Goldstein 369tr, Ifeelstock 425c, Konstantinos Moraitis 456fbl, 456-457cb, 457bl, Pavel Losevsky 380cl, Manaemedia 425cra. **Ebenezer Pictures:** J.Browne 383crb; **Ecoscene:** 449tc; **ESA:** ATG medialab 51cl; **E.T.Archive:** 284bc, 464tr, National Maritime Museum 282tl, bl, V.&A. Museum 251cr; **Mary Evans Picture Library:** 284l, 285tr&b, 287b, 314tr, 357cl, 376clb, 422clb. **Gary Farr:** Photo appears courtesy of New Line Cinema Corp. 317crb; **Chris Fairclough:** 313tr, 330bl, 447tc; **Ffotograff:** Patricia Athie 369crb; **Fine Art Photographic:** 286bl; **Focus, Argentina:** 358-9c; **Michael & Patricia Fogden:** 77br; **Foods from Spain:** 337bl; **Ford Motor Co.Ltd.:** 456tr; **Werner Forman Archive:** Asantehene of Kumase 279crb, Plains Indian Museum, Buffalo Bill Historical Centre, Wyoming 276; **Fotolia:** Stocksnapper 355ca; **French Railways Ltd.:** 461tr; **Fullwood:** 331c. **Gary Gaiscoigne:** 265tr; **John Paul Getty Museum:** 262cr; **David Gillette, PhD:** 137tl; **Getty Images:** Ebrahim Adawi/AFP 319tc, Oleg Albinsky 355, Andia 453cla, Chabruken 248-9, Gianluca Colla/ Bloomberg 426cb, Charles Crowell/ Bloomberg 451bl, John Crux 357cr, DreamPictures 386-7c, E+/Mie Ahmt 366tr, E+/Yuri_Arcurs 364-5bc, ESA/ Rosetta/MPS 51br, Flightlevel80 453ca, Romeo Gacad/AFP 389cr, Gallo Images/Motivate Publishing 451cla, Chris Gorgio 224-225c, hadynyah 387bc, The Image Bank/ Martin Child 450c, iStock Editorial/ csakisti 364bc, Jesusdefuensanta 310tl, Johner Images 366c, Jason Kempin/ WireImage 426-7, Kimimasa Mayama/Bloomberg 457cra, mrbfaust 314fbr, Bill Nation/Sygma 457tl, Nordroden 350tr, nycshooter 457bc, olrat 453bl, Joaquin Ossorio-Castillo 385cr, Photographer's Choice RF/ Franz Aberham 367tc, Pictorial Parade/Archive Photos 425tc, Monty Rakusen 441tr, Rastan 53tl, RichLindie 351cr, Robert Harding World Imagery/Eurasia 450ftl, Joel Saget/AFP 450ftr, sankai 332bl, Sankei 427tr, Science Photo Library 245tr, sdbower 61crb, Stone/Arnulf Husmo 366-7, suwich 130cr, Time Stopper 442bc Yoshikazu Tsuno/AFP 427c, Universal Images Group/ Environment Images/UIG 424clb;